Whose Welfare?

STUDIES IN GOVERNMENT
AND PUBLIC POLICY

Whose Welfare?
AFDC and Elite Politics

Steven M. Teles

 University Press of Kansas

© 1996 by the University Press of Kansas
All rights reserved

Published by the University Press of Kansas (Lawrence, Kansas 66049), which was
organized by the Kansas Board of Regents and is operated and funded by Emporia
State University, Fort Hays State University, Kansas State University, Pittsburg State
University, the University of Kansas, and Wichita State University

Library of Congress Cataloging-in-Publication Data

Teles, Steven M.
    Whose welfare? : AFDC and elite politics / Steven Michael Teles.
        p.   cm. — (Studies in government and public policy)
    Includes biliographical references and index.
    ISBN 0-7006-0801-X (alk. paper)
    1. Aid to families with dependent children programs—United
States.   2. Public welfare—United States.   3. Elite (Social
sciences)—United States.   I. Title.   II. Series.
    HV699.T45   1996
    362.7'13'0973—dc20   96-12351
                                                                    CIP

British Library Cataloguing in Publication Data is available.

Printed in the United States of America

10 9 8 7 6 5 4 3 2 1

The paper used in this publication meets the minimum requirements of the American
National Standard for Permanence of Paper for Printed Library Materials
Z39.48-1984.

Contents

Preface

Despite the relatively modest amounts the nation spends on AFDC, welfare is one of the most ideological, emotional, and contentious issues in U.S. politics today. Welfare is loaded down with a huge amount of moral baggage. If one studies the soul of a nation through its policies toward its poorest citizens, then the soul of America is troubled and unsettled. It is divided between a broad, consensual public that wants authoritative yet compassionate reform and elites cut off from this consensus, who prefer to use welfare to wage a vicious cultural war. In this book I argue that the behavior of cultural and intellectual elites is the key to the ongoing deadlock of welfare policy, a deadlock that prevents fundamental change the public wants.

Perhaps it is best to start out by establishing what this book is not. It is not policy analysis: those hoping for a study of "what works" in welfare reform should turn to the voluminous, and for the most part depressing, evaluation research literature. It is not a study of a particular institution, although the functioning of most of the major institutions of U.S. politics is examined. It is not pure political theory, presenting a vision of a just welfare system based on abstract moral principles. And it is not hard social science, despite the fact that some new analyses of primary data are presented to make certain arguments, and the findings of a series of interviews are discussed.

This study attempts to seek and interpret knowledge; it is frankly, and unapologetically, synthetic. I have attempted to make sense of a broad range of literature, data, and argumentation on welfare and its place in American politics, drawing from a variety of social science literature and methods. I am not particularly interested in giving the book a disciplinary label, although I have been trained equally in American government, public policy, and political theory. I hope the reader will judge my work not by the narrow standards of any single discipline but by its success or failure at drawing together a mass of information into a coherent and plausible argument.

A strong ethical commitment to what I call cultural integration, or the effort to bind together strains in American culture that have been unfortunately torn asunder, informs the book's argument. This approach is centrist, or moderate, only in the sense that I believe it is essential to the basic principles of U.S. government and public policy to integrate our commitments to liberty, equality, and order rather than pull them apart. I have abandoned the frustrating task of trying to find a name for this tendency, except to say that it is consistent with American liberalism, especially the strong government tradition of Hamilton, Lincoln, and Theodore Roosevelt.

Although I take the unfashionable approach of arguing that ideas matter in American politics, I do not mean that interests are irrelevant; in fact, it is my opinion that ideas are rarely more important than interests. If one wants to understand why the deficit is so large, or why diffuse interests usually lose to concentrated ones, some form of rational choice theory is indispensable. The dispute between "institutionalists" and "rational choice theorists" is, in fact, quite misled. The important question is: When and in what combination do interests, institutional design, and political ideas matter? This study attempts to show that, at least in one case, ideas are predominant.

Finally, I place a great deal of emphasis on political elites, of whom I am highly critical. It is worth establishing at the outset that I am not a populist, and I do not dream of a government directly ruled by the people. Machiavelli was right when he observed, in the *Discourses,* "How useless a crowd is without a head." The people, if they are to guide the political system, must do so only through intelligently designed institutions and through a wise and well-trained elite. Every attack on the idea of elites is, in reality, an effort to substitute one elite for another. I ignore this gesture in the direction of populism and conclude with a suggestion of what the principles of an integrative elite would look like, and what sort of welfare principles it would support.

Acknowledgments

The weight of acknowledgment is especially heavy upon this, my first book. I begin where I began, with my parents, who were with me through every step, every doubt, every time I questioned myself or the work I was struggling with. Without them, this book would never have been written. All is owed to, and nothing blamed on, my parents—to whom I dedicate this book.

Equally responsible and without culpability are my wonderful advisers at the University of Virginia. This is a book written by a liberal under the patient tutelage of three conservatives, Martha Derthick, Steven Rhoads, and James Ceaser. They made being a liberal just as difficult as it should be, and no more. They asked all the right questions and were sublimely tolerant when my answers were not the same as theirs. In our ideological age, they gave me something more important than ideology, which is wisdom. To Martha Derthick, in particular, I owe a debt beyond my ability to pay. She supervised the dissertation on which this book is based, and extended herself above and beyond the call of duty in the period when it was being revised. Finally, Steve Nock, of the University of Virginia's sociology department, rekindled my interest in poverty and welfare, guided me through the early stages of writing the dissertation, and wet-nursed me in the manipulation of the General Social Survey.

Fred Woodward, my editor at University Press of Kansas, was more patient than duty required, always helpful, never pushy. A special thanks is due to my two reviewers. Jennifer Hochschild and a second, anonymous reviewer helped make this book, especially Chapters 1 and 4, much more coherent and defensible.

The Harry and Lynde Bradley Foundation helped pay for much of my graduate studies, including summer fellowships. In addition, the Bradley and the John M. Olin foundations supported a nonteaching fellowship at Harvard University, part of which I used to complete this study. Their support offers more evidence that lines of left and right are, and should be, permeable.

Special thanks also to the scholars who read and commented on parts of the manuscript, especially Lawrence Mead. Professor Mead's work, along with that of Aaron Wildavsky, is the central intellectual inspiration of this book. Thanks must also go to Stanley Rothman of Smith College, who provided me with an advance copy of his book *American Elites,* the research of which is crucial to the argument in Chapter 4. A debt is owed to all those individuals who agreed to be interviewed, both on and off the record. Special thanks go to Chuck Hobbs, without whom Chapter 7 might never have been written.

Finally, thanks must go to the friends and colleagues who got me through the struggle to write this book: Cary Federman, John Coumarianos, Marshal Zeringue, Beth Dougherty, and Steven Bragaw at the University of Virginia; David Paris, Bonnie Urcioli, Gwen Dordick, Alan Cafruny, Joseph Dorsey, Frank Anechiarico, and Christoph Cox at Hamilton College; everyone at the Gordon Public Policy Center, especially Marc Landy and Martin Levin; Lucius Outlaw at Haverford College, my friend at a difficult time; and Harvey Mansfield at Harvard University, who saved me from teaching during the 1995–1996 academic year and thus made possible the timely publication of this book.

My brother, Thomas Teles, helped preserve my sanity with his humor, friendship, and sympathy. Finally, all is owed to Maria Deknatel, my dearest friend and shrewdest critic.

1
AFDC: Consensus or Dissensus?

On August 14, 1935, the modern American welfare state was founded.[1] The president signed the Social Security Act, which established programs of cash assistance to the aged (Old Age Assistance, a program of grants to the states, and Old Age Insurance, an entitlement financed by a payroll tax), the unemployed, the blind, and dependent children. Since that time, the program for the aged has been extended to include widows and widowers of working people and has been transformed into a quasi-annuity entitlement program. Unemployment insurance has been moderately nationalized, and along with the programs contained in Old Age, Survivors, and Disability Insurance (OASDI), it provides a popular and reasonably generous safety net for those with a history of work. Aid to the blind has been nationalized as well, and along with aid to the non-OASDI disabled and elderly, has evolved into the Supplemental Security Income (SSI) program. Although there are occasional political debates about these parts of the original American welfare state, they are for the most part uncontroversial and politically stable.[2]

The one part of the American welfare state that has not been substantially nationalized, and which is perpetually politically contentious, is aid to dependent children. Aid to Dependent Children (ADC), or Aid to Families with Dependent Children (AFDC), as it was later christened, has retained much of its original federal character,[3] has meager benefits (compared to both programs serving different populations and the public's assessment of minimum needs[4]), and has resisted almost all efforts to transform it into an entitlement. Checks are delivered to the other classes established under the original Social Security Act on a regular, programmed, national basis, but AFDC recipients must deal with a caseworker on a regular basis to get their money. Since the mid-1960s, AFDC has been the subject of regular and emotionally charged efforts at reform; in contrast, SSI was created in 1974 with almost no debate, and during this period, OASDI

1

and Unemployment Insurance have seen virtually no change. AFDC is different. Why?

The key concept that will be used to explain this anomaly in America's welfare state is "dissensus." Although the other major parts of the U.S. welfare state are governed by a consensual opinion structure, that is, their fundamental justification is treated as a given and debate occurs only at the margins, AFDC has not, at least since the mid-1960s, had anything near this level of agreement. Nearly every aspect of AFDC is controversial: its standards of eligibility, level of benefits, federal structure, and obligations for receipt of assistance. Its impact on recipients is a matter of constant dispute: Does welfare cause dependency and a reduction of work effort, does it break up families, does it cause people to move across state lines in pursuit of more generous benefits? AFDC has a budget in the tens of billions but is at the same time unpopular across the political spectrum. No other program of the American welfare[5] state is so unpopular and yet so resistant to change.

The theory of dissensus is the intellectual tool that can help us understand why AFDC is such an outlier. Dissensus describes the nature of elite conflict and the way that elite conflict relates to popular ideas and desires. I believe that AFDC is so persistently unpopular, and yet so resistant to fundamental change through the legislative process, because it has been used as a proxy issue in the U.S. elite cultural conflict.

ALTERNATIVE EXPLANATIONS FOR THE NATURE OF THE AFDC SYSTEM

The heart of my explanation for the development, politics, and policy of Aid to Families with Dependent Children is a theory of cultural and ideological conflict. Before I articulate that theory, it is useful to investigate an alternative approach, which explains AFDC as a manifestation of cultural consensus. Although there are not an enormous number of studies of the politics of the AFDC program in particular, three sets of authors provide a reasonably clear and coherent alternative to the approach that I take.

In *The "Deserving Poor,"* Joel Handler and Ellen Hollingsworth analyze welfare administration in the United States around 1971. Their approach emphasizes administrative decentralization, which they trace to pre–welfare state notions of moral deservedness and the institutions that detect and establish that status. They observe that "with rare exceptions, the major policy questions in the AFDC program have been decided at the local level. When moral blameworthiness is not at issue, there are different allocations."[6] Although the names have changed, society has always deemed it of the greatest importance that the deserving poor be distinguished from "paupers," who are responsible for their plight and must be stigmatized. This stigma on the pauper class was important, for there existed the ever-present danger that this class would expand at the expense of the "deserving" poor. These distinctions were important not only to contain the size of the pauper class but also to prevent the erosion of the moral stature of the socially functional poor. Even as the welfare state expanded, including larger groups of people in the class of deserving, the distinctions were perpetuated. National and state administration was established for Civil War veterans and their families and for the mentally and physically incapacitated, but "the county and local systems were for the paupers—the undeserving."[7]

The key aspect of Handler and Hollingsworth's analysis is the continuity between the past and the present, and the past they describe is long indeed, extending not merely to the Social Security Act, or to the nineteenth century, but as far back as the English Poor Law. Handler and Hollingsworth concisely summarize the matter:

> The most striking characteristic of welfare legislation, from 1935 to the present, is how very little has changed. At least at the legislative level, the basic structure and substantive decisions that were made on the state level before 1930 remained in the ADC statutes for the next 35 years.[8]

This basic continuity has been maintained as a result of the political value that decentralization has for those at the top. Handler and Hollingsworth observe:

> Thus far the legislatures (whether federal or state) have been able to delegate the basic policy questions in AFDC through the use of broadly worded statutes. It has avoided getting into the business of resolving the moral dilemmas raised by the welfare program ... The delegations have been successful from the legislature's point of view. A successful delegation is one that stays delegated in the sense that no conflicts arise to demand legislative action. So far this has been the case with the AFDC program.[9]

Although Handler and Hollingsworth's analysis emphasizes the function that decentralization plays in preserving political stability, it is contingent upon another, cultural foundation. Conflicts can only be kept at the local level as long as there is enough of a cultural consensus to prevent certain issues from becoming matters of national concern. The great continuity in their system is the distinction between the worthy and the unworthy, which is broadly shared and historically grounded and which provides the moral justification for local control.

A second, related analysis is furnished by historian Michael Katz, author of *In the Shadow of the Poorhouse: A Social History of Welfare in America*. Katz attempts to explain welfare broadly, including public provision for all classes and categories of the poor; but his analysis is particularly apt when applied to dependent children and their mothers. Before the nineteenth century, most of the poor were assisted by some form of outdoor relief (that is, aid provided outside of residential public institutions). This form of assistance had become highly controversial by the beginning of the nineteenth century, as the introduction of wage work replaced subsistence farming as the primary form of economic activity. Advocates of indoor relief (assistance provided within residential public institutions) faulted existing assistance to the poor for causing innumerable social dislocations.

> Despite immigration, the growth of cities, and drink, to many observers the great source of pauperism lay within poor relief practice itself. For private charity and outdoor relief encouraged idleness by undermining the relation between work and survival. To nineteenth century observers, the poor laws interfered with the supply of energy available for productive labor by draining the working class of its incentive. Paupers were living proof that a modestly comfortable life could be had without hard labor. Their dissipation was a cancer demoralizing the poor and eroding the independence of the working class.[10]

The poorhouse would prevent this demoralizing effect by rendering pauperism a hard and undesirable business, by reducing the freedom of paupers, and forcing them to suffer the ministrations of religious and other moral authorities.

The poorhouse was, however, a failure. "A preoccupation with order, routine and cost replaced the founders' concern with the transformation of character and social reform. Everywhere, reform gave way to custody as the basis of institutional life."[11] And yet, the concerns that caused the poorhouse movement persist. The public and the helping professions continue to suspect that outdoor relief diminishes work effort and undermines character. Public assistance has concentrated ever since on making life on the dole uncomfortable and embarrassing; welfare reform arises with such frequency because the public's concern about the moral effects of welfare is never removed. The public is not willing to see poverty as a function of larger social causes, and welfare as a way of cushioning its effects, but insists on searching for a characterological explanation. Welfare reform is, therefore, a vicious cycle. The public sees the poverty in front of it, reaches back to a moral explanation, creates policy on that basis, the policy fails, and thus poverty persists and causes the cycle to begin again. The source, once more, is in the view of "American society" on the subject of the poor. Change is only possible if, as in the Great Depression, a sufficiently large portion of the public is forced into poverty, making it difficult to see that condition as anything other than the consequence of social structure. Once those periods are over, however, the cycle reasserts itself.

Perhaps the most controversial theory of public welfare politics is that put forward by Frances Fox Piven and Richard Cloward in *Regulating the Poor*.[12] Although Piven and Cloward were key participants in, as well as scholarly observers of, the welfare rights movement (their participation will be discussed in Chapters 5 and 6), it is their contribution of a Marxist interpretation of changes in poor relief that is most relevant to this discussion. For Piven and Cloward, welfare has one overarching function: the stabilization of the capitalist mode of production.

It fulfills this function in two ways. First, reflecting Handler and Hollingsworth, and Katz, Piven and Cloward maintain that the punitive nature of welfare legitimates even the most exploitative work: "To demean and punish those who do not work is to exalt by contrast even the meanest labor at the meanest wages."[13] In good times, this aspect of welfare is sufficient to stunt the growth of proletarian consciousness by emphasizing the distinction between work and pauperism.

Piven and Cloward's important contribution to the literature is, in contrast, their explanation for how welfare operates in times of economic distress. Capitalism is in a constant state of expansion and contraction, boom and bust, and within certain bounds it can prevent political disorder from occurring as a consequence of these patterns. However, when economic distress is widespread, the capitalist class is incapable of maintaining its legitimacy though the operations of the market.

> There is no harvest or paycheck to enforce work and the sentiments that uphold work; without work, people cannot conform to familial and communal roles; and if the dislocation is widespread, the legitimacy of the social order itself may come to be questioned. The result is usually civil disorder—crime, mass protests, riots—a disorder that may even threaten to overturn existing social and economic arrangements. It is then that relief programs are initiated or expanded.[14]

The critical problem with relief as the totality of the state's response is that it fails to replace the social control previously provided by the market. In its place the state must provide "a surrogate system of social control," where the work norm is preserved by giving the poor assistance "only on the condition that they labor, whether in public workhouses and labor yards or by being contracted and indentured to private entrepreneurs."[15] The rise of mass enfranchisement has not changed this dynamic substantially; now the state recognizes public disorder not through riots but through shifts in voting patterns. Disorder causes certain groups of voters to become disaffected: "It is this objective—the political 'reintegration' of disaffected groups—that impels electoral leaders to expand relief programs at times of political crisis engendered by economic distress."[16]

In addition to reintegrating mass voting blocs into the political system, this particular form of welfare statecraft also buys off the protest of individual radical leaders by integrating them into the body of the state. This strategy was key to the operation of the Great Society:

> Although the federal government did not fully anticipate and could not fully manage all of the varied activities it had set in motion, it nevertheless shaped the over-all course of these events, and in very traditional directions. If civil rights workers often turned federal dollars to their own purposes in the short run, in the longer run they became model-cities directors, or community-action executives—that is, they became government employees or con-

tractors, subject to the constraints of federal funding and federal guide-lines.[17]

The crux of Piven and Cloward's theory is a Marxist understanding of the state and the role of ideology. In this frame of analysis, the state is merely the reification of the capitalist class, called to do its bidding in hard times and leave it be in good times. The state is capable of strategic action and self-consciousness. The state can only be understood as a whole, whose ideology is one and whose policies are merely adjustments to circumstance, not the result of fundamental alterations in the justification for state power. Although there are classes in so-ciety, those classes are economic, and only the ruling class, that is, capital, has ac-cess to the state. Welfare policy can, therefore, only be understood as the opera-tion of welfare statecraft in the service of capitalist stabilization.

These three theories have certain aspects that commend them, but they all bump up against a few nagging, unexplained facts. All three attempt to establish a virtually unbroken consensus on the treatment of the nonworking poor that reaches back to the Republic's earliest days. This attempt to link older ideas about the punitive nature of poor relief with modern proposals for linking work and welfare is obviously intended, at least partially, to serve emotional and ideo-logical purposes. If one can demonstrate that current proposals are organically linked to ideas from an earlier, pre–welfare state era, the novelty and seeming connections with contemporary values can be broken and the ideas stripped of their legitimacy.

The mistake that this sort of approach makes is that it examines public atti-tudes only through the highly problematic perspective of governmental action and policy. In this view, government is seen as completely functional, incapable of misperceiving, misadministering, or twisting public values for its own purposes. As I show in Chapter 3, there is a much more complex underlying public consen-sus on welfare than any of these authors imply, one that reflects a much different set of principles than those that informed the English Poor Law and its progeny, different even than that which informed Aid to Dependent Children. All three approaches assume that public values are expressed in our nation's policies, but when, whether, and how they get expressed are precisely the questions that need to be answered.

At the same time, however, there is much that is valuable in these authors' approaches. Handler and Hollingsworth correctly point to the relation between federalism and issue-avoidance on the national level, a theme I address in Chap-ter 7. However, I believe that they fail to capture the causes for this devolution of responsibility and how it has changed in character over time. In 1935, local con-trol was preserved not only because of pressure from southern members of Con-gress but also because of a strong belief that poor relief was, like education, an inherently local function. Poor relief is no longer conceived by the public at large as an inherently local function, and yet substantial decentralization endures. Why has the institutional character of programs representing a very different time persisted when public opinion has changed? Why is public policy nonfunctional in terms of public attitudes?

Piven and Cloward properly call attention to the insurgent movement represented by the National Welfare Rights Organization (NWRO) and the litigation strategy that supported it; the groups in the movement play a key role in my discussion of the Supreme Court and the failure of radical reform. However, Piven and Cloward fail, as did the welfare rights groups, to see that public opinion, when appealed to in the appropriate manner, can serve to support claims for humanitarian social policy. Piven and Cloward's lens can only focus on oppressed minorities struggling against an intransigent public, which has no other option than to use the public's institutions against itself. They miss the big picture, which is the substantial change in public values about poverty, and which could have been addressed in such a way as to create a more humane welfare system. Piven and Cloward's way of looking at America's welfare system not only creates a jaundiced view of the past but also obscures real opportunities in the present. It leads to a political attitude of confrontation rather than conciliation and acceptance of opportunities as they present themselves.

Furthermore, Piven and Cloward's Marxist framework forces them to see only an unyielding state that must be tricked into doing the bidding of the poor, not a multiplicity of power sources and ideologies that can be pieced together in any number of ways. The best evidence that Piven and Cloward misunderstand the interaction of ideology and the state is their explanation for the Great Society. It is difficult to reconcile their explanation of welfare as regulative in bad times with the substantial planning and concern that began years before the first riots (the Watts riots did not occur until August 1965) and a full decade before the slowdown in the American economy. In the early 1960s, there was no economic crisis. In fact, rates of economic growth were at historically unprecedented levels. What was the state defending itself against? Only a change in ideology can explain the utterly new political landscape of antipoverty policy that began in the early 1960s and continues today. In fact, it is my contention that despite the success that all these authors may have in explaining poverty policy prior to the 1960s, their explanations fail utterly to account for the political landscape after that point. The alternative theory that I sketch in this chapter explains the politics of this new era.

Finally, Katz is right in emphasizing the continuing fear that Americans have toward the effects welfare has on work effort and dependency but is wrong to dismiss these views as irrelevant or immoral. He seems to suggest that such a concern can only lead to punitive strategies for welfare reform. However, it is not that difficult to demonstrate, as I hope to in my conclusion, that concern for dependency can be woven into an ideology of welfare that emphasizes generosity rather than niggardliness. Again, looking at one public value apart from the full scope of American culture can result not only in bad history but in unwarranted skepticism about the public's desire for change.

In the end, these authors' insistence that welfare has a central political dynamic, different from that which governs other policy areas, is their most important contribution. They are also right to notice the centrality of issues of dependence and order in welfare politics, even as they are wrong to stigmatize these concerns as somehow illegitimate, as evidence of mass psychopathology. Welfare has a politics of its own, with questions of value at the center. The difference between my argument and that of the consensus thinkers is that they believe the public's values are imbedded in America's welfare policies while I wonder why they are not.

The object of my theory is to provide a way of looking at AFDC that can demonstrate how public action can fail to represent public values. This lack of connection, and the consequences associated with it, is the main subject of this work. The theory that follows provides the framework for our later discussion of specific aspects of welfare policy and politics in America.

AN ALTERNATIVE FRAMEWORK:
ELITE CONFLICT AND DEADLOCK

Despite their generally left-wing orientations, all of the consensus thinkers agree that public values determine public policy. American culture emphasizes a punitive attitude toward the poor, and that culture is shared both by society's influentials and the average citizen. Accordingly, the conveyor belt between the public and public policy is smooth and, with a very few exceptions, unbroken.

I differ from the consensus thinkers on two levels. First, I dispute their assessment of American culture, seeing it as substantially less punitive and more open to opportunity-enhancing policy than they do. At the same time, however, I recognize that generosity is not all there is to the public consensus, that there are strong strains of individualism and respect for order and competency mixed in with the desire to help. To be frank, I believe that the outlines of this public consensus are reasonable and decent, while the consensus thinkers believe that they are irrational and punitive. In Chapter 3, I discuss in detail the nature of the public consensus over welfare and the academic controversy that accompanies it.

Second, I dispute their image of the relationship between policy and public ideas. Although there are many cases in which the relationship is clear, welfare is not one of them. In fact, welfare manifestly does not reflect public values, either in its meager benefits or its loose enforcement of behavioral standards. What needs to be explained is how this disconnect is possible.

Both politically and substantively, AFDC is an aberrant policy area. Lawrence Jacobs argues that "public opinion is most influential in directing policy deliberations when it is unambiguous and strong."[18] Echoing Jacobs, Benjamin Page and Robert Shapiro find in a more statistically oriented study, "substantial congruence between opinion and policy (especially where opinion changes are large and sustained, and issues are salient)."[19] In fact, welfare represents exactly the kind of policy area that these two sets of studies suggest should respond to public opinion. And yet, policy has continued to stray far from what Chapter 3 demonstrates is, perhaps, the strongest public consensus on any major political issue. How, then, to explain this anomaly? To understand it, we must distinguish welfare politics from other kinds of politics.

Welfare politics is like—and unlike—two other types of politics with which social scientists are more familiar: (1) interest group conflict, which has traditionally been explained either by pluralist theory or public choice/economic approaches, and (2) religious, "culture war" politics, which is the province primarily of sociologists. The differences between AFDC politics and culture war politics are less severe and will be dealt with first.

In his important study, *Culture Wars,* sociologist James Davison Hunter attempts to come to terms with the devastating and divisive issues of education, abortion, and the nature of media in a free society. He suggests that only a framework of "cultural conflict," defined as "political and social hostility rooted in different systems of moral understanding,"[20] can account for the spirited and uncompromising nature of the debate surrounding the complex of questions he investigates. For Hunter, what distinguishes the conflict is that the competing value systems "always have a character of ultimacy to them," leading him to characterize the difference between the combatants as between "orthodoxy," the belief in inerrant and eternal standards of justification, and "progressivism," the idea that the good is unstable and evolving through time and across cultures.

It is the absence of ultimacy that sets welfare politics off from the culture conflict that Hunter describes (and for which his framework successfully accounts). In culture war politics, conflicts occur over metaphysical matters (What is the nature of reality?) and epistemological matters (What is the nature of truth and how can we come to know it?). In welfare politics, the issues are not ultimate but relate to these worldly questions: What is the value of work? What are one's obligations to others in an orderly society? To what degree does structural inequality justify violation of social norms? and so on. Although the public is highly divided on many of the metaphysical and epistemological issues Hunter studies, it is quite consistent on the political questions that welfare asks. Still, there are similarities between the issue areas, which Hunter suggests by observing that "public discourse, then, is largely a discourse of elites. This is the first reason why the vast majority of Americans who are somewhere in the middle of these debates are not heard."[21] By pointing to the conflict between elite ways of seeing the world and those of average Americans, Hunter identifies a critical element of modern society—one with important ramifications for welfare politics.

The second, and more common, form of politics is interest group politics. In the classical pluralist model of politics, the fundamental unit of the community is the group. All (or almost all) individuals are represented by groups, which jockey for advantage and resources. This competition among groups for social resources eventually results in "equilibrium," a steady state that represents the bargains struck between the various groups. Public policies are, therefore, the ultimate results of group competition.

In the pluralist model, the fundamental division within society is between groups. An alternative tradition suggests that the fundamental schism is between rulers and the ruled, and that pluralist theory, by attempting to trace policy outcomes to the results of democratic bargaining, covers up the more fundamental nature of political conflict. This tradition has two elements: those who see the ruling part of society as unified and those who see it as in conflict. Those who see it as unified are divided between the Marxists, who see society as divided between capital and labor,[22] and elite theorists, such as Vilfredo Pareto, Max Weber, and Gaetano Mosca, who are more willing to see variation in the dominant element of society.[23] There may be competition for supremacy and a certain degree of circulation within elites, but society is always ruled by a small cadre of men. Machiavelli states this point succinctly: "For in all states whatever be their form of government, the real rulers do not amount to more than forty or fifty citizens."[24] Standing between these two perspectives is C. Wright Mills, whose "power elite" blends elements of Marxist class analysis and elite theorists' power approach,[25] arguing that American society is ruled by a coalition of the highest elements of the military, large multinational businesses, and senior bureaucrats.[26]

The Marxist and the unified elite perspective are joined not only by their emphasis on a single governing element in society but also by the certainty with which they assume that this element rules in its own interests. For these thinkers, the ruling element is set apart from the rest of society and extracts resources from the masses in order to fuel its own ambitions. Therefore, this perspective sees the ruling group as having an interest, that is, a knowledge of what it wants as a coherent entity, and that interest is by definition contrary to that of the public.

If the pluralist model treats democracy not as an aspiration but as an accurate description of how things are (necessarily?), then strong elite theory assumes the same for oligarchy. Against both of these perspectives is the theory of "strategic elites," which Susan Keller develops in her important book, *Beyond The Ruling Class*. For Keller, the essence of modern society is the differentiation of social functions and the increasing fracturing of elements of social power. Although agreeing that rule by elites or those with the greatest competency is the nature of politics, Keller argues that there are many elites in modern society and that all do not necessarily have the same interests. This conflict within those who rule distinguishes the theory of strategic elites from that of a power elite or ruling class.

This theory is further developed in Daniel Bell's two classic works, *The Coming of Post-Industrial Society* and *The Cultural Contradictions of Capitalism*.

Bell argues that the social complexity inherent in modern society was creating a "disjunction in realms," with competing elites fighting not so much over tangible social resources as over cultural meanings. A "new class," which possessed a strong belief in the virtues of "modernity" (defined by the aesthetic of abstraction and an ethics of self-expression) was now competing with the traditional classes in society in a battle over the governing principles of society. An elite driven by rationality, order, and self-discipline was in competition with one driven by emotion, flux, and authenticity. Bell, it should be noted, suspected that the governing ideas of both elites needed to be overcome, or at least supplemented, by the ancient idea of the "public household."[27]

Although the competing elite theory of Keller and Bell does not explain all politics, or perhaps even most politics, it is quite useful in explaining the politics of AFDC. Unlike the meat and potatoes issues of economics, AFDC politics is not organized by a conflict of well-defined interests and groups to represent them. AFDC politics is dominated by "advocates," those who claim to speak for those without voices, rather than representatives, who have a regular and structured relationship to those they claim to speak for. This pattern of advocacy means that there is more opportunity for AFDC politics to express the priorities of elites (who are not disciplined by a rank and file that can remove them from their positions), who can use the issue as a way of furthering their positions on the larger cultural conflict.

It is this conflict between elites, on matters of crucial symbolic and ideological significance, that I take to be the fundamental fact of AFDC politics, the one that determines its basic contours and that sets it off from most other areas.

CONSENSUS POLITICS

Is there such a thing as consensus politics? That is, when I suggest that AFDC politics is driven by elite dissensus, am I doing nothing more than suggesting that it partakes of the political form characteristic of all other policy areas?

Comprehensive change involves the overcoming of "normal" political forms, which in the American context means incrementalism and dominance by interest groups. When comprehensive change does occur, it is typically because there exists an alignment of elite opinion and public opinion that is sufficiently strong, persistent, and mature to act as a counterweight against interest-group agreements. This alignment is what I mean by "consensus politics."

It would be fair to say that with the single exception of changes driven by transitions in party control (and even then unevenly), consensus politics is the only formula for comprehensive change in the American context. Deregulation of the airlines in the 1970s, and tax reform in the 1980s are the best examples of this phenomenon. In both cases, there existed a public receptivity to change, a desire motivated by the impression of interest-group driven corruption.

This impression would have been empty and without political significance, however, had it not been for a remarkable confluence of elite opinion. In the case of airline deregulation, consumer advocates, ideological conservatives, and especially academic economists agreed on the need for comprehensive change. Derthick and Quirk observe:

> Within the academic world the convergence was interdisciplinary, and within the political-governmental world it cut across political parties, ideological groupings, and branches of government. Perhaps most important was the convergence of the two worlds when analytic prescriptions, instead of depending upon technical and abstruse arguments, proved adaptable to political rhetoric and position taking.[28]

Timothy Conlan, David Beam, and Margaret Wrightson find an almost identical phenomenon in tax reform. They note that "the movement for tax reform rested above all on the shared conviction of knowledgeable experts in and outside of government that the federal income tax system had grown indefensible from the standpoint of professionally salient values."[29] Although substantial change may be difficult in many areas of American politics, it is not because of the invincibility of interest groups.[30] There are reasons to believe that this pattern will accelerate and may cease to be seen as aberrant.[31]

What consequences does this pattern of comprehensive reform have for AFDC? Clearly, if elite consensus can drive policy change, even over the screams of powerful interest groups, then elite dissensus may have the inverse effect: Blocking change even where there is popular support and no powerful interest group opposition. Elaborating the theory of dissensus that I use to explain AFDC politics is, therefore, our next challenge.

THE THEORY OF DISSENSUS

The theory on which this book is based is not intended to explain welfare policy throughout American history, and it cannot necessarily be extended to other policy areas. I hope to show that AFDC is a special case, with no clear parallels. AFDC is an almost pure case of cultural and intellectual politics. To understand it, therefore, one must have a theory of culture as a grounding.

In their 1990 work, *Cultural Theory,* Michael Thompson, Richard Ellis, and Aaron Wildavsky present a grid-group schema for analyzing political culture. The group dimension describes "the extent to which an individual is incorporated into bounded units,"[32] while the grid dimension "denotes the degree to which an individual's life is circumscribed by externally imposed prescription." Put another way, the first dimension is concerned with the degree to which decision-making power within the group is highly structured, while the latter describes the amount of social and moral regulation that exists in a particular culture.

When the two dimensions are combined, they result in four cultural tendencies. One, which is high grid, low group, is not of particular relevance to our study because it mainly concerns alienated and disjointed cultures, such as those ruled in empires or as slaves.[33] The three important groups are hierarchists, individualists, and egalitarians.

Hierarchists are, in Thompson, Ellis, and Wildavsky's terminology, high group and high grid. Their most important values are order, discipline, tradition, continuity, and structure. The central social institution is the family, followed by the church and the local community. For a hierarch, the role of the state is to support and protect the legitimacy of lower-level social institutions and to maintain order. The most important elites associated with the hierarchist position in American politics are leaders of conservative religious organizations, farmers, and senior military officials.

The individualists are low group and low grid. Their most important values are liberty, autonomy, and self-determination. The central social institution is the market, followed far behind by courts (whose purpose is to vindicate claims of rights). The role of the state is to support and defend the legitimacy of the market and to protect individuals from coercion from lower-level social institutions. The most important elites associated with the individualist position in American politics are those in business, economists, and civil libertarians.

Egalitarians are high group and low grid. Their most important values are equality, dignity, adequacy of social provision, and protection of minority group rights (as opposed to individual rights). The central social institution is the polity, followed by ethnic, gender, and sexual orientation groups. The role of the state is to redistribute power from those who possess it to those who do not and to protect minority groups (as groups) from the majority. The most important elites associated with this position in American politics are artists, much of the foundation and academic world, and large elements of the media, social work, and legal services (defined narrowly) professions.[34]

In a culturally homogeneous context, one of these three cultural patterns dominates, structuring the way that individuals conceive of themselves and their political role, and typifying the way that decisions are made and the ends they are made for. There are two ways that a nation may be culturally heterogeneous. In the first, its members may come from a variety of contexts, as in a nation with a large number of unassimilated immigrants.[35] In this scenario, there are large groups of individuals with different cultural patterns, which they will exercise in more or less pure forms within their subgroup and (in some cases) attempt to make the dominant form in the nation as a whole. In the second type of cultural heterogeneity, a nation attempts to reconcile a multiplicity of cultures from the moment of its founding. The homogeneous culture is consensual in form, the first type of heterogeneous culture is dissensual by nature, while the third (and I believe American form), can be either dissensual or consensual, depending upon the political context and issue area.

The second type of cultural heterogeneity is, as I have already suggested, characteristically American. Our founding documents and our later political and social history are characterized by attempts to reconcile three very different political cultures, none of which the American public as a whole has been willing to dispense with. Americans believe in liberty and the freedom of the individual, and this conviction is embodied in American capitalism and freedom of conscience. Americans believe in equality, and our society's numerous struggles to include its out-groups, from the Jacksonian struggles over suffrage through the black civil rights movement, indicates America's conviction that it is an unfinished experiment until all its people possess the equality embodied in citizenship. Americans are hierarchists in that they support strong moral regulation in their private lives, a commitment typified by the nation's unique (in the West) level of church-going and its emphasis on local government (which because of its proximity to citizens is more attuned to and capable of regulating personal behavior with civic consequences) and preservation of national origins.

These three coexisting cultures within the American mind can lead either to a politics of consensus, or, as in the case of welfare, a politics of dissensus. A simple democratic theory would argue that if the American people and their political traditions support policies and programs that blend these three cultural traditions, democratic institutions would generate consensual outcomes. There would be arguments about how best to balance these three cultures and, as always, distributional conflicts over who should bear the burdens and benefits of policy. However, agreement about the legitimacy of the three cultural tendencies and the need to reconcile them would constrain conflict within fairly narrow limits. The main elements of the American social welfare state, particularly old-age assistance and unemployment insurance, are examples of this kind of politics. Comprehensive changes, discussed earlier in this chapter, are another.

How can this same structure of opinion be capable of moving in the opposite direction of the consensus politics that characterizes most of the American social welfare state? That is, how can a relatively consensual public opinion and political tradition generate a dissensual politics? For the purposes of this work, dissensus is defined as a form of politics marked by a high degree of conflict on the level of fundamental moral questions. It is characterized by a politics of extreme moral and ethical claims, as opposed to one oriented to reconciliation of differences and debate within narrow ethical constraints.

Because of the nature of the American tricultural system, direct claims of representing one cultural tendency to the exclusion of the others are not, except in the most culturally homogeneous political jurisdiction, likely to constitute a successful political strategy. The alternative is, however, quite close in its effects to the monocultural strategy. Its key component is to use a particular issue to demonstrate fidelity to one of the three cultures and then demonstrate that one's opponent lacks such fidelity, thus placing the opponent outside of the political mainstream. The form of political rhetoric that is typical of this strategy would be: "I have worked hard to force those on welfare to work, while my opponent has consistently resisted mandatory work for welfare recipients. I believe in the value of work; my opponent has consistently voiced opposition to this crucial American value." Conflict emerges out of consensus because of the composite nature of American political culture:

> The unsystematic and unideological character of this Creed is reflected in the fact that no theory exists for ordering these values in relation to one another and for resolving on a theoretical level the conflicts that inherently exist among them. Conflicts easily materialize when any one value is taken to an extreme: majority rule versus minority rights; higher law versus popular sovereignty; liberty versus equality; individualism versus democracy.[36]

American political culture needs an elite to reconcile its parts and is therefore highly subject to conflict and disorder when its elite ceases to be culturally integrative.

The objective of the disintegrative strategy is to place one's opponent outside of the political mainstream by the use of a (usually small in policy significance) proxy issue that carries significant symbolic moral weight. A consensual mode of debate, in contrast, might still use proxy issues but would put them in the context of an overall effort to reconcile the different parts of the public mind. For example, a consensual form of rhetoric would have to place a single issue, such as work requirements, in the context of its implications for the rest of the cultural consensus: Does it reduce individual rights? Does it foster greater social and economic equality? In consensus politics, political debate would concern itself not with fidelity or its absence on a single cultural form but with whether a policy position represents an excessive reliance on one cultural pattern to the detriment of the others.

The absence of such a structured debate is the key element of dissensus politics. Issues are sought for their symbolic moral value. A single aspect is focused on, and an issue is presented as a matter of acceptance or rejection rather than one of balance in light of other priorities. The issue is not important for its own sake or for the consequences on the experience of individuals that it will have but as an indicator of larger ideological patterns.

Welfare is an ideal issue for dissensus politics for a number of reasons. In contrast with most high-profile social issues, such as health reform, economic regulation, and fiscal policy, few individuals who will actually be affected by the issue are organized or represented by membership organically linked with them. If a bill is before Congress to raise the minimum wage, for example, workers will be represented by the AFL-CIO and the views of business will be made clear by the Chamber of Commerce. Both these groups are the creation of those who will be ultimately affected by a change in the law. Their leadership structure, although hierarchical, eventually leads back to individual workers or business owners who will be helped or harmed by an adjustment of the wages paid to employees.

What of welfare? A congressional committee considering changes in AFDC is likely to hear from unions, who will oppose work requirements (as likely to lower the prevailing wage for labor) but will support an increase in welfare benefits. The Children's Defense Fund might be there, supporting increased centralization and higher payments. Representatives of local and state government might attend, hoping to prevent any increase in their financial obligations. Bureaucrats in charge of the program will certainly attend, and although they may be more knowledgeable than any other group involved in welfare reform, they may also be more likely to avoid making their opinions known, lest they offend the White House, state administrators, or the committee itself. Finally, a broad range of intellectuals from think tanks and universities will be asked to attend and will propose changes ranging from complete elimination of the program to a guaranteed income.

Who will not be in attendance are representatives of the poor. Of course, a number of individuals will say that they represent the poor, and in the case of a few inner-city representatives this claim may have some validity. However, there will not be any large organized group of welfare recipients because no such group exists. Only one such group (the National Welfare Rights Organization) has existed in this nation's history, and it was short lived and as much a creation of its leader, George Wiley, as the welfare mothers who made up its (very small) membership. As a general rule, the poor play no direct role in the politics of welfare in America.

Because of the absence of any interest group or other organized political role for the poor in the politics of welfare, the vacuum is filled by those who either claim to speak for the poor or who possess some form of expertise or higher understanding that permits them to know what a properly functioning welfare system would look like. The poor have advocates, not representatives. Welfare politics is thus a matter not of interest aggregation or conflict but of ideas and symbols. Symbols and ideas are carriers and surrogates for cultural forms, the means through which cultural conflict is joined. The interests at issue in welfare policy-making are only tangentially those of recipients themselves; the more important interests are those of the nonpoor.

Welfare policy, which is sharply estranged from the interests of those directly concerned with the actual structure of the program on the ground, is thus exceptionally dominated by issues of morality. Even if the interests of welfare recipients were represented in the political process, this high level of moral intensity would still be present, for the simple reason that any policy with welfare's recipient population would face a staggering set of "regime-level issues." A regime-level issue, as I use the term, connotes a matter of public policy that touches on the basic issues of citizenship and social system maintenance. A regime-level issue concerns fundamental matters of how a polity chooses to organize itself politically, socially, and economically, how it reproduces itself (not merely in the biological sense), and how it distributes rights and obligations. It concerns not merely who gets what, when, where, and how, but why a particular community exists and for what ends it is organized.

Almost every aspect of welfare policy touches on these regime-level issues, which explains why the program is so controversial and, paradoxically, so resistant to change. It is controversial as a result of the presence of regime-level issues because interests cannot simply be traded off on the basis of comparative power, as they are in most other areas of politics. Not only are concrete interests absent in the making of the policy but these differences of opinion are highly resistant to bargaining. Welfare policy is resistant to change because many of those involved are not interested primarily in welfare as such. The debate exists as a forum for issues unrelated to welfare, for social and value conflicts that would exist with or without the poor. Welfare has become more contentious since the 1960s as the elite moral consensus on the issues that relate to it has broken down and as the broader public consensus has changed.[37] Because change in the program is not, for the most part, the main issue at hand, few participants are willing to move from their position in order to change matters in the lived world of those on welfare.

Welfare is extraordinarily susceptible to dissensus politics because it permits issues of social value to be debated without directly judging the behavior of the majority of citizens. Family decomposition, the decline of the work ethic, and the erosion of personal responsibility are social trends occurring throughout American society. However, to discuss them directly would inevitably lead to fingers being pointed at a large group of American citizens. The politics of morality are generally more effective when the finger can be pointed at someone else. Welfare and the population it serves provide that someone else. The use of the welfare population in this manner reduces the psychic strain that declining social morality causes by pushing its responsibility off onto a politically weak and intellectually ill-represented population. It is a highly effective strategy for blame avoidance on the part of politicians, who do not have to address the complex and fundamental causes of wider social decline, and on the part of the public at large, who can avoid looking in the mirror to see the cause of the nation's changed social mores.

CONCLUSIONS

Dissensus politics is most likely to occur (1) in an environment in which the issue in question does not have experiential consequences for those who are debating it; (2) when a policy can be used to address in proxy form a larger matter of moral and ideological significance; and (3) when there are strong reasons to avoid debating those same larger matters directly. Dissensus itself is characterized by an effort to split apart the elements of the public consciousness and to pose each cultural pattern as a take-it or leave-it proposition rather than a matter of balance and reconciliation.

American welfare policy was not always characterized by dissensus. In fact, the rise of dissensus politics in the AFDC program is less than a thirty-year phenomenon. In the following three chapters I discuss the origins and early history of AFDC; the rise of a new public consensus on welfare, work, and the family; and the elite cultural conflict that has led to dissensus politics. This background will render the events discussed in Chapters 5, 6, 7, and 8 intelligible as part of the larger process of dissensus politics. In the concluding chapter, I will summarize my findings, consider whether America's welfare dissensus can be broken, and discuss the ideological transformation necessary to establish a new, humane, and politically sustainable alternative to AFDC.

2

The Development of the AFDC Program

An adequate history of the Aid to Families with Dependent Children program would be much longer than this volume. Consequently, although that task is a worthy one, I will instead, in this chapter, strive toward two more modest goals. The first is to provide a broad view of the relevant historical statistics on the program and an in-depth exploration of two crucial changes in the program during its sixty-year history: the explosion in participation in the late 1960s and early 1970s and the change in the program's racial composition. The second goal is to describe the program's founding and its roots in earlier state-level efforts and to provide a gloss on the era of limited controversy in AFDC that came to a close at the beginning of the 1960s. Overall, I will attempt to provide the reader with a sufficient background in the history of AFDC to render my study comprehensible and to make clear the significance of the changes that have occurred since the early 1960s.

AN INCREASING RECIPIENT POPULATION

The most important fact for understanding AFDC is that it has grown in terms of total recipients and that this growth has been enormous and discontinuous. Figure 2.1 presents the basic statistics on the growth of the recipient population of ADC/AFDC from its first year of operation, 1936, to the most recent year for which statistics are available, 1991. The growth of the recipient population was steady between 1936 and 1966, exploded between 1967 and 1972, and has been relatively flat since then. Our first task, then, is to explain this dramatic expansion in the rolls.

Although the increase in the welfare dependent poor has been a central issue in academic circles for years (with a variety of explanations, ranging from the

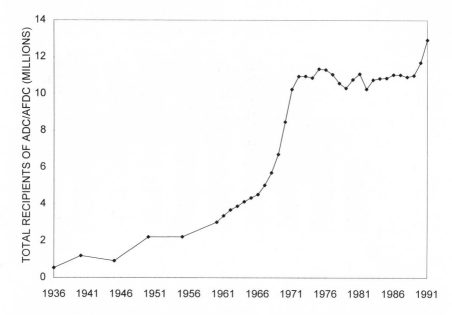

Figure 2.1. Growth in AFDC Rolls, 1936–1991. *Source:* U.S. Bureau of the Census, *Statistical Abstract of the United States* (Washington, D.C.: G.P.O., 1949, 1972, 1993), pp. 246–247, 299, 366, 371.

living arrangements of poor mothers to the state of the American economy), Figure 2.2 suggests that these explanations are incomplete or at least of relatively little import. Using a sophisticated microsimulation statistical model, researchers at the Urban Institute have estimated the total population eligible for AFDC and have calculated from that a participation rate: the number of those eligible for the program who are actually receiving assistance.[1] The researchers discovered that the participation rate for AFDC was 42 percent in 1967, 64 percent in 1970, and its current level, 87 percent, in 1973.[2] Using these estimates of the eligible population, I recalculated what the AFDC population would have been had the 1967 participation rate held steady. Figure 2.2 presents the results and demonstrates in dramatic fashion the degree to which the welfare explosion of the late 1960s and early 1970s was only marginally a factor of such extra-program factors as increases in poverty or single-parent families. If such factors had been the driving force behind the increase in the AFDC rolls, the rate of increase with the participation rate held constant would closely approximate the actual numbers of AFDC recipients. The participation-rate constant estimate increased from 1.138 million in 1967, to 1.344 million in 1970, to 1.445 million in 1973 and 1.819 million in 1983, which would have amounted to an approximately 60 percent increase in the rolls. As it was, the rolls increased by an astounding 299 percent during this period. In the same period, the population of the United States increased 19 percent.

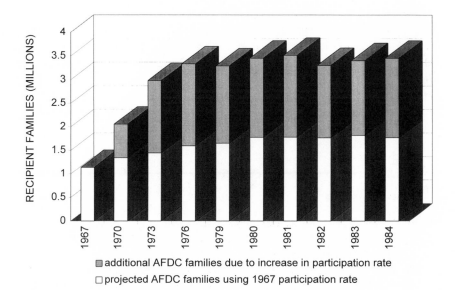

■ additional AFDC families due to increase in participation rate
□ projected AFDC families using 1967 participation rate

Figure 2.2. Effect of Participation Rates on AFDC Caseload, 1967–1984. Recalculations based on data from Patricia Ruggles and Richard Michel, "Participation Rates in the Aid to Families With Dependent Children Program: Trends for 1987 Through 1984," Urban Institute, unpublished manuscript, April 1987.

There are only two logical means by which the participation rate could have increased: Either administrators were becoming more lenient (that is, the supply of AFDC increased) or more single parents in poverty felt that it was worth their time, effort, and humiliation to receive assistance. Robert Moffitt has done a regression analysis of the various factors that may have fed into the rise of the total participation-rate increases (that is, the percentage of all single-parent families receiving assistance) and found that only the increase in the benefit reduction rate (the rate at which increasing earnings cause a reduction in assistance) and the addition of food stamps to the overall benefit package explain a significant percentage of the increase. Even these two factors, however, cannot explain more than one-fifth of the increase. Moffitt concludes that on the matter of whether measurable economic variables can explain the increase in welfare participation,

> the overwhelming answer . . . is that such variables cannot explain the explosion; there was, by implication, a structural shift in the nature of welfare participation in the United States. The major nonquantifiable alternative explanation are two: (1) attitudes toward welfare changed over the period and the stigma of welfare receipt fell; and (2) a series of court and legislative decisions that liberalized eligibility during the period made participation easier.[3]

AFDC increased dramatically during this period, therefore, largely as a result of changes that were not created by the popular branches of government (such as benefit levels, treatment of earned income, and additions to the benefit package) or primarily by larger social changes. Instead, the transformation of the rolls was the result of the behavior of welfare recipients and the organizations and ideological forces that influenced them combined with a change in administrative practices that did not come about by legislative means. This explains a great deal of the increasing unpopularity of AFDC: It was transformed dramatically in its scope and coverage without the instigation or blessing of popular institutions and thus, indirectly, without the agreement of the people.

BENEFIT LEVELS: VARIABILITY ACROSS TIME, STATES, AND PROGRAMS

AFDC has never been a generous program, whether the measure of generosity is a comparison of its level of benefits to other programs serving similar demographic groups or to the basic needs of its recipients. Moreover, the gap between AFDC and programs serving similar population groups has grown markedly over the past forty years, and the real purchasing power of its benefits stagnated and then declined over the past twenty-five. The survey data in Chapter 3 show that support for AFDC has declined dramatically over the past thirty years, and this declining level of support has been reflected, slowly but surely, in the amount of assistance that goes to poor women and their children.

Figure 2.3 presents the basic facts starkly. In 1950, AFDC benefits and those of its closest counterpart, OASDI survivors insurance, were considerably different, with survivors insurance benefits approximately one-quarter more than AFDC. Since 1950, however, the assistance provided to those under the survivors insurance program has grown dramatically, increasing two and one-half times in real terms. Change in AFDC benefit levels, compared to that seen in survivors insurance, has been almost nonexistent, with the exception of a small increase in the late 1960s and a slightly larger downswing since 1980. With the exception of the 1980s, survivors insurance has not only kept up with inflation, it has regularly surpassed it. AFDC benefits, however, have been consistently eaten away by inflation since 1980. Given that AFDC benefits are not indexed for inflation, this slow whittling away of the purchasing power of its assistance is a clear sign of its political weakness; this attack on AFDC is the easiest possible: Simply do nothing.

Benefits for AFDC recipients have gone down at the same time as the number of those needing such assistance has gone up. For example, in 1970, 10 percent of families with children at home were headed by a woman; by 1992, the percentage had climbed to 22 percent.[4a] In 1970, 14.9 percent of all children were in families below the poverty line; in 1991, 21.1 percent were living in poverty.[4b]

What accounts for the disparity between the AFDC and survivors insurance benefits? The difference lies in the nature of the two populations served by these

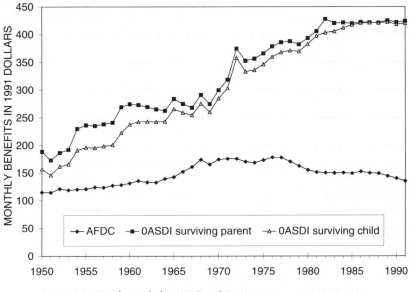

Figure 2.3. Benefit Levels for AFDC and Survivors Insurance, 1950–1991.

programs. The women receiving survivors insurance are in need of aid because of the death of a spouse. Popular judgment rarely weighs heavily on someone left to bring up a child alone because of the death of her husband. But many may grumble about women who bear children with men who desert them or refuse to marry them. Death is random and unpredictable; the victims are thus blameless. Giving birth to a child outside of marriage is (at least to some degree) considered an intentional act on the part of the woman, the result of her free will choice. Although the children in both populations are living in a single-parent, female-headed household, there is a fundamental difference in the mother's role in the circumstances leading to that fact, and this difference is significant to those who control benefit levels.

The second important reason for the differential is simple: Survivors insurance is considered just that—insurance. The matter of desert is barely even a question, since on some level it is thought that the benefit checks represent the recipient's own money, held in trust by the government and then returned at a later date. Although this belief is not precisely valid, there is enough truth to it that survivors insurance, like the rest of OASDI, has been rendered politically sacrosanct. AFDC, however, involves redistributing money not across time (horizontal) but across classes (vertical). Almost everyone will receive some form of Social Security in their lifetime, but only 25 percent of the population are likely to receive welfare, of which a smaller percentage will be enrolled in AFDC.[4c] Most

Americans are not on AFDC, and they never will be. Therefore, AFDC appears to them to be a matter of giving their money to someone else, with the consequence that the character of those getting the money, what they do with it, and what is expected of them in exchange for getting it are all highly salient issues that do not pertain to any of the purely federal income security programs.

Although AFDC benefits have not varied dramatically over time, they have consistently varied across space, that is, between the various states. In only fifteen of the fifty states do combined AFDC and food stamp benefits amount to more than 80 percent of the poverty line.[5] (All of those states are either on the West Coast, near the Great Lakes, in the northeast, or outside the contiguous 48 states.) In eight states, the welfare package is between 40 and 59 percent of the poverty line. When AFDC is taken alone, the differences are even more stark. Alabama's benefit levels amount to only 14 percent of the poverty line, whereas California's are 84 percent.[6] Depending upon the size of the family, the differences between the maximum AFDC payment in the highest benefit and lowest benefit states are as much as eightfold. Only seventeen states pay 100 percent of need standards they set for themselves.

THE RACIAL COMPOSITION OF THE AFDC ROLLS

One explanation for the decreasing popularity of AFDC is the racial composition of the program. Although a number of studies focus on the relative poverty rates of blacks and whites,[7] few if any discuss the actual racial composition of the AFDC rolls. As we shall see, the statistics on poverty and welfare receipt have substantially different trajectories.

As Figure 2.4 shows, in 1937, just two years after the passage of the Social Security Act, whites accounted for 85 percent of the AFDC rolls while blacks accounted for 13 percent.[8] These rates remained stable for the next few years but then began to converge dramatically to the point that by 1961 the number of black and white children on the AFDC rolls was nearly the same. The shift in the racial composition of the AFDC rolls occurred before the Great Society, before the Civil Rights Act of 1964, and before the creation of the Office of Economic Opportunity.

The differential change in the poverty rates between white and black certainly played a part in this shift, but white poverty was not going down and black poverty was not going up fast enough to account for this change. Changes in the differential illegitimacy rates of blacks and whites cannot account for this difference either: Between 1940 and 1960, the illegitimacy rate among whites went from 3.6 births per thousand to 9.2 per thousand, while the rate for blacks went from 35.6 per thousand to 98.3 per thousand.[9] The increase in the number of households by race is roughly equal during this period as well.[10] Given the limited change in other potential causes, a change this dramatic could only be accounted for by a structural shift in the program, that is, a change in the basic assumptions

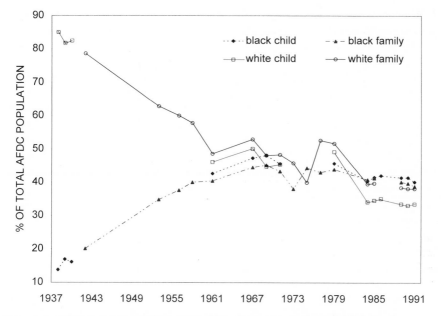

Figure 2.4. AFDC Racial Composition, 1937–1991. *Source:* Family Support Administration, Office of Family Assistance, Division of Program Evaluation, Information and Measurement Branch.

underlying its administration. Clearly, at the genesis of the ADC program, its assistance was intended for and enjoyed by whites overwhelmingly. It was this assumption that changed.

Research conducted by Richard Sterner for Gunnar Myrdal's *American Dilemma* provides evidence that at least in a number of southern states, the lower number of blacks who received ADC was clearly due to discrimination. In North Carolina in 1935, for example, there were 7,426 black families eligible for ADC and 7,914 eligible white families; but for a number of reasons the black eligible population was probably higher. Despite the equal or greater eligible black population, blacks accounted for only 25 percent of the ADC acceptances in that year.[11] The figures for Georgia were even more dramatic: 23,974 white children versus 29,100 black children were eligible for ADC. Despite the black overrepresentation in the eligible population, only 439 black children received assistance in contrast to 3,458 white children, for a 1.5 percent black against a 14.4 percent white participation rate.[12]

Like the shift in the AFDC participation rate in the 1960s, something dramatic occurred to the racial composition of AFDC that cannot be accounted for by factors outside of the program in larger social trends. Blacks who in 1938 would have been denied assistance were getting it, somehow, in 1961. It is remarkable that this shift occurred years before the changes in the participation rate.

How did blacks get on the rolls at an increasing rate before they attained wide-spread political power or the legal support of the Supreme Court and the Civil Rights Acts? The best explanation may be that the change occurred as a result of blacks moving from more to less discriminatory jurisdictions. Between 1940 and 1960, the black population of the South increased from 9.9 million to 11.3 million, while the black population in the Northeast went from 1.1 million to 3 million, in the North Central from 1.4 million to 3.4 million, and in the West from 171,000 to slightly over a million.[13] These black migration rates were all far in excess of those for whites. Furthermore, blacks were moving in large numbers to urban areas.[14] Since the change in ADC occurred simultaneously with the great black migration to northern cities, this shift in population probably accounts for much of the increase in the number of blacks on the welfare rolls.

AFDC: A PRE-HISTORY

Can one accurately say when the modern system of welfare was founded? At the very least, the creation of the Aid to Dependent Children program in 1935 would probably not qualify as the founding moment. "Welfare" was not created in 1935—cash aid to the poor in the United States preceded the Social Security Act by at least twenty years in a form recognizable to us today—and was present in other forms during the early years of the republic. The modern era is the focus of our discussion, however, and as such our story begins with the creation of what were then called mothers' pension programs.

The state programs that were supplanted by Aid to Dependent Children in 1935 were called mothers', or widows', pensions. The crucial fact is that ADC was not simply a creation of the Great Depression or the New Deal. The programs for which it established federal funding were in existence decades before the creation of the Social Security Act and came into being as a result of a significantly differ-ent political dynamic than that which led to retirement insurance or unemployment compensation. Furthermore, these programs were based on a conception of public provision that seems, at this time, simultaneously progressive and highly conservative. I will examine two aspects of the program that are particularly crucial to an understanding of later developments: first, the moral basis of the program and, second, the overall design of the program, in order to determine precisely what changed when a federal financial role was established in 1935.

Before 1911, no state in the nation had a mothers' pension program. By 1934, every state in the nation, with the exception of South Carolina and Georgia, had such a program, with the overwhelming number of states creating one before 1920.[15] States set up these programs without financial assistance from the federal government, and yet the rapidity with which they were established is remarkable. How did it happen?

It did not happen spontaneously, and it did not occur without the involvement of the federal government or organizations with national scope. The federal government was involved through the personal support of President Theodore Roosevelt and his sponsorship of the Conference on the Care of Dependent Children, held in Washington, D.C., in January 1909. The conference was graced with a national distribution of attendees, including such historic figures as Jane Addams, Theodore Dreiser, and Booker T. Washington and most of the important figures in public and private charity in the United States. Roosevelt set the tone of the conference, which was echoed, virtually without dissent, by every other participant:

> There are half a dozen different types of children for whom we need to care. There is first of all the complete orphan, the child who has lost both mother and father. For this child we wish to make permanent provision. My own belief is that the best kind of permanent provision, if feasible, is to place that child in a home. We then meet the case—one of the most distressing of cases—where the father has died, where the breadwinner has gone, where the mother would like to keep the child, but simply lacks the earning capacity. Surely in such a case the goal toward which we should strive is to help that mother, so that she can keep her own home and keep the child in it; that is the best thing possible to be done for that child. How the relief shall come, public, private, or by a mixture of both, in what way, you are competent to say and I am not.[16]

In the decades preceding the conference, what can only be called a revolution in the relationship of the state to parents and children had occurred. Of greatest importance was the establishment of the principle that children had interests above and apart from their parents and particularly their fathers. This principle began to emerge first in state courts, where the principle of father right (wherein children were conceived as the property of the father) was supplanted in custody cases by that of the best interests of the child, and a preference for the mother as custodian. The earliest application of this principle that I have encountered is the 1813 case of *Commonwealth v. Addicks,* in which the Pennsylvania State Court found that children's interests should be considered paramount in deciding which parent should be granted custody. "It is to them, that our anxiety is principally directed," the court argued, finding that the children's interests were intimately connected to "the kind of assistance which can be afforded by none so well as a mother."[17] In all the cases that overturned the British tradition of father right, it should be noted, the primacy of the mother was a subsidiary principle to the independent rights of the child.

By the turn of the century, however, the practice of child protection had turned decisively against placing children with their mother or, in fact, in any family whatsoever. For example, the New York Society for the Prevention of Cruelty to Children, the first organization of its kind in the United States, and one that was given broad police powers by the state, had placed 2,413 children by

1900, only six of whom were put in private homes.[18] Although many of these children were taken out of their homes because they were victims of battery or other acts of violence, many were removed because of the financial circumstances of their widowed mother.

By 1909, the number of children placed in institutions had grown to staggering levels and had become a matter of acute public concern. The image of a child taken out of the arms of its mother and put in an orphanage, where it faced the grave danger of becoming delinquent and a burden on society, for no other reason than the financial incapacity of the mother, had become a powerful symbol in America. Virtually every participant in the 1909 conference made reference to this symbol, which supported its first, and highly instructive, recommendation.

> Children of parents of worthy character, suffering from temporary misfortune and children of reasonably efficient and deserving mothers who are without support of the normal breadwinner, should, as a rule, be kept with their parents, such aid being given as may be necessary to maintain suitable homes for the rearing of the children. This aid should be given by such methods and from such sources as may be determined by the general relief policy of each community, preferably in the form of private charity, rather than of public relief. Except in unusual circumstances, the home should not be broken up for reasons of poverty, but only for considerations of inefficiency or immorality.[19]

This passage is revealing because it suggests, in concise form, the general justification for mothers' pension. First and foremost, aid was defended as an alternative to placement out of the home, driven by the conferees' belief in the superiority of a home supervised by the mother of the children against institutional care. The attendees had seen the results of such care and sought to avoid them by making the conservation of the family after the loss of a husband economically feasible. The conference attendees, however, did not wish to provide aid indiscriminately to all mothers upon the loss of the husband. Institutional or foster care was still an option, which would be available if the mother did not meet the standard of providing a "suitable home." (This standard would be carried over to most state programs under ADC and would be the center of controversy when the Supreme Court became involved in the program in the 1960s, as we shall see in Chapter 6.)

While the conference provided presidential support, a base of professional acclamation, and a strong intellectual justification for mothers' pension, the political drive behind the creation of state programs came from a number of national organizations of women, with the cooperation and occasional intervention of family court judges. Theda Skocpol discovered that the first mothers' pensions were intrastate affairs: that is, one part of the state, in this case judges, petitioned another part of the state for the authority to grant pensions rather than commit minors to institutions.[20] The early involvement of the courts had a substantial institutional impact on the structure of mothers' pension programs; in many cases, it was the court, rather than an executive agency, that had the authority to approve mothers' pension payments.

Quite rapidly, however, the mothers' pension movement became more than an intrastate affair and began to involve a new kind of interest group in American society; organizations of women organized around their status as mothers. Skocpol found that the most crucial event in this early history was when "a number of prominent social settlement women, including Mary Simkhovitch, Lillian Wald, Jane Addams, Florence Kelly, Julia Lathrop, and Edith and Grace Abbott, broke ranks with most charity people and social insurance advocates to give early support to mothers' pensions."[21] These women, who had seen firsthand the difficult task of raising children in institutions, provided intellectual and organizational expertise to the wide-ranging coalition of mothers groups who embraced mothers' pensions as part of their agenda. These organizations, including the two-million-strong General Federation of Women's Clubs and the National Congress of Mothers, had previously concentrated their efforts on child and maternal health and education programs, protective labor statutes, and the establishment of the Children's Bureau. Mothers' pensions were both in keeping with these organizations' previous activities (because they promised to keep families together) and something of a departure (because they involved the delivery of cash, as opposed to the regulatory and service programs they had previously sought).

The coalition that the mothers' movement was able to pull together is, to this day, quite remarkable. In addition to the mothers' organizations, the coalition included "juvenile court justices, notable politicians such as Roosevelt and [Robert] La Follette, local labor unions, and mass circulation magazines such as the *New York Evening World,* the *Nation,* and especially the *Delineator,*"[22] as well as the American Federation of Labor (AFL), which endorsed mothers' pensions in 1911.[23] Mark Leff argues that although the organizational strength of the movement was important, it was the societal consensus it represented that was the truly effectual factor: "No individual or group of individuals was vital to it. The consensus that it created depended largely on the ease with which it meshed with developing American attitudes. By adopting the name, 'widows pensions,' it even exploited the public support given to pensions for families of war veterans."[24] The important point in Leff's analysis is that the consensus for mothers' pensions was created rather than preexistent. The values that supported it did exist before the organizational and intellectual work was done by reformers and mothers' groups, but it was their work that gave that latent consensus policy content. As we shall see in Chapter 5, it was the failure of later advocates for the poor to put the public's values together in a consensual way that caused much of the conflict that came to characterize welfare politics.

Arrayed on the other side were private charitable organizations that were opposed to mothers' pensions because they would introduce wasteful and corrupt bureaucracies into an area where "scientific" private charity was already doing an acceptable job. These organizations were quite unsuccessful in restraining the movement for mothers' pensions, however, as a result of their lack of any broad-based popular support. By 1913, nineteen states had passed mothers' pension programs, and by the Great Crash of 1929, all but four (New Mexico, Alabama, Georgia, and South Carolina) had created some type of program to give cash assistance to widows.[25]

The first mothers' pension programs were enacted in a rush of enthusiasm, which was not to last. The task of ensuring that the programs as actually financed and administered matched the framer's ideas was much more daunting than the movement to simply get legislation passed. Three challenges were apparent early on, and they remain fixtures in welfare politics: the amount of the grant, the breadth of coverage, and the tone of administrative behavior. The first two elements are politically highly connected. As with any government program, funds for mothers' aid were limited, and there were only two ways to keep the cost of the program down: Reduce the money given to each recipient or shrink the recipient pool. In various combinations, both strategies were used by most states. Skocpol notes that concerning the adequacy of mothers' aid grants, "funding never came anywhere close to meeting the needs of eligible persons or actual recipients—even at statutorily defined levels, which were themselves pitifully inadequate to the real needs of families."[26] As of 1931, only two states, Massachusetts and New York, provided monthly amounts of more than $40, and in a number of southern states benefit levels were below $15.[27] On the matter of breadth of coverage, the story was similar: Only nine states aided more than 15 families per 10,000 as of 1931, with a similar geographic inequality as beset grant levels. States restricted access to the program through a number of processes, the most common of which were asset limits and morality tests. Christopher Howard notes that "in Massachusetts, one of the more generous states, a single mother was ineligible if she possessed more than $200 in liquid assets, more than $500 in home equity, or any other property worth more than $500. Nor was she eligible if the assessed value of her home were greater than $2500."[28]

The second strategy for restricting access to the rolls was also connected to the final challenge of mothers' aid implementation: the moral tone of the program. A certain amount of discretion was built into mothers' aid programs at their conception through the agency of the "friendly visitor." However, the friendly visitors were conceived by the early mothers' aid advocates less as administrators who would sort the worthy from the unworthy and more as " 'an advisor and friend' who would supervise and [make] suggest[ions] . . . to the lonely mother."[29] The friendly visitors would serve as an extension of the other purposes of the mothers' movement, providing recipients with parenting and nutrition advice, as well as softer services such as solace in hard times. These visitors were, however, soon transformed into agents who determined eligibility and who removed women from the rolls who could be defined as "unworthy" of assistance. As the old enemies of mothers' pensions, scientific social workers, gained a foothold in the administration of those programs, " 'scientific charity,' the guiding principle of private charities, soon became the guiding principle of the first American case-workers. With it came distinctions between the worthy and unworthy and an emphasis on moral uplift."[30] Although neither the scientific social workers nor the original proponents of mothers' aid supported anything like what we would now call an entitlement conception of public assistance, there were differences in their idea of the moral role of the program. The mothers' aid movement was based upon the idea of the solidarity and similarity of all mothers and was more likely to attribute parenting problems to a lack of information and education and less to a bad character in need of reforming. Scientific social workers had no such solidaristic idea and were deeply committed to the idea of separating and categorizing the poor. The former idea leads to more capacious eligibility standards, since it would be easier to provide education once a friendly visitor had access to a mother, while the latter leads to strict eligibility standards, since it is important to keep the worthy from bleeding into the category of the unworthy. The capture of the administration of the program by social workers ensured that the latter, strict, idea of eligibility won out.

MOTHERS' AID NATIONALIZED: THE CREATION OF THE AFDC PROGRAM

It was the establishment of mothers' aid programs, rather than the creation of the Aid to Dependent Children program as part of the Social Security Act, that was the real founding of modern welfare.[31] The moral content, the administrative structure, and the basic contours of conflict and consensus were established in the decades before the Act was passed, and although the Act did have a number of significant consequences for the administration of aid to unmarried women, those developments are generally less profound than those that came before. The transition from mothers' aid to Aid to Dependent Children was a smooth one, much less significant in its implications than it might have been.

Aid to Dependent Children was created as a small part of the much larger structure of public assistance established by the 1935 Social Security Act. The Act created two separate old-age programs—the first, a system of grants to the states for their current programs, the second providing for regular contributions during the years of productive work and retirement benefits related to prior contribution. The Act also established grants to states for unemployment compensation, for maternal and child welfare services, for public health services, and finally for grants to states for aid to dependent children.

The Social Security Act states that funds are provided for grants to aid dependent children, "for the purpose of enabling each State to furnish financial assistance, as far as practicable under the conditions in each State, to needy dependent children."[32] The Act places few regulations on the states and, with a few exceptions, it does not touch the bedrock of the financial or control functions of the states.[33]

The main exceptions to this rule, as stated in the Act, were the requirement of a fair hearing when aid was denied and the prohibition of residence requirements longer than one year. Insofar as control is concerned, the hearing requirement has the possibility of transforming the relation of welfare officer to client, changing what may previously have been an informal and nonrebuttable relation to a formal and challengeable one. To some degree the demand of a hearing has the possibility of breaking down the authority of the state. An even stronger encroachment on state authority is present in the residence requirement. If an essential element of political sovereignty is the ability to determine who is a member of the state (and thus eligible for its largesse) and who is not, the Act demands that anyone otherwise eligible who has resided in the state for more than a year is a member. Thus, although it may be said that the Act envisions a decentralized system of support, it cannot be said that the essential control function is completely given over to the states; even in the beginning, the federal government was reducing the scope of state autonomy.

These restrictions, of course, paled in significance to the wide latitude granted to the states in regard to the control function of AFDC. Although the language of the Act is somewhat ambiguous about coverage in the eligible population being tantamount to a claim of statutory entitlement, the accompanying congressional reports leave little doubt that broad freedom was granted to the states. The language of both the House and Senate reports was similar. Both reports repeatedly declared that a state could "impose such other eligibility requirements—as to means, moral character, etc.—as it sees fit."[34]

The issue of the devolution of the control function to the states is not cut and dried, however. The report of the Advisory Council to the Committee on Economic Security (CES) stated that

> it is very important to retain the gains which have been made in the administration of public assistance in the last few years. . . . These gains cannot be made permanent without the revision of the so-called "poor laws" in most of the States. It is rarely that such an opportunity comes to change a whole group of antiquated and sometimes inhuman laws.[35]

The CES's final report did not explicitly discuss morality tests. However, the report clearly suggested that reforms in state administration of mothers' aid programs would lead to a more "humane" environment for aid recipients. It indicated that three administrative reforms (all of which made it into the bill) would have this effect: unitary state control of ADC (referred to as the "single state agency" requirement); the establishment of this agency (which did not have to handle only ADC) on a permanent basis; and an "administratively as well as financially" unified program. Finally, it made the crucial observation that in the case of "most of the children on relief lists . . . nothing is wrong with their environment but their parents' lack of money to give them opportunities which are taken for granted in more fortunate homes."[36]

One reasonable interpretation of this statement is that although the committee understood that states would impose morality tests and that politically there was little it could do at the time to forbid them, raising the administrative level upward (away from the localities) would make such tests less likely and the standards of administration more uniform and less punitive. This interpretation fits into Joel Handler's finding of a correlation between degree of localism and the punitive nature of social interventions.

> The control of deviant behavior is primarily a local matter. Juries, prosecutors, police—the guts of criminal law enforcement—are local. The moral issues, the dilemmas, the fears, the hatreds, the passions and compassion that arise out of close contact with deviant behavior are most keenly felt at the local level. Welfare has always involved great moral issues—work, moral redemption, pauperism, vice, crime, delinquency, sex, and race. The anger and hostility among classes and categories is most keenly felt among those who are the closest in proximity. As a general rule, the more deviant the government program, the social category, the more local the program.[37]

The Act can be read as an attempt at a jurisdictional solution to the punitive practices of local mothers' aid programs. This way of looking at the Act (often overlooked by those boggled by how a program seen originally as simply a way to funnel money to needy state programs could become largely nationalized) should change our way of seeing later events. The process of moving the locus of authority toward the federal government was inherent in the Act, first by the requirement of a state agency and then by making that state agency answerable to the federal bureaucracy. The future development of the program can be seen as movement on a trajectory that, far from perverting the intentions of its founders, extends their logic.

The most we can say about the contemporary understanding of the AFDC program was that in regard to its control function, it often pushed in opposite directions. Although the Act forbade certain means of controlling AFDC clients (in particular giving aid-in-kind rather than in cash), it left ambiguous all other possible means. Indeed, the same Congress that passed the act later contradicted its own provisions. The Senate report, for example, states that "this program does not represent an attempt to dictate to the States how they shall care for families of this character, but is recognition of the fact that many States need aid to carry out the policy which they have already adopted."[38] Of course, those congressmen had to know that they were changing the way that states would organize their mothers' aid programs. If they did not seek such a change or oversight, the provisions for federal approval of state plans would have been without purpose.

Echoing the understanding of the Act expressed by the Advisory Committee on Economic Security, the Social Security Board would express an even more activist understanding:

> In some places it has been the traditional practice to give mother's aid only to selected applicants and to leave to the overseer of the poor or other local official the families in which serious social problems existed. Modern practice in the State[s] recognizes that the major consideration must be the welfare of the children rather than the conduct of the parents and that the existence of social problems in a family group usually indicates the need for more intensive service rather than for curtailment of aid.[39]

The board encouraged states to remove laws specifically related to the conduct or morals of the parent and, taking their cue from substitute provisions suggested by the American Public Welfare Association, replace them with the less obviously punitive standard of "a suitable family home meeting the standards of care and health."[40] These standards, of course, existed in a measure of contradiction with the Senate report's own understanding that "through cash grants adjusted to the needs of the family it is possible to keep the young children with their mother in their own home, thus preventing the necessity of placing the children in institutions. This is recognized by everyone to be the least expensive and altogether the most desirable method for meeting the needs of these families that has yet been devised."[41] The tension between these two elements—caring for the child in its own home, on the one hand, and the desire for "suitable home" provisions, on the other—provided much of the subject matter for the welfare controversies of the late 1960s. It is sufficient at this point to observe that the Act and its supporting interpretations can buttress either a narrow or broad use of control standards. Those seeking authoritative guidance on the intent of the framers of the Act are likely to be disappointed.

THE ERA OF NORMALCY: ADC FROM 1939 TO 1962

The years between the founding of the Aid to Dependent Children program in 1935 and the beginning of what I call the "modern era" in 1962 are bracketed by two important changes in the program. The two changes, the creation of the survivors insurance program in 1939 and the 1962 amendments to the Social Security Act, mark the beginning and the end of a period in which ADC was, for the most part, politically invisible. In fact, one of the most important histories of welfare in America, Michael Katz's *In the Shadow of the Poorhouse,* moves directly from the passage of the Social Security Act in the 1930s to the planning for the War on Poverty in the 1960s. Much of the important activity in this period was administrative, operating below the observation of all but the most interested participants, with little impact on the national political scene. It was this invisibility that made the political emergence of the program in the mid-1960s so dramatic and which left the political system so bereft of knowledge—and thus reliant on ideology—when it was forced to deal with the issue.

Only four years after the passage of the Social Security Act, Congress revisited its handiwork and found it to be in need of some fine-tuning. In the case of aid to indigent mothers and their children, however, the implications of the 1939 amendments were more substantial than for other categories of recipients. The 1939 amendments are the key marking-off point between the era of mothers' aid and modern welfare, in that they established decisively that the old practice of dividing the worthy and the unworthy would remain. This decision meant higher benefits and better treatment for some (in this case, widows) and lower benefits and more punitive treatment for others (mothers of illegitimate children).

This pattern, it must be noted, occurred not because of any change in the ADC program but as the result of the creation of an entirely new program: survivors insurance. The original Social Security Act did not, except for a small lump-sum payment upon the death of a husband, provide any insurance support for single mothers and their children. This group was supported under the ADC provisions in the Act; decisions as to whom to support within the class of single mothers were left to the states.

The 1939 amendments extended Old Age Insurance to the wives and children of deceased workers qualified for retirement benefits, as well as to those below retirement age who met certain qualifications. This change meant that a large group of those eligible for ADC, a relief program, were now covered by an insurance program. Whereas before the 1939 amendments, widows were primarily the subject of state discretion, now they were the subject of federal authority. The Advisory Council on Social Security, in its report recommending the changes that became the 1939 amendments, expressed clearly the normative understanding that informed this change: "While public assistance is now being provided to a large number of dependent children in this country on a needs-test basis, the arguments for substituting benefits as a matter of right in the case of children are even more convincing than in the case of aged persons."[42] The distinction suggested here, between state and federal, and thus between welfare and insurance, is at the center of the American welfare state. Linda Gordon finds that "the federal programs have higher standards, more generous stipends, a bigger tax base to support them—and dignity. State programs are far more vulnerable to political attacks, declining tax bases and interstate competition."[43]

The 1939 amendments meant that widows had, for the most part, escaped from relief. Although this was good for them (as Figure 2.3 shows), it was unfortunate for those who remained under the coverage of ADC. It is important to remember that mothers' aid, the precursor to ADC, was alternatively called widows' insurance, and it was the plight of the widow that caused the greatest public sympathy. Without the image of the destitute widow, unable to care for her child because of the unexpected death of her husband, there was no political symbol that could successfully connect the concerns of mainstream America with those in need. A dead father could elicit sympathy. But what about an absent father? ADC was politically viable at its creation because it helped all single mothers by connecting their plight to that of widows. With the widows gone, the program was left in a politically precarious condition.

Although the 1939 amendments may have hurt the ADC program in the long run, its short-term effect was to put the program on a more stable financial footing. The most important modification was made to the federal share of ADC benefits, which was increased from 33 percent to 50 percent, up to a maximum of $9 per child per month. There was pressure for an even more generous federal share of public assistance costs, as indicated by the introduction by Texas senator Tom Connally of an amendment to share two-thirds of the program's costs up to $15 and one-half of the benefits up to $40. Although the amendment was not successful, it does suggest that the pressure for change in the program was in the direction of greater generosity, a factor that might be accounted for by ADC's consideration as part of "public assistance" rather than as a category unto itself.

The story from 1939 until the passage of the 1962 Social Security amendments is a very slow and, with a few exceptions, a quite boring one. Most of the changes made during this period were adjustments to the federal matching formula, which are summarized in Table 2.1.[44] Although the changes are not particularly relevant to the moral foundation of the ADC program, they do suggest a few interesting points. First, support for the program was fairly strong, as evidenced by the consistent maintenance of benefit purchasing power during this period. Second, the federal government took increasingly greater responsibility for the financial support of ADC mothers, a factor that may reflect federal support for the states more than compassion for dependent children. Finally, by changing the match from a fixed 50 percent to an initial higher match and a lower one for more generous benefits, Congress made a decision that protected the federal treasury but created something of a disincentive for higher benefit levels. Henceforth,

Table 2.1. Trends in ADC Federal Match, 1946–1958

Year	Initial Match	Match for First Child for Remaining Amount	Match for Second Child
1946	2/3 of first $9	1/2 up to $24	1/2 up to $15
1948	3/4 of first $12	1/2 up to $27	1/2 up to $18
1952	4/5 of first $15	1/2 up to $30	1/2 up to $21
1956[a]	14/17 of first $17	1/2 up to $32	1/2 up to $23
1958[b]	Same as 1956		

[a]Added 1/2 up to $32 for one needy adult.
[b]Variable matching established, whereby the overall federal match could not be more than 65 percent or less than 50 percent.
Source: U.S. Department of Health and Human Services, Administration for Children and Families, *Overview of the AFDC Program: FY 1992,* "Summary of the Legislative History."

states with the highest benefit levels would be saddled with the highest costs in the ADC program, while those with relatively ungenerous benefits would have a much higher percentage of their costs picked up by the federal government. This unequal treatment has been the source of high-benefit state complaints ever since.

In relation to other changes to the program, the story is even thinner. Almost all of the legislative action was concerned with amplifying provisions present in the 1935 Act. In 1950, Congress forbade ADC for any recipients of Old Age Assistance;[45] in 1951, it extended the fair hearing provision to include those whose claim was not processed with "reasonable promptness";[46] and in 1952 it tightened somewhat the one-year maximum on state residence requirements.[47] In other words, this period was one of quite minimal congressional involvement in the issue.

EARLY SIGNS OF THE VOLATILITY OF WELFARE POLITICS

Despite the overall lack of interest in ADC during this period, there were signs that all was not well with the program and that its popular support was far from solid. James Patterson observes that the overall spirit of the program was becoming punitive almost from the start, leading to conflict with the program's administrators in Washington.

> Many states denied aid to families with "employable mothers," dawdled in processing applications, established lengthy residence requirements (usually a year or more), and intimidated prospective applicants—sometimes by stationing police outside relief offices. Irritated officials in the Bureau of Public Assistance issued endless regulations to force states to comply with federal guidelines: by the 1960s its Handbook of Public Assistance Administration was more than five inches thick. But this effort resulted mainly in heaps of paperwork for case workers.[48]

Two cases in particular, although not characteristic of the politics of the nation as a whole, illustrate the nature of the conflicts during this period. In Louisiana, 23,489 children on AFDC were declared ineligible because they were deemed to be living in "unsuitable homes." Not coincidentally, 95 percent of those removed were black.[49] The second case occurred in New York State in 1961. The city of Newburgh "promulgated a thirteen-point code of welfare regulations that included in one package many of the devices being used across the country to control the size of the welfare rolls and to reduce welfare expenditures."[50] Both jurisdictions were, for the most part, forced to backtrack on these policies, but these two cases demonstrate that the unexpected rise in the rolls was beginning to have political consequences.

In response to these cases and others across the country, Arthur S. Flemming, the secretary of Health, Education and Welfare (HEW) put forward the

"Flemming rule," which stated that state conditions on AFDC could be rejected by HEW when they "imposed a condition of eligibility that bears no just relationship to the Aid for Dependent Children program."[51] Flemming's rule was not novel. The department had already been using a standard called "Condition X," which was an informal rule of thumb that embodied the substance of the Flemming rule. In 1954 the Federal Security Agency (the predecessor to HEW) "refused to fund an Arizona welfare program excluding reservation Indians from coverage."[52] The justification for the rejection was not that it was discriminatory, but that it was arbitrary in light of the purposes of the Act.[53]

The promulgation of the Flemming rule, along with Condition X, signaled that a new federal-state relationship was evolving: Instead of "approving any plan which fulfills the conditions specified in subsection (a)" of the Social Security Act, the federal government was now judging state plans in light of how they furthered the "larger" purposes of the Act. This standard began to be used simultaneously with, and was supported by, the passage of the 1961 and 1962 Social Security amendments. The nation was embarking on a new era in the politics of welfare.

THE 1962 AMENDMENTS: A FAILED EFFORT TO STEM THE TIDE

In announcing changes in AFDC in 1962, President John F. Kennedy directly addressed the punitive approach taken by states like Louisiana. Kennedy laid the groundwork for the approach that would dominate AFDC for the next twenty years: Cash without punishment and supplemental services that, it was hoped, would lead to independence.

> Today, in a year of relative prosperity and high employment, we are more concerned about the poverty which persists in the midst of abundance. . . . Communities which have—for whatever motives—attempted to save money through ruthless and arbitrary cutbacks in the welfare rolls have found their efforts to little avail. The root problems remained. But communities which have tried the rehabilitative road—the road I have recommended today— have demonstrated what can be done with creative, thoughtfully conceived and properly managed programs of prevention and social rehabilitation.[54]

Kennedy proposed programs for locating deserting parents, reducing fraud, permitting those on the rolls to save money without affecting their grant, increasing services, and improving training of personnel. The last two provisions were probably the most important, since they aimed to change the character of the program, moving it in a more therapeutic direction.

It should be recognized that these changes were based on a dramatic shift in the expectations of the program. Whereas the purpose of the program prior to the act was to permit women who had been widowed or deserted to stay at home with their children (and thus dependency was not a primary concern—if anything it was expected), the new approach saw the fact that a family was on the rolls as a result of social dysfunction. This new approach was signaled by Kennedy's statement that "we must find ways of returning far more of our dependent people to independence. We must find ways of returning them to a participating and productive role in the community."[55] Unlike the original ADC program, which sought to prevent women from having to enter the workforce, the new program emphasized a new set of values.

This change had two aspects, which led in somewhat opposite directions. The first, having to do with reducing the stigma of welfare, led to fewer conditions on the receipt of welfare, such as man-in-the-house rules, and provided the foundation for the Supreme Court decisions we will look at shortly. The second aspect, concerning the desire to reduce dependency, led in the opposite direction: toward more conditions, such as training programs and mandatory work, instead of restrictions on the basis of sexual practices or residency. Again, AFDC was characterized by expectations that led in opposite directions.

The most lasting reform in AFDC created by the 1962 amendments is embodied in name change, from Aid to Dependent Children to Aid to Families with Dependent Children. Starting in 1962, under very strict conditions, intact families that were poor as a result of the husband's unemployment were made eligible for welfare assistance (at the option of each state). Although the service components of the amendments suggested that work was becoming an important issue in welfare politics, the creation of AFDC-UP (Unemployed Parent) signaled the rise in public concern over illegitimacy. It was thought that providing welfare to broken families while denying it to those that are intact created an incentive for family dissolution. Although AFDC-UP has never accounted for a very large percentage of those on the AFDC rolls (between 1983 and 1991, AFDC-UP recipients were between 6.2 and 8.8 percent of the total rolls), the creation of the program was a sign that AFDC had moved even further from mothers' aid.

The 1962 amendments firmly established the two issues that would tower over AFDC politics to the current day: work and illegitimacy. No one could have anticipated in 1962, however, how soon welfare would become a central issue in American politics. With the report of a rather obscure subcabinet official in the Department of Labor, welfare and family break-up were to burst onto Washington's consciousness and the politics of AFDC would never again be the same.

CONCLUSIONS

From the statistical overview with which this chapter began, a few basic facts are important to keep in mind. First, the dramatic increase in the rolls that precipitated and drove the political conflict that began in the 1960s and continues to the present was largely a function of changes in the AFDC participation rate. That is, although changes in American demographics certainly played an important part in the increased numbers of persons assisted by AFDC, it was the creation of a "structural shift" in the program that may be the most important cause. Second, AFDC benefits have never been large compared to the cash assistance to similar demographic groups, to the poverty line, or to AFDC need standards. Finally, the racial composition of AFDC changed dramatically between the creation of the program and the early 1960s, a change that, when combined with the absorption of many widows into survivors insurance, changed the character of those assisted by the program.

This survey of the history of ADC, from the establishment of mothers' aid to the enactment of the 1962 Social Security amendments, shows that support for single mothers was originally based upon a moral consensus that, by the early 1960s, was beginning to unravel. Mothers' aid was based on a powerful ethical principle: Women who were unable to support their children because of the death of their spouse should be able to care for their children at home. Although this principle was never fully implemented in practice, the existence of this ethical foundation provided mothers' aid, and ADC in its early years, with a consensual moral foundation that gave it a certain degree of political strength.

This moral foundation started to unravel almost as soon as mothers' aid programs became Aid to Dependent Children, largely as a result of the enactment, in 1939, of the survivors insurance program. By supporting widows through a larger program of insurance and leaving those incapable of supporting their children because of desertion or other causes in ADC, the legislation stripped away the moral cover these latter families were given by the presence of widows. By the 1950s, many states were experimenting with various methods to keep women off the rolls, practices that were struggled against, mostly in vain, by administrators in Washington. As Chapter 6 demonstrates, this pattern of discrimination would provide the opportunity for legal activists to bring the Supreme Court into AFDC policy-making.

If there is a larger point that the early history of ADC demonstrates, it is the primacy of ethical and moral issues in the politics of welfare. The success of the early mothers' activists was based upon their ability to link the public's basic moral principles with the needs of the poor and disadvantaged. Mothers' aid was not the creation of radicals; this group of activists took society's basic principles as a given. This very conservatism, ironically, made mothers' activists capable of directing their nation in a more progressive direction. They fused various aspects of the public's mind and the nation's political traditions into a few basic ethical principles and then connected them with a practical policy program. A basic point of my work is the necessity of culturally integrative political thought as a foundation for social policy-making. Although the creators of mothers' aid may not have known much of what we have learned about fighting poverty since the early 1900s, they knew about the necessity of that foundation; that awareness made them more successful welfare reformers than their modern counterparts.

3

The Collapse of One Consensus, the Rise of Another

What support there was for the early mothers' aid programs and Aid to Dependent Children was based on a clear moral ideal: the desirability of keeping women out of the workforce and in their homes caring for their children, as an alternative to placing children in public institutions. This chapter investigates the collapse of that moral ideal and along with it support for AFDC and the rise of a new set of public values.

The new ethical foundation, which emphasizes the obligation of all citizens to work, now claims overwhelming public support. Although the public consistently supports efforts to alleviate poverty, it wants to do so by replacing unlimited cash payments to single mothers with paid work, either in the public or private sector. Support for welfare has declined, but this trend does not indicate that the public has become more conservative on matters of social justice. Rather, the public sees welfare as a flawed weapon in the fight against poverty. In this chapter I demonstrate that there exists a broad public consensus on welfare, one that the nation's institutions have, as yet, failed to establish as public policy.

PUBLIC OPINION AS A PROBLEMATIC CONCEPT

American politics is suffused with public opinion. Polls have become to the business of politics what the stock exchange is to the business of, well, business. It is virtually impossible to witness a debate about a major public issue without learning of the "unprecedented level of support" that the public gives to a particular position. Welfare is no exception.

Despite the rise in the use of polls in public debate, the normative status of public opinion remains problematic. In *Federalist* No. 10, James Madison wrote that the advantage of a representative system was that it would "refine and en-large the public views by passing them through the medium of a chosen body of citizens, whose wisdom may best discern the true interest of their country and whose patriotism and love of justice will be least likely to sacrifice it to temporary or partial considerations."[1] For Madison, although public views were relevant, and indeed the starting point for deliberation, they were not conclusive. The people as a whole could be wracked by temporary enthusiasms, irrational preju-dices, or fleeting romances with eloquent orators. Public opinion was important for Madison, but he made a distinction between temporary enthusiasms and in-formed, persistent preferences, and he was confident that even a normatively de-fensible public opinion could be in need of "refining."[2]

One need not look far for examples of public opinion in need of refining, not to mention enlarging. The public wants a balanced budget but is unwilling to accept more than marginal changes in entitlement programs. Americans want health care reform that will reduce costs and ensure security but without wide-spread institutional change. They are against "regulation" but in favor of almost all areas in which it is used, such as environmental protection and workplace safety. These are issues with substantial informational content and slim cultural resonance. The public's views, therefore, should be of relatively less significance in these areas than in welfare, where information is less important than basic so-cial principles in shaping program content.

On many issues, it is hard to argue that the public has an opinion, if by that we mean a stable, coherent position. It is widely accepted that on many issues people's responses fluctuate within the context of a single interview, that most people do not have sufficient information to powerfully anchor their beliefs on specific issues, and that their responses are highly sensitive to the way questions are worded.[3] Rejecting most of this tradition is Benjamin Page and Robert Shapiro's impressive *The Rational Public,* in which they argue that the "incoher-ent public" tradition was a remnant of a particularly politically uninspiring time in American history and that "for the most part, the public reacts consistently, in similar ways to similar stimuli."[4] If the public is not well informed about particu-lar issues, it is a function of a failure of formal political education, elite manipu-lation, or the lack of easily accessible information.[5]

Both of these traditions have much to commend them, but both generally overreach, attributing to the public either too much or too little consistency. Paul Sniderman and Michael Hagen put the issue succinctly: "Under what conditions is a minimalist model useful, and under what conditions is a maximalist one ap-propriate?"[6] For the most part, the minimalist model (low coherence) explains most political issues. However, when issues involve "salient groups" and tap into what Sniderman calls "folk ideology," or what I call political culture, the public's ideas can display high levels of organization. It is my argument that although opinions on welfare recipients may or may not be strong, welfare taps directly into the most important and vibrant parts of American political culture. For that reason, we can be relatively comfortable in stating that there is an American public opinion on welfare and that it is rich enough to guide public policy.

However, it is important for a number of reasons not to depend upon a single point—or even a few data points—in identifying public opinion. Public opinion on welfare is richest when illuminated by the broadest possible base of data, both across time and in response to different ways of asking similar questions. We shall see that public opinion about welfare has changed over time, for fairly clear and identifiable reasons. Furthermore, we shall see that opinion about welfare is complex and not reducible to "ideology." The public is nonideological but not disorganized. Rather, it displays support for a number of positions that can be reconciled. In this chapter I show how a general position on the basic welfare issues can be divined from the welter of data on the subject.

THE DECLINE IN SUPPORT FOR WELFARE

Since 1960, the popularity of welfare has declined substantially. Figure 3.1 shows the change between 1961 and 1993 in the public's response to the question, "Are we spending too much, too little, or about the right amount on welfare?"[7] Especially prominent in the figure is the dramatic shift in public support for welfare between 1961 and 1973, when the proportion of Americans supporting more welfare spending dropped from a bit more than 60 percent to approximately 20 percent. None of this change was the result of a shift to the belief that government was spending the right amount. As the figure shows, the number of Americans supporting the "right amount" option has changed marginally over time. Instead, the percentage of Americans who felt that the government was spending too much on welfare increased almost eightfold between 1961 and 1973.

A different set of data, presented by Fay Cook and Edith Barrett in *Support for the American Welfare State,* suggests that the term "welfare" overstates opposition to AFDC. In their study, conducted in 1986, 32.6 percent of respondents were in favor of increasing spending for AFDC, 51.9 percent thought it should be maintained, and 15.5 percent believed it should be decreased.[8] With the exception of food stamps, AFDC was the most weakly supported component of the welfare state. Still, Cook and Barrett's findings show stronger support for AFDC than the term "welfare" would indicate, a finding that if valid would call into question AFDC's purported unpopularity.

An indication of why the term "welfare" as used by the General Social Survey (GSS) is a more accurate indicator of public support for the program can be found in the explanation the Cook and Barrett survey provided for the AFDC program. As we have already seen, it is widely accepted that the public has limited knowledge of the specifics of government programs or institutional design. Therefore, it is important to avoid relying on survey questions that assume more information than the public could reasonably possess.[9]

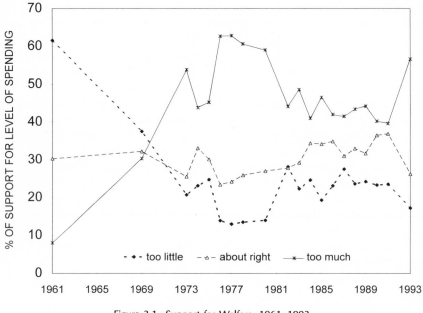

Figure 3.1. Support for Welfare, 1961–1993.

Cook and Barrett, recognizing this problem, provided an explanation of the program as part of the questionnaire: "income assistance for low-income mothers, and sometimes fathers, who have children under 18."[10] The problem with this explanation of the program should be obvious; it could just as easily describe the Earned Income Tax Credit, since it provides no indication that AFDC is primarily a substitute for, rather than a supplement to, earnings. This description of the program does not signal (intentionally or not) a number of characteristics of AFDC that the term "welfare" does quite successfully. However, Cook and Barrett clearly show that the public is not necessarily opposed to supporting this demographic *group*. But since other studies suggest that the problem with AFDC is less the group it supports than the way it supports them, Cook and Barrett do not provide a compelling case against the contention that AFDC is widely unpopular.

Many of the reasons for the change in AFDC's popularity will be discussed later, but I will comment on a few now. First, poverty was a prominent issue at the end of the 1960s in a way it had not been when the decade began, and the impression of an explosion of spending was widespread.[11] Some of the change could be the result of a shift in the public's impression of how much the government was actually spending rather than underlying support for any given level of welfare spending.

A second explanation for the shift in support is the changing image of welfare recipients. One obvious aspect of this movement is the racial composition of the welfare rolls, which was discussed in depth in Chapter 2. In addition to the changing racial composition of the AFDC rolls was the perception that welfare was "out of control." This perception goes beyond the mere fact that greater numbers of people were receiving welfare, which was causing great fiscal distress in many large cities.[12] It may be that beginning in the late 1960s, the public began to suspect that no control was being exercised over who was on the rolls and what they were doing once on them. The exploits of the welfare rights movement were receiving great attention,[13] which when combined with the combustible atmosphere created by urban riots, may have caused the public to respond to a perceived threat both to their security and their values. This reaction can be conceptualized as a public impression that the hierarchical side of the civic culture was being ignored, thus throwing policy off-center.

These shifts continued in the 1970s, when the level of opposition that developed in the 1960s rose even further. The next important shift occurred between 1980 and 1982, when the "too much" response dropped substantially, from 59 to 44.1 percent. One obvious interpretation of this drop is that it was less a change in underlying support for welfare than a belief that a substantial shift in policy had already occurred. The Reagan administration's assault on social welfare programs was highly publicized; one can surmise that this spotlight caused a number of those who had believed that the government should spend less to conclude that it was spending about the right amount, and some of those who thought that it was spending about the right amount to move to the "too little" category. One other interpretation is that the recession caused a number of Americans to feel economically destabilized or to know persons who had gone on public assistance, which increased the perceived need for more welfare spending.

The validity of the recession explanation for shifts in public support for welfare is cast in doubt by the next, and last, major shift in public opinion, which occurred between 1991 and 1993. The dip in antiwelfare sentiment between 1980 and 1982 was maintained throughout the 1980s, when there was virtually no statistically significant change in support for welfare. Then, between 1991 and 1993, antiwelfare sentiments exploded, from 39.6 percent in 1991 to 56.6 percent in 1993, a level near the historic highs of the mid-1970s.

A 1987 study by James Kluegel, based on sophisticated regression analyses of the relation between welfare and a variety of economic insecurity measures, found that "there is no evidence here that the public finds the poor more personally blameworthy or that it is more likely to attribute poverty to structural causes following the economic difficulties experienced during the 1970s than in previous times."[14] Although this phenomenon held true during the time of Kluegel's study, it does not stand up as a routine trend in American public opinion, based on the changes in the 1991–1993 period.

What could explain the change between 1991 and 1993? One possible explanation is the increase in attention that the issue received in the popular press and the prominent place the issue had in the campaign of Bill Clinton. Clinton campaigned on a promise to limit welfare recipients to two years of support, and the shift in opinion from 1991 to 1993 suggests that the public took this as a promise to lower spending on welfare (despite the fact that Clinton's promise was to spend more money on welfare, not less). This shift also casts doubt on the recession explanation for shifts in support for welfare. The period between 1991 and 1993 saw a prolonged, if rather shallow, recession, and yet antiwelfare sentiment went up—the opposite of the trend in the early 1980s and mid-1970s.

There are two possible interpretations of this anomaly. First, the decrease in welfare opposition that occurred in those two previous periods may not have had anything to do with the state of the economy. Second, and I suspect more accurately, those two previous recessions were accompanied by a more solidaristic, or at least self-protective, belief in the need for government action. The most recent recession, however, was accompanied by antisolidaristic, group-directed responses, such as outcries against immigration and a diversion of anger at those whom, at a time when many Americans were working harder to support themselves through the recession, were seen as surviving on government largesse.[15] These impressions may have been reinforced by the dramatic antiwelfare rhetoric and policy changes in states such as California, New Jersey, and Wisconsin. This rhetoric, along with the legitimation that these sentiments may have received (albeit unwittingly) from then-candidate Clinton, could explain the gush of antiwelfare sentiment.

Another possible interpretation of these changes is that they represent a fundamental shift in the public's attitudes toward spending on social welfare programs as a whole. Figure 3.2 suggests that this interpretation is unsupportable. It shows that opposition to welfare is far in excess of what one might think are linked issues: opposition to aid to big cities and aid to blacks.[16] Opposition to the latter types of social spending is consistently low throughout the twenty-year period in which polling on these issues has been done, and these issues appear to be linked to each other far more closely than they are connected with welfare. Opposition to welfare vacillates during this period, but there was virtually no statistically significant change in support for aid to cities or blacks. The figure also suggests that opposition to welfare is not highly connected to racial animosity, since aid to blacks remains fairly popular even as one particular form of aid, welfare, remains highly unpopular.

Another view on the relationship of race and welfare can be found in a 1977 study conducted by political scientist Gerald Wright. Wright found that it "appears that public support for welfare is systematically related to underlying racial attitudes."[17] He backs up this claim by demonstrating that in states with low AFDC benefit levels, opinions hostile to blacks are strongest. An essential part of Wright's analysis, and that of academics who argue that welfare is a racial proxy issue, is the assertion that the public has become much less willing to express explicit hostility to black interests (through such means as answers to the

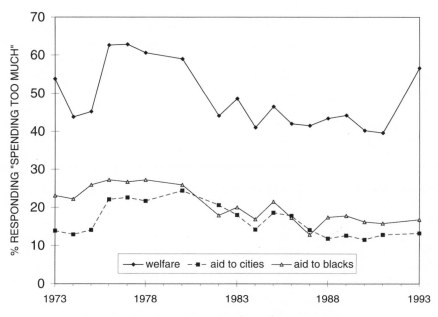

Figure 3.2. Opposition to Social Spending, 1973–1993.

"aid to blacks" question on the General Social Survey) and has sought other, more indirect means for registering such feelings, such as support for busing and welfare.

This argument is a difficult one to address, primarily because it dismisses a class of data (direct questions on racial feelings) that, if accurate, would be the most appropriate means by which to answer the question of the relationship between prejudice and support for welfare. Even so, it is possible to analyze the argument, if in an indirect way. The principal problem for the racism explanation is how to reconcile the sharp decline of support for welfare during a period (1960–1994) when the racial attitudes of whites, at the least, have not become more hostile and have, in many areas, become substantially less virulent.[18] Wright looks only at data for a single year: Time series data make his argument more difficult to sustain. This argument also fails to take into account the other changes that have driven attitudes toward welfare, especially impressions of the level of government spending, opinions on the role of women and of the moral authority of AFDC administration.

In the most careful and sophisticated public opinion study of racial attitudes yet attempted in the United States (Paul Sniderman and Thomas Piazza's *The Scar of Race*), the authors found that opposition to welfare was not primarily a matter of submerged racism. Instead, they found that "opposition to social welfare assistance, our results make plain, goes beyond the ranks of bigots. . . . So how do whites make decisions about whether blacks are entitled to more social welfare assistance? By judging according to the 'effort principle.' "[19] The "effort principle," which combines the circumstances that face a person and her willingness to exert herself to take control of those circumstances, is a fundamentally race-neutral principle, and one rooted deeply in American culture.[20]

That said, there is an important racial component of attitudes on welfare spending. Over time, the racial composition of the welfare rolls has evolved, with blacks composing an increasing percentage of AFDC recipients. Furthermore, media attention to the program has focused primarily on black recipients, supporting the impression that the rolls have become "blacker." The American public might have supported welfare when the rolls were "whiter" but became more hostile as the program became less closely aligned, in the mind of the public, with majority group members. Inferring a quite modest degree of causal force to race in explaining opinions on welfare may, therefore, be warranted. One recent study, by Donald Kinder and Tai Mendelberg, has shown that although prejudice has a substantial impact on the racial policy views of Americans on a variety of issues, it has the least direct effect on welfare.[21] The relation between opinions on welfare and race is difficult to quantify, but I would argue that the evidence, on balance, indicates that it is simplistic to look at welfare simply as a proxy issue. There are too many other inputs that feed into support for welfare spending, and the link between race and opposition to welfare is too indirect to sustain such a position. Furthermore, there is always the possibility that opposition to welfare may be causing racial tension rather than the other way around.

Aid to blacks remains significantly more popular than welfare, suggesting that there is a great deal more animosity directed toward those on welfare than to individuals who are black. This interpretation is somewhat flawed as well, however. Figure 3.3 suggests that although the public feels warmer toward blacks than those on welfare, the differences are rather slight.[22] The larger differences exist when the questions are phrased, "How do you feel about the program?" as opposed to "How do you feel about the people supported by the program?" Opposition to welfare is probably not a function of feelings about its recipients, or, at the least, the perception of the program itself is more of a factor than perceptions of those it assists.[23]

Figure 3.3 also suggests another fact about welfare. The level of warmth felt toward poor people is substantially higher than toward those on welfare, despite the fact that one would think that the two groups were highly correlated. Figure 3.4 emphasizes this point.[24] The opinion category of "assistance to the poor" draws levels of support twice or more those of welfare. These data suggest that although people support programs to fight poverty, they believe that welfare is not the right tool.

What is the reason for the level of opposition to the particular tool of welfare as opposed to other social programs to aid the less advantaged? Figure 3.5 presents the results of a 1986 poll on the public's view of the effects of welfare.[25] One

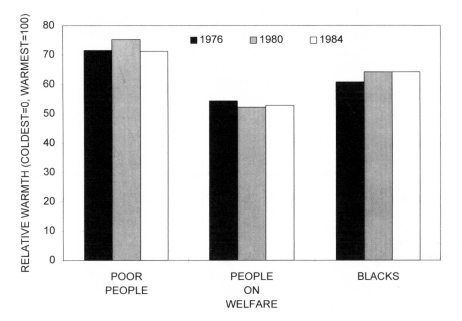

Figure 3.3. Feeling Thermometer Toward Groups.

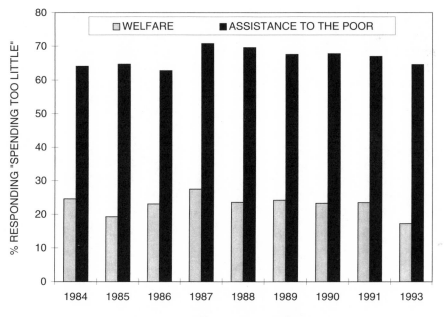

Figure 3.4. Welfare vs. Poverty-Fighting.

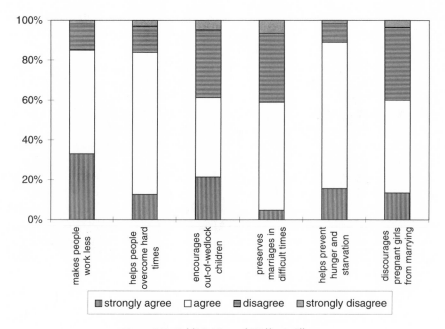

Figure 3.5. Public's View of Welfare's Effects.

clear finding of this survey is that the public suspects that welfare is efficacious, that is, that welfare has consequences on social outcomes. Every possible effect receives at least a 60 percent "agree" response. This data is interesting to a social scientist, partially because those of us who study poverty have had such a hard time finding data to support the effects that the public is convinced exist.[26]

The public overwhelmingly believes that welfare performs its basic security purpose, a finding reflected in the strong support that is given to two options: "helps people overcome difficult times" and "helps prevent hunger and starvation"; the findings also indicate that there is lesser but still strong majority support for the option "preserves marriages in hard times." At the same time, there is very strong support for the idea that welfare affects work effort, which is indicated both by the high level of overall support for the idea that "welfare makes people work less," but particularly by the level of "strongly agree" responses, more than for any other proposed consequence. Majority levels of support are also found for the two family-consequences options, "encourages out-of-wedlock children" and "discourages pregnant girls from marrying," the first of which received a large number of strongly agree responses. Figure 3.5 suggests, then, that although the public believes that welfare successfully performs its security functions, it does so at the risk of encouraging deviant and self-destructive behavior.[27]

These opinions are particularly important given that the public suspects that behavioral factors are highly related to the incidence of poverty. Figure 3.6 pre-

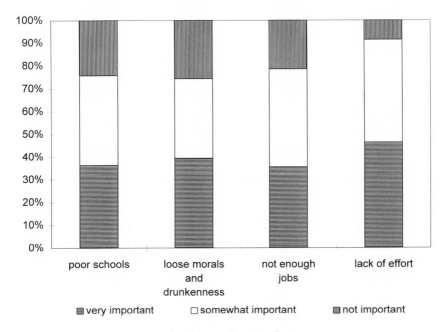

Figure 3.6. Public's Explanations for Poverty.

sents the findings of a 1990 poll on the public's explanations for poverty.[28] Virtually all of those polled found "lack of effort" to be a contributing factor in poverty, a finding that is probably related to the high levels of support for the proposition that welfare makes people work less. Together, these two polls suggest that
the public finds lack of personal motivation to be a key element in regard to poverty and suggests that welfare is a important factor in reducing effort in one particularly important area: work. In addition, Figure 3.6 shows that large numbers
of those polled agree that "loose morals and drunkenness" contribute heavily to
poverty, a result that might be surprising, given that this question is phrased in a
highly inflammatory fashion.

That the public is capable of supporting strongly individual-level explanations for poverty, and is also willing to support more structural explanations, is
consistent with research investigating the role of issue-framing and the role of the
media in shaping public attitudes. Shanto Iyengar has found that how the media
frame stories on poverty has a profound impact on Americans' attributions of
responsibility.[29] Iyengar's findings could be used to argue that the public does not
have a strongly held set of beliefs about poverty and that the views that they do
have are shallowly held and capable of elite manipulation.

I would suggest a contrary interpretation. If the public's view is that both
structural and individual factors influence poverty, one would expect that concentrated exposure to one or the other approach would exercise a substantial degree

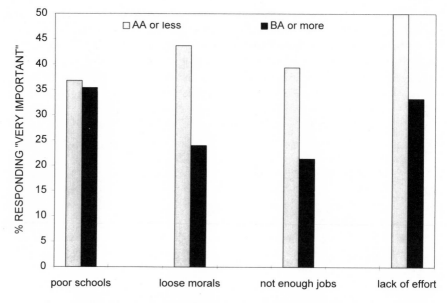

Figure 3.7. Explanations for Poverty by Educational Attainment.

of short-term influence. People do engage in social learning, and fresh information certainly should have an effect on political opinions. Elites may be able to
temporarily push public opinion in one direction or another. Over the long term,
however, public opinion is susceptible to being pushed back toward the cultural
center by new information, a conclusion also consistent with Iyengar's findings. If
the public is capable of accepting either a structural or an individual explanation,
it is certainly capable of accepting both.

There is a strong class dimension in the public's explanations of the cause of
poverty, as shown by Figure 3.7.[30] Every proposed cause, except for poor schools,
is highly stratified by the educational class of those questioned. Lower-class individuals are much more likely to connect poverty with the two behavioral explanations, which would suggest that lack of educational socialization results in
more individual-level explanations for poverty. At the same time, however, lower-
class respondents found lack of jobs to be a very important factor in poverty, a
result that may be related to this group's direct experience in the poor's low-skill
labor pool.

WELFARE AND POVERTY: THE PUBLIC'S ANSWER

Some interpretations of these data would suggest that the public and, especially,
the lower-class segment are revealing a contradictory set of opinions. They support individual-level explanations, such as lack of effort, but at the same time they

provide strong support for what social scientists would identify as "structural" causes, such as lack of job opportunities. Although there may be some degree of internal contradiction in these findings, a better interpretation is that the public thinks in terms that differ from those of academic social scientists. Academic social scientists tend to view the world through a prism that sharply discriminates between individual and structural causes; and when a strong preference for one or the other is not chosen, they interpret the response as waffling or contradictory. Either the individual is to blame or the system is. The public thinks that it is possible to have it both ways.

Against the views of the punitive consensus theorists discussed in Chapter 1, the public supports quite generous levels of public provision. Utilizing a methodologically innovative 1987 survey of the public's opinions on welfare, Jeffry Will found that when a variety of poverty scenarios were provided, in only 6.3 percent of cases did the public support reducing a family's award below its current level.[31] In contrast, 37.3 percent of the public kept awards at the status quo, and 55 percent increased them. Overall, the public awarded an average weekly income of $255 per family, approximately two-thirds of the median monthly AFDC award during that year.[32] This award amounted to an average $75 per week increase over the status quo, which would require doubling AFDC payments.[33] This study gets around some of the methodological problems of other studies of the public's preferred level of support by presenting actual cases of individuals and their current level of support instead of inquiring as to an abstract poverty level, which the public may or may not support raising everyone to and which does not allow people to use current policy as an aid to calculation.[34]

There is a great deal more consistency in the public's views on this subject than academics tend to recognize. The public opposes welfare but supports aid to the poor and blacks, primarily because people believe that welfare causes an unacceptably high level of deviant and self-destructive behavior. The public knows, however, how it would choose to deal with the problem of poverty: with jobs. There is no finding as consistent or as overwhelming in all of the survey data I have seen than the support the public gives for guaranteed government jobs programs and other efforts to expand employment.[35] The public is willing to have inflation rise in order to expand employment, thinks government should do more to expand employment, and agrees that "the government in Washington ought to see to it that everybody who wants to work can find a job,"[36] all by very strong margins. Underlying this belief in the need for government programs to support employment is the belief that hard work is the key to advancement in the American system. A 1987 poll found that 89 percent of Americans thought that hard work was either essential or very important to getting ahead, a higher percentage than any other factor.[37]

This complex of beliefs explains why Americans oppose welfare but support assistance to the poor: They believe that work is of supreme importance, both for its own sake and because of its connection to upward mobility. Work is the primary means through which the public desires to help the poor. Americans oppose welfare because they believe that it represents the negation of the work ethic. A number of polls taken across a range of years and worded in a variety of ways suggest that the public wishes to narrow the difference between work and welfare by transforming the current welfare program into one that pays people for work. The margins are staggering. Even when the question includes the difficult issue of making women who have preschool children work, the same results are found. No way of wording the basic question results in approval ratings below 68 percent, and most are in the high 80s.[38]

These figures are buttressed by Will's analysis, which addressed the question in a somewhat different way. When the vignettes of poor families were presented to the public, families in which the mother or father were presented as actively looking for work were given higher benefit awards.[39] However, for those who were not looking for work, "could not work because of a lack of transportation," or "were unemployed because the only work available paid minimum wage," substantial reductions in benefits were made.[40] Of particular interest to the matter of core welfare values, "one important volitional characteristic which was not significant in determining overall levels of generosity was marital status."[41] Once again, work, not sexual or marital behavior, is the central American behavioral norm.

These numbers appear even in polls of one of the most liberal states in the nation—New York. The June 1994 Empire State Survey found 93 percent support for government proposals that "require job training for those on welfare and after two years require them to work" and similar levels of support for other work-oriented questions.[42] To support this policy, nearly the same level of support emerges for assistance for child care and transportation (82 percent support) and guaranteed health care (83 percent support). These figures do not represent blanket hostility to social provision: Only 6 percent of those polled supported scrapping welfare entirely. These near-consensus figures exist even though those polled had somewhat divergent explanations for why people are poor or on welfare.[43] These data suggest that the work strategy represents an overlapping consensus, bringing together those who tend more in the direction of one cultural position or another.[44]

Americans oppose welfare because they believe that there is only one legitimate means of upward mobility and income support: work. Page and Shapiro nicely sum up this finding: "Most Americans don't like the idea of welfare programs that give payments to people, some of whom may not be truly helpless and may thereby be discouraged from helping themselves. . . . But most Americans want to give jobs to everyone who can work."[45] They are willing to spend more on the poor, and indeed on blacks in particular, but only if they are sure that the method will be effective and consistent with their basic values. This view may be partly based on a purely moral position: Everyone should work because it is immoral not to work. One fairly old survey found that 75 percent of Americans believe that "there is something wrong with a person who is not willing to work"[46] and 66 percent supported a view that work has value apart from its economic benefits.[47] Apart from this moral position, I suspect that people are upset by "free riders." Work is the central means by which our society provides for itself and to avoid work is to survive on the efforts of others. Work programs, regardless of how they are explained, are popular because they seem to engage all sides of the public's mind: its egalitarian desire to help those in need, its hierarchical desire to enforce a central societal norm, and its individualist desire to foster independence and self-reliance. Work for those on welfare is a popular issue because it is seen, at least at the level of slogan, as the kind of program that connects all sides of the nation's political culture.

Work is indeed a central societal norm and a crucial variable for welfare programs. But work, like most other norms, is not applied equally across time and social categories. Some classes of individuals are excepted. Social security continues to be popular because it allows older people to avoid having to enter the workforce, and child labor laws are consensual because children, like the aged, are seen as outside of the group to which the work norm is applicable. AFDC was created, as Chapter 2 demonstrated, to support the American value that women are outside of the moral community for which work is normative. How did public opinion shift so dramatically that 85 percent of Americans could support requiring women with preschool children to work in order to receive public assistance (see note 38)?

The original set of public beliefs that supported Aid to Dependent Children was a blending of hierarchical ends (maintaining the stability of the family as a central social institution by keeping families together and women in the home) and egalitarian means (cash redistribution). AFDC has lost much of its political foundation because of the drying up of social support for what had been the hierarchical leg of the coalition and a shift in coalitional sympathies of egalitarians toward individualists. That is, the percentage of those who supported the idea that women should stay out of the workforce diminished dramatically and along with it the central justification for AFDC. Furthermore, those who sought greater social equality began to define equality not just between upper-class men and lower-class men but between men and women as well, an overlap with the individualist position.

The structure of opinion that supported mothers' aid and, later, Aid to Dependent Children had two crucial components: the idea that women whose husbands could support them should not work and the belief that mothers' employment adversely influences the moral and emotional development of their children. Both of these ideas were supported by the concept of a separate, domestic sphere within which women were supposed to find their place, and the related idea that attempts to enter men's commercial, industrial, and political sphere was harmful to both public and private order.[48] All of these ideas, strongly in place at the time of the passage of the Social Security Act of 1935, had been substantially eroded by the 1970s.

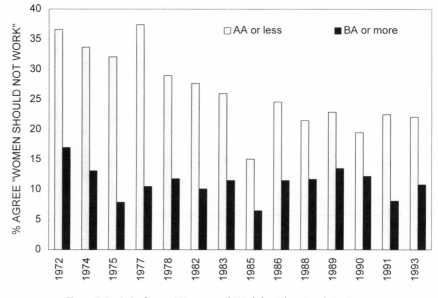

Figure 3.8. Attitudes on Women and Work by Educational Attainment.

When the Gallup organization asked the public in 1936 whether "you approve of a married woman earning money in business or industry if she has a husband capable of supporting her," only 18 percent of respondents approved while 72 expressed disapproval.[49] By 1969, the situation had changed dramatically: 55 percent approved, while only 40 percent disapproved. Since 1969, this shift in opinion has solidified. Recent polls show that 80 percent of the public approves of women working outside the home. The results for the period between 1972 and 1993, stratified by class, are shown in Figure 3.8.

Other polls conducted in and around 1935 show that the same set of beliefs about women's work were widely held, regardless of question wording or special conditions. Fifty-six percent of Americans supported prohibiting married women from working at state and local government positions paying more than $1,000 a year, and 67 percent supported a proposal to forbid women from working in business or industry if their husbands earned more than $1,600 a year (both polls 1939).[50] A 1945 poll that asked, "If there is a limited number of jobs, do you approve or disapprove of a married woman holding a job in business or industry when her husband is able to support her," elicited a remarkable 86 percent opposition to women working.[51]

Changes in the wording of these questions did have an effect, however. A 1946 survey found that 34 percent of men and 42 percent of women thought that "a married woman who has no children under sixteen and whose husband makes enough to support her" should be allowed to take a job.[52] Other surveys that did

not address the issue of the husband's ability to support or the presence of children also found fairly strong support for women's right to work. Even more dramatic was the acceptance of women working in wartime industries. Support was
as high as 60 and 70 percent but as low as 32 percent when the question allowed
for the possibility of "operating a machine."

One very instructive poll, conducted in 1946, allowed respondents to support
three separate statements about women's work and divided the results on the basis of sex. It found that 22 percent of men and 29 percent of women believed that
"all women should have an equal chance with men for any job in business or industry regardless of whether they have to support themselves or not," while 46
percent of men and 49 percent of women felt that "only women who have to support themselves should have an equal chance with men for jobs in business or
industry," and 28 percent of men and 17 percent of women believed that "a man
should have preference over all women for any job that he can fill satisfactorily."[53]

The common opinion of women's work in the 1930s and 1940s was fairly
strong support if the woman was single, weak support if the family had no children or if the husband could not bring home enough money to support his family,
and strong opposition if the couple had children. Work was seen as tangential to
a woman's true responsibilities and to be avoided at all costs when she became a
mother.

Although it is difficult to determine whether the shift in opinions on
women's work determined the change in the number of women in the workforce
or vice versa, the two trends certainly went hand in hand. The labor force participation rate for single women changed only marginally between 1960 and 1992
(from 58.6 percent to 66.4 percent), but married women's participation in the labor force surged (from 31.9 percent to 59.2 percent).[54] The change was even more
dramatic for women with children. The rate for married women with children
(data for single women with children are not available for the pre-1980 period)
went from 39 percent to 75.4 percent for those with children ages six to seventeen,
and from 18.6 percent to 59.9 percent for those with children under six.[55] Even in
the absence of poll results, the revealed preference of American society on the
subject of women in the workforce underwent a very clear change in this period.
Women with children are no longer expected to stay at home, and when the children are of school age, staying at home is an option chosen by a minority of
American women.

The set of beliefs that formed the moral foundation for the mothers' aid and
Aid to Dependent Children programs has utterly collapsed. By the mid-1970s,
the public was evenly split on whether a mother's working was harmful to her
children, and by the most recent year for which we have polls, 67.1 percent of the
public had come to accept the absence of harm position.[56] By 1974, 64.4 percent
of the American public disagreed with the statement that "women should take
care of the home, not country," and by 1993 that position had reached 85.2 percent acceptance.[57] By 1977, 38 percent of women and 47 percent of men disagreed

with the belief, which was strongly supported in the previous surveys we have looked at, that "it is more important for a wife to help her husband's career than to have one herself," and by 1986, 62 percent of women and 64 percent of men disagreed.[58] Support for equal pay for equal work is now almost complete, receiving support in the mid-1990s.[59] Finally, a strong majority of the public now supports "most of the efforts to strengthen and change women's status in society today," with 73 percent of women and 69 percent of men in the favorable column.[60]

Quite simply, in the mid-1930s, when ADC was created, large majorities opposed women entering the paid labor force, especially when a woman was also a mother; the majorities are now strongly on the other side. Women are no longer expected to subordinate their work desires to men, are not stigmatized because of the effect their work has on their children, and efforts to enforce these beliefs are well supported. The flip side of this shift in opinion, of course, is that programs that are based upon the assumption that society has an interest in keeping women out of the workforce are based upon an obsolete moral foundation, leaving the program "suspended in air." There is no longer public support for AFDC's central historical justification. Increasing support for one part of the individualist cultural system, the autonomy and freedom of women, has come in conflict with an egalitarian program of support for single mothers.

As Chapter 6 indicates, these changes in public opinion have been accompanied by substantial, and for the most part nonlegislative, and thus nonpopular (in the sense of the institutional processes that create them) transformations in the Aid to Families with Dependent Children program. The moral foundations of the program were being corroded at the same time that the composition of the welfare rolls was becoming increasingly unpopular among the majority of the American people and as the number of recipients and the cost of the program skyrocketed. This transformation has left an intensely unpopular program, but one that has been highly resistant to change.

Finally, it should be noted that AFDC is unpopular not only with the public at large but with the one group not discussed so far in this chapter, welfare recipients themselves.[61] In a study of welfare recipients in New Haven, 61 percent of those questioned said they felt stigmatized either always or sometimes by receiving AFDC.[62] One of the participants in the study seemed to encapsulate the views of the welfare mothers surveyed:

> Judy was very ambivalent about her position as a welfare client. On the one hand, she felt degraded and stigmatized by a society that saw her as a failure for being on welfare and ashamed because she, like most Americans, believed that anyone who tries hard enough can succeed. Unable to buy new school clothes for her children each fall, forced to borrow each January to pay for her heat, she felt she was failing her children. She also felt guilty for collecting welfare. Even though she knew that she and her children were entitled to AFDC benefits because they had no other means of support, she still felt

she was begging. . . . In spite of her ambivalence, Judy was optimistic that she would soon leave welfare behind for good.[63]

As indicated in Judy's comments, welfare recipients feel that receiving AFDC has a negative impact on their family life, a view supported by studies that are more systematic.[64] Welfare recipients rarely blame structural conditions for their poverty, attributing it instead to personal problems that keep them from entering the paid workforce, such as "their own lack of education or skills, lack of child care, lack of transportation and health care."[65] Welfare recipients, in their day-to-day behavior, indicate a desire to make mainstream behavior a greater part of their experience on AFDC; a study by Christopher Jencks and Kathryn Edin found that public assistance only made up 57 percent of the income of most mothers on AFDC.[66] The rest was made up by generally unreported sources, such as jobs, aid from relatives, friends, and boyfriends, and vice.

CONCLUSIONS

AFDC (at the time, ADC) was premised upon the moral value of women remaining out of the paid workforce and at home caring for their children. Public support for this ideal has collapsed since the 1960s, as millions of women from every social class have combined work and parenting. The world has changed, and the public has come to demand that welfare change as well. The public expects that the values that regulate life for the majority of citizens apply equally to those currently on welfare.

Support for welfare has declined because although public values about the application of the work norm have changed, the structure of the nation's welfare programs has not. Although the public strongly supports efforts to integrate the poor into the mainstream of social life, to raise their income and their life chances, they suspect that welfare is incapable of serving these ends. They oppose welfare because it is seen as inconsistent with the value of work. The public desires to see poverty programs emphasize paid work and deemphasize cash payments unrelated to social obligations. I have shown that the public has become more hostile to welfare because its basic values about work and the social role of women have changed, but the nation's welfare programs have not.[67]

The obvious question is, Why has such a clear shift in the public's beliefs not translated into a change in public policy? Why does AFDC continue to reflect one set of public values when those values have clearly been rendered obsolete? The next chapter shows that although the public is of one mind on welfare, the nation's elites are not. The public looks at issues of personal responsibility, generosity, work, and family as matters to be reconciled, but elites see them as either-or choices, to be decided one way or another.

4

The Nature of the Elite Cultural Conflict

This chapter establishes the basic contours of the conflict within America's cultural elite, with particular attention to those aspects of the conflict that are relevant to AFDC. Unfortunately, investigating elite opinion is not as easy as examining public opinion. Numerous polls that span a number of years have been conducted on the public's views on welfare, and these polls have been closely scrutinized as to wording and methodology. Problems in the area of public opinion are more a matter of interpretation than absence of data.

In contrast, divining elite opinion on any subject, and welfare in particular, meets with problems of interpretation and the absence of data. As James Q. Wilson points out, "Our shelves are filled with books on public opinion but not with ones on elite opinion."[1] There are a handful of elite opinion studies, but they are marked by serious methodological problems. For one, defining an elite is not as easy as defining the public. The public, after all, is everyone. Who are the elites? Selection of subjects is obviously of the greatest import. Second, these studies are not repeated, as are the public opinion surveys. Therefore, it is difficult to determine whether elite opinion at one time is representative of those elites at another time. Finally, many studies are not comprehensive. Of particular importance to my inquiry are two major surveys: One is by Stanley Rothman and his collaborators[2] and the other by Sidney Verba and Gary Orren. These researchers do not directly ask any questions about welfare or AFDC, as does the General Social Survey. Getting at opinions on these topics is, therefore, a process of approximation and indirection.

Even so, political scientists, regardless of the professional incentives to do so, cannot select their subjects strictly on the availability of pristine data sets. When the data is not perfect, a combination of ingenuity, creativity, and instinct must serve as a substitute. One must build from what is reasonably well known to what is less well known, letting the reader know where judgments are characterized more by speculation than certitude.

Fortunately, much of what is necessary to demonstrate is on the side of the reasonably well known. I will begin by establishing that elites have a different opinion structure than the public, one characterized by high levels of ideological thinking. Second, I will show that within American elites, there are strong and serious cleavages on fundamental cultural issues, and I will give some indication as to the content of those divisions. Third, I will discuss the institutional manifestations of elite dissensus, looking at charitable foundations and think tanks. Finally, I will examine the consequences of elite dissensus in the intellectual sphere, examining the poverty and welfare literature in the light of Wildavsky's cultural theory.

I will show that the more intellectually involved our elites are, the more they become divided on a cultural basis and the less they are divided in a traditional, bipolar way. Professional elites, at the least intellectually involved end of the scale, are divided on a fundamentally ideological basis, between traditionalist conservatives (such as the military and business) and modernist, culturally "experimental" liberals (such as the media and public interest lawyers). Politically active think tanks and foundations are divided ideologically as well, along a bipolar scale, although there are signs that many of them are becoming more culturally unitary with the progress of time and thus more likely to fit into Wildavsky's hierarchist-egalitarian-individualist division rather than the left-right dichotomy that more accurately fits professional elites. Finally, I will show that the conflict between intellectuals, where the need to integrate one's ideas into a coherent whole are most pressing, can be best understood only in Wildavsky cultural theory terms. At each level of American elites there are strong, durable splits with substantial consequences for welfare.

THE WAY ELITES THINK

In "Ideological Thinking Among Mass Publics and Political Elites," M. Kent Jennings analyzed the only directly comparable data set for elites and mass opinion, the National Election Studies and the National Convention Delegate Studies. Jennings notes that "overall, it is patent that political party elites have a vastly more constrained and stable set of political preferences and perspectives than does the mass public in general, a conclusion that applies whether the test is a demanding one based on opinions about policy issues or a less stringent one based on appraisals of sociopolitical groups and prominent political actors."[3] To say that a group's opinions are constrained means that they generally conform to some ordering principle (in Jennings's study that principle is liberal-conservative). For example, we ask people four questions, the answers to which translate easily into a liberal or conservative stance. A person who answers all four questions with the liberal response or all four with the conservative response would be said to be highly constrained, while those who split evenly between the two ideologies would be said to be minimally constrained. Jennings found that party elites exhibited much higher levels of constraint than the public at large, whether the questions concerned issues or responses to sociopolitical groups.[4]

The difference between elites and the mass public, in short, is that elites have well-constrained ideological structures that rank-order political values and ensure that positions on various issues will cohere. The beliefs of the public, however, are not well-constrained, which means they are either incoherent or indicative of an underlying set of cultural values that does not fit into the liberal-conservative continuum (or any ideological structure). This finding is similar to that of W. Russell Neuman, who notes that approximately 5 percent of the American public are politically "sophisticated" and actively involved in politics.[5] Neuman, however, describes the difference between the "activist" stratum and the rest of the public as one of "literacy," which is connected to the relative costs of collecting information. I suspect that the difference, although highly related to information, has more to do with a fundamentally different way of seeing the world, one that is an important consequence of advanced education.

Using a different set of methods and a different data set, Rothman also found that elite opinion was more constrained than public opinion. However, he and his researchers found that the increased constraint was generically applicable only to issues of "collectivist liberalism," which concerns the state's activities to equalize income and to regulate business, but not for "expressive individualism," which focuses on the degree to which personal behavior should conform to traditional social norms. However, when the elites in Rothman's study were further disaggregated into those with graduate degrees in such areas as the humanities, social science, and medicine, the level of ideological constraint jumped substantially. Thus, when one looks at the intellectual elite of the overall elite, a similarly ideological and constrained pattern emerges.[6]

To be ideological in the American context means to emphasize one element of the American experience, and the multiple strands that make up American political culture, over and against the others. A person with an ideological approach is culturally disintegrative. That is, she seeks to pull apart the elements of American political culture and pit them against each other. This approach is in sharp contrast to the pattern we saw for the American public in general, which is culturally integrative; the integrative pattern translates into a nonideological, nonconstrained opinion structure and those who use it pay attention to politics only when one element of the national culture seems to be pushing out the other elements. This conflict of approaches is the fundamental divide between elites and the public and is the basis for the politics of dissensus.

This division between public and elite, or activist, opinion has been uncovered in descriptive studies of cultural policy activists. Kristin Luker, in her careful study of the politics of abortion, cautioned that

> we should recall that motherhood is a topic about which people have very complicated feelings, and because abortion has become the battleground for different definitions of motherhood, neither the pro-life nor the pro-choice movement has ever been "representative" of how most Americans feel about abortion. More to the point . . . neither of these groups will ever be able to be representative.[7]

A similar distance in approach between elite and public opinion was uncovered by Jane Mansbridge in her study of the politics of the Equal Rights Amendment. Mansbridge attributes this distance to the political necessities of policy activism, which drive those most involved in politics into "doctrinal purity."[8]

One could argue that although American elites are ideological, they are basically in agreement. This position would be more consistent with the ruling-class model of politics and would be true regardless of whether that class is seen as consisting of "new class intellectuals," East Coast Ivy League old money, or the wealthy elements of society generically.[9] This approach may be valid, particularly, in the area of foreign affairs, where elites seem to be much more cosmopolitan and internationalist than the public at large,[10] but it does not seem consistent with the evidence on welfare-related issues. There are areas that America's elites agree upon, but for the most part they are divided and sharply so. This divide is primarily professional, with different "strategic elites" composing parts of the broader cultural elites.

Rothman found that the degree of dissensus on collectivist liberalism mirrored the level of constraint. That is, elites are both highly ideological and sharply divided one from another.[11] For example, on issues relating to the legitimacy of government authority, such as criminals' rights in court, there is a great deal of dispersion. Verba and Orren's findings also support the argument that elites are highly dispersed ideologically. They find:

> Group affiliation, in short, is closely related to the leaders' views on equality. The distinctive positions of leaders in different groups are linked to their institutional roles. In this sense, the potential conflicts over equality may be understood as being structured by the various sectors of society reflected in the leadership groups.[12]

Furthermore, when American elites are compared to foreign elites on social welfare issues, Americans are likely to be divided equally between right and left, whereas foreign elites are all substantially to the left.[13]

Of particular importance to my work are Rothman's findings comparing newer, cultural elites to older traditional elites. On the two measures that are most important to welfare issues, alienation and expressive individualism, the new elites and the old ones were extremely divergent.[14] Because system alienation is crucial to determining whether one is willing to enforce traditional American behavioral norms, and expressive individualism measures the degree to which one accepts those norms as morally compelling, this enormous difference between elites is strong evidence of an elite culture war with relevance to AFDC.

THE SUBSTANCE OF ELITE CONFLICT

If elites do think "ideologically," what is the content of their ideology? This question is not easy to answer, partially because of a dearth of sophisticated polling and also because of difficulties in creating categories that illuminate without distorting. The data problem can be partially, but only partially, remedied. Since the early 1980s, Stanley Rothman and his colleagues have undertaken a massive study of the ideology of American elites, interviewing members of virtually every major "strategic elite" in American society. Although Jennings demonstrated that at the very least, party elites have constrained ideologies, Rothman has shown that a broader set of American elites is both ideological and sharply divided internally. Similar findings, albeit with a more restrictive set of elites and a less culturally driven set of questions, can be found in the elite studies of Sidney Verba and his collaborators.[15]

Rather than relying on a simple right-left, conservative-liberal dichotomy, Rothman divided up America's elites on the basis of four dimensions: collectivist liberalism, expressive individualism, system alienation, and regime threat.[16] Collectivist liberalism supports the regulation of business and the redistribution of income. System alienation expresses fidelity to or estrangement from mainstream society. Expressive individualism measures the degree to which personal behavior should be governed by the expression of personality or by conformance to traditional norms.[17] Finally, regime threat measures the level of perceived danger to American society, both internally and externally.

As it happens, although there are very high levels of ideological dispersion among America's elites, certain elites appear on one end of the scale on some of these measures but not on others.[18] Labor leaders are very liberal on measures of collectivist liberalism and system alienation but are among the most conservative on expressive individualism and regime threat.[19] Religious leaders are liberal on all dimensions except expressive individualism, where they are the most conservative group. The position of labor and religious leaders can be best described as hierarchist-egalitarian, which is similar to the position of Christian Democratic parties of Europe and, for that matter, to New Deal liberalism. This pattern may be a function of the low levels of exposure of these groups to elite education: Only 6 percent of labor leaders and 19 percent of religious leaders attended an elite college. Furthermore, only 38 percent of labor leaders completed a college degree, by far the lowest of any of the elites surveyed.

When the Christian religious elites were broken into Catholic, mainline Protestant, and fundamentalist, the differences between the groups were extremely stark.[20] On economic and foreign policy issues, Catholic and mainline Protestants were far to the left of the fundamentalists. On social issues, however, Catholics and mainline Protestants diverged, with the Catholics moving to the right and the mainline Protestants going to the left. These divisions explain why, on most welfare-related issues, the fundamentalists line up with the conservatives and the Catholics and mainline Protestants affiliate with liberals. We can see, thus, that Catholics can serve as a swing force, given their more conservative position on social issues. Jewish elites (not the principal religious figures, as with the Christian elites, but Jews among all the professions), meanwhile, were substantially to the left of non-Jewish elites on virtually every measure, which suggests that they are one of the most egalitarian segments of American society.[21]

Movie and TV elites are moderate on collectivist liberal issues but highly liberal on system alienation and expressive individualism. Those in the media are similarly inclined, with a lower level of alienation. This pattern suggests that although the major culture-producing elites are nonideological on economic issues, they are highly inflamed when it comes to cultural and personal expression. This pattern could be considered egalitarian-individualist, with a strong emphasis on the latter. Lawyers are more conservative on economic issues and more liberal on regime threat and expressive individualism. It is interesting that they are the least alienated of the American elites, perhaps because of their central roles in government, corporate law, and the justice system. Lawyers are therefore closer to pure individualism than the culture-producing elites.[22] Public interest group leaders are the most liberal group on all dimensions, consistent with a strong egalitarian orientation. Many public interest group leaders are lawyers, which indicates that they represent the egalitarian wing of the legal profession, while the nonpublic interest lawyers represent the individualist wing.

Military leaders are the flip side of public interest groups, suggesting a hierarchist-individualist (leaning more to hierarchist) fusion consistent with traditionalist conservatism. A similar pattern, leaning this time in the individualist direction, characterizes executives in American business. One elite that Rothman did not interview (that has rocketed to cultural significance since the mid-1980s) are producers and executives in the area of advanced technology. A *New York Times* article on a recent conference of high-tech producers and their attendant intelligentsia described the group: "Much as the newly formed United States rejected monarchy and embraced democracy, the founding fathers of cyberspace (who, like their forbears, were white, male, middle-aged and privileged) came together in Aspen to denounce unnecessary regulation and to endorse, in effect, libertarianism as their core political system."[23] If this view and the recent flap over porn on the Internet are any indication, the new high-tech elite would be America's purest individualistic elite, combining strong support for the free market with hostility to moral regulation.

Although America's professional elites show indications of the Wildavsky-style cultural splits, they are somewhat less hardened into this structure than intellectuals, as we shall see later in this chapter. Of greatest salience to the study of welfare, the "new class" elites, such as members of the media, TV and movie producers, and public interest officials, are highly split from the traditional elites, such as those in business and the military, on expressive individualism. This measure is critical for a study of welfare because it addresses directly the willingness of elites to enforce the "bourgeois virtues," such as work and family.[24] If this split is central to the conflict between the traditional and the new elites, then one would expect that this aspect of welfare would come to dominate the politics of the issue. We shall soon see it has.

Although elites are divided on a broader, cultural level, they are also divided on some issues of relevance to welfare. Verba and Orren found that when elites in their sample were asked whether poverty in America was the fault of the poor or the fault of the system, Republicans, farmers, and people in business were all strongly supportive of individual attributions of blame.[25] Labor, intellectuals, the media, Democrats, blacks, feminists, and youth were supportive of the contrary opinion: The "system" is to blame for American poverty. It is interesting that for every elite except labor and blacks, shifting the question to the responsibility for black poverty dramatically increased system attribution, suggesting that nonracial factors may drive elite opinion on poverty in the same fashion as public opinion. A similar breakdown of elites was present in most of the responses to Verba and Orren's other questions, which have more relevance to non-AFDC distributional issues.

ELITE DISSENSUS IN ORGANIZATIONS AND INSTITUTIONS

The idea of competing elites is not merely a public opinion construct, a way of describing the most intelligent or sophisticated portion of the population. Elites are also an organizational and institutional phenomenon. At the top of the organizational ladder are charitable foundations, on a step down are think tanks, and at the bottom are individual intellectuals clustered by cultural tendency. As one goes from top to bottom, the idea orientation shifts from ideological and partisan (liberal versus conservative, Republican versus Democrat[26]) to cultural. The difficulty of maintaining ideological divisions in the face of cultural splits becomes ever more clear as conservatives are split between those with a focus on social issues (hierarchists) and those with a focus on economic issues (individualists).[27] Liberals too have been split, between those who emphasize free trade, deregulation, race neutrality, and civil liberties (individualists) and those who support mercantilism, affirmative action, and what has come to be called "political correctness."

The situation in American foundations clearly supports the contention that America's elites are sharply divided. Most major foundations that are oriented toward public policy issues have a discernible ideological tendency; among those that do, very few support research that is not in line with their ideological predispositions. Nagai, Lerner, and Rothman found that among the twenty largest politicized foundations ("one in which politicized grants dominate that foundation's funding"[28]), almost all gave more than 90 percent of their financial support to kindred ideological spirits.[29] The division of the foundation world, within the more focused area of public policy research, is just as stark. On the liberal side we find the Ford, MacArthur, Rockefeller, and Carnegie foundations, while on the conservative side, we see the Olin, Smith Richardson, Amoco, Scaife, and Bradley foundations. All of these organizations, which are the largest supporters of public policy research, give more than 95 percent of their support to researchers of their own ideological persuasion.[30]

Since the mid-1970s, these programmatic foundations, which are driven by a particular ideology rather than a diffuse philanthropic instinct, have risen in power and influence. This trend is clearest on the right: Conservative foundations have flourished in response to the impression of left-wing hegemony in the world of ideas. Furthermore, conservative foundations have directly addressed this impression by creating a counterestablishment of intellectual conservatives through the medium of think tanks.[31] This shift is particularly evident of "the Olin Foundation, which had, prior to the 1970s, directed its money primarily to antilabor organizations and to educational programs on free enterprise in undistinguished colleges. But in the 1970s, its patterns of giving became more sophisticated and more closely attuned to the potential of grantees for influencing debates on national policies."[32] This pattern was seen among other conservative foundations, as can be illustrated by the fact that "think tank support comprises almost one-fifth of all conservative grants but only 5 percent of all liberal grants," with conservative foundations focusing most of their money on ideological, conservative think tanks.[33]

It is at the think-tank level that the cultural division of the American elite starts to become clear. Although it is difficult to divide the foundation world on a cultural basis,[34] at the think-tank level, the job becomes much easier. Of the major think tanks that work on social policy, only a few can be said to be culturally integrative, such as the Urban Institute, the Progressive Policy Institute, and the Brookings Institution. Think tanks with a predominantly individualist streak include the American Enterprise, Cato, Manhattan, Hudson, Reason, and Hoover Institutes, and the Institute for Contemporary Studies. Among the most prominent egalitarian think tanks are the Center on Budget and Policy Priorities, the Economic Policy Institute, the Institute for Policy Studies, and the Joint Center for Political and Economic Studies. Finally, among the more prominent hierarchical think tanks are the Heritage Foundation, the Ethics and Public Policy Center, the Rockford Institute, the Family Research Council, and the Christian Coalition.[35]

Through the 1960s, most foundations and think tanks were sharply tilted toward the left. More accurately, it could be said that think tanks reflected the moderate liberal consensus of the time, which combined New Deal economic reform with deference to the fundamental institutions of American society.[36] As liberals were dragged toward the left, the consensus broke and conservatives began to organize more actively. By the 1980s, the conservative movement was splintering into its individualistic and hierarchical wings, creating in the arena of think tanks a structure along the lines of the larger elite division in the United States. The consequence, as James Allen Smith observes, is that

> The experts seem unable to agree, and debate becomes inconclusive. Thus, no consensus on policies can be reached. In the ideologically charged environment of the 1980s, that old complaint seems ever closer to the mark. . . . All research begins to look like advocacy, all experts begin to look like hired guns, and all think tanks seem to use their institutional resources to advance a point of view.[37]

The dissensus that began in the 1960s, with an attack against the liberal consensus by the radical egalitarian left, has settled into a cultural split, with no clear establishment to rebel against. In this world of clearly defined cultural divisions, reaching a culturally integrative consensus becomes ever more difficult. The consequences of this division reach their sharpest and most rigid level when intellectuals themselves are examined.

ELITE DISSENSUS AMONG THE INTELLECTUALS

> American politics has become more ideological. There is no question that as politics becomes more ideological, intellectuals become more significant. That is the reason intellectuals like ideological politics. The ideological energy has left the center and has either gone to the right or to the left.[38]

With the exception of the work of a few culturally integrative thinkers, who have only recently become influential (and who will be discussed in Chapter 9), most of the popular and influential works on poverty and welfare can be divided among three approaches. The first, which is derivative of the hierarchist approach, is known as the behavioral, or culture of poverty, school. The second, which is derivative of the individualist approach, is known as the incentive, or economic, approach. The third, which is derivative of the egalitarian approach, is known as the structural approach. Although there may be questions at the margin as to who belongs where, there is a logic to these categories.

The Hierarchist Approach: The Culture of Poverty

The culture of poverty school, while not hierarchist in its infancy, became so almost as soon as it could walk. Its founder, Oscar Lewis, coined the phrase to describe the vicious and reinforcing cycle of poverty that affected the poor he studied in Mexico and Puerto Rico in the 1950s and 1960s. Lewis wanted to know why pockets of intense poverty did not dissipate as the conditions that called them into being weakened. He concluded that the high level of present-orientation (a weak sense of the connection between action in the present and consequences in the future), alienation from core societal processes (such as marriage, political activity, and education), and anger at major social institutions were the consequences of long-term deprivation. Most critically, because these behaviors become embedded in culture, they did not disappear even when structural conditions changed. Cultural patterns that were adaptations to structural conditions could themselves become causes of social outcomes, especially intergenerational poverty. Lewis, in sharp relief to later culture of poverty theorists, suggested that events that caused high levels of group solidarity, such as the civil rights movement in the United States[39] and the socialist revolutions in the Third World,[40] could transform the culture of poverty into nonbehavioral deprivation.

Those who followed in Lewis's footsteps threw out most of his consideration of the causes of the culture of poverty as well as his implicit suggestion of radical political mobilization, leaving only the self-reinforcing cycle of poverty. This approach is clearly seen in Edward Banfield's controversial work *The Unheavenly City Revisited.* Subtly changing Lewis's terminology, Banfield identified the urban poverty and welfare problem with "lower class culture." Those who possess lower class culture are "present-oriented" and "therefore radically improvident."[41] Lower class culture is marked by high levels of social disorganization, single-parent families, low levels of work, violence, and poor health, all of which can be seen as consequences of present-orientation. Banfield was not sanguine about the possibility of alleviating poverty, given its essentially behavioral nature. He prefaced his suggestions for change with a long discussion that explains why "solutions" are generally of little use.[42] Anticipating future behavioral theorists, Banfield suggested programs that would change the social milieu of poor children (to expose them to "normal culture"), and he advocated strict crime control measures to make the costs of crime more clear and direct.[43]

As Machiavelli is the unspoken, the unspeakable, father of modernity, Banfield is the unmentioned source of all later behavioral analyses of poverty and welfare. The most important contemporary advocate of the behavioral approach is Lawrence Mead. Mead emphasizes the role of public authority in explaining low levels of conformance to core social values: "A commonsense explanation for crime is simply ineffective law enforcement; for fatherless families on welfare, it is weak enforcement of child support; for nonwork, it is the failure of welfare programs to require employable recipients to work."[44] Mead observes that "resistance to low-wage jobs and a sense of defeatism appear to be the main deterrents to work in the minds of the poor."[45] It is behavior, driven by culture, that explains why large segments of the poor remain dependent. Because those in the underclass are unable to motivate themselves to conform, public authority must demand conformity from them rather than expecting it to emerge as a result of changed incentives or from a defective, and for the most part irredeemable, cultural environment. Again, behavior is seen as the essential cause of social condition; the ultimate cause of behavior is, from a policy perspective, irrelevant.

A somewhat different school of hierarchists emphasizes the role that public programs have had in weakening the ability of low-level social organizations to enforce desirable, future-oriented behavior. On one extreme are those who emphasize the role of religion and spiritual values in the rise of the underclass. Previous generations of the poor married, went to work, obeyed the law, and contributed to their community because they possessed a belief in a higher power, one who provided hope in this life and judged in the next. Most social provision in this previous era emphasized the spiritual needs of the poor even more than their physical needs and focused on ministering to the poor individually rather than giving them goods by right.[46]

In a less religiously driven context, Nathan Glazer emphasized the role that public interventions have had in eating away at "the traditional constraints that still played the largest role in maintaining a civil society. What kept society going, after all, was that most people still felt they should work—however well they might do without working—and most felt they should take care of their families—however attractive it might appear on occasion to desert them."[47] Hierarchists, like Glazer, may believe that incentives are important, but they believe that in a good society, people will do the right thing regardless of its impact on their short-run financial advantage. Previously, society's upper classes reinforced this attitude. This link, however, has become undone, and the underclass is the consequence. Arguing against the idea that the underclass is the consequence of economic inequality, Myron Magnet suggests that "underclass culture is a much larger, deeper reality. It is formed in the total historical experience of the groups that compose the underclass—and especially their close and complicated interrelationship with the totality of the larger culture."[48] Ultimately, hierarchists believe that poverty is a condition of the soul, and the care of the soul can only be conducted in the proper moral environment. Individualists disagree.

The Individualist Approach: The Power of Incentives

Individualism, as an intellectual construct, finds its grounding in Thomas Hobbes, John Locke, and above all, Adam Smith. In the modern day, the preeminent individualists are economists or those influenced by economic approaches to social science.[49]

The intellectual manifestation of individualism in the realm of poverty and welfare is the incentive approach, which sets aside such things as culture, power, and race and asks simply: "What pays?" Individuals are rational actors, sensitive to price signals. An expensive behavior will be avoided; a cheap one will be pursued. If the poor do not work or do not marry, one must investigate the self-seeking roots of their behavior. For the individualist, there is no such thing as "pathology"; all behavior is rational. The trick is to make what is good for society rational for the individual.

The quintessential, and in a sense the founding, contemporary individualist is Milton Friedman. Friedman may not have been the originator of the negative income tax (NIT),[50] but he was certainly its most popular early proponent. Friedman accepted that poverty was a consequence of the free market, and although he was ambivalent about the desirability of redistribution, he saw the negative income tax as the least incentive-distorting method for reducing poverty. In *Capitalism and Freedom*, he argued that "like any other measures to alleviate poverty, [the negative income tax] reduces the incentives of those helped to help themselves, but it does not eliminate that incentive entirely, as a system of supplementing incomes up to some fixed minimum would. An extra dollar earned always means more money available for expenditure."[51] Redistribution is an inherently problematic enterprise, Friedman warned, but there are better and worse ways of redistribution. The negative income tax was the worst possible method—except for all the other ones.

A somewhat later, and equally compelling, argument for the individualist approach to poverty and welfare is advanced in Arthur Okun's *Equality and Efficiency*. Addressing the behavior-centered approach to poverty, Okun agreed with Banfield that the poor had a different orientation toward the future. "But I believe that he wrongly views present-orientedness as a psychological mystery requiring some deep explanatory structure. As I see it, many of the poor act like there's no tomorrow because their main problem is surviving today. Saving and investment are hardly rational at the cost of survival."[52] Behavior is a consequence of relative prices. If saving for the future is expensive, people will spend today. The goal of policy, therefore, is not to change psychology (which for economists is a fixed commodity[53]) but to change incentives.

Both Okun and Friedman accepted the idea that redistribution, in the form of a negative income tax, would have some negative consequences for overall efficiency and individual work effort. Charles Murray, operating from the same incentive-based approach that Friedman and Okun used, came to quite a different conclusion: The incentive effects of redistribution, either in the current system or as a result of an NIT, are huge and encompass not only work but also family structure. Drawing on evidence from the 1960s and 1970s, Murray developed the following maxims:

> Premise 1: People respond to incentives and disincentives. Sticks and carrots work.

Premise 2: People are not inherently hard working or moral. In the absence of countervailing influences, people will avoid work and be amoral.

Premise 3: People must be held responsible for their actions. Whether they are responsible in some ultimate philosophical or biochemical sense cannot be the issue if society is to function.[54]

These are all core individualist beliefs. Murray found that these maxims were even more valid than Friedman and Okun believed. In fact, any cash redistribution had perverse effects, reducing desirable social behavior among not only the class receiving assistance but also those susceptible to being attracted into that class.[55] Far from being merely ambivalent about the desirability of redistribution, individualists should be positively hostile. George Gilder summarizes the consequences of this thinking: "In order to succeed, the poor need most of all the spur of their own poverty."[56]

Behind all of the individualists' arguments is the primacy of the market. All forms of redistribution are deviations from market rewards and thus inherently treacherous. For some, like Murray, it is so treacherous that it should not be attempted at all. All individualists, however, believe that social policy must conform to the needs of the market: The best policy deforms market incentives least. The argument for incentives is ultimately an argument for the individual as the core of social reality, for the market as the central social institution, and for freedom as the highest value.

The Egalitarian Approach: Alleviating Need, Weakening Social Control

As an intellectual movement, egalitarianism is grounded in the philosophy of Jean-Jacques Rousseau and Karl Marx and in the antiestablishmentarianism of Tom Paine.[57] Egalitarians are committed to democracy as the preeminent social principle, one with consequences far beyond the sphere of government. Democracy is seen as a principle guaranteeing social citizenship and a right to participation in all spheres of society.[58] For egalitarians, rights without the means to exercise them are simply the window-dressing of power, a way of concealing the advantage of a few by presenting the image of a benefit to all. As Herbert Gans argues, "Liberty has become the ideology of the more fortunate to be as free as they were in the past to keep the less fortunate in their place."[59]

The substance of the egalitarians' critique of welfare has been discussed in Chapter 1. Michael Katz, Joel Handler, Frances Fox Piven, and Richard Cloward all agree that the essential function of welfare in a capitalist state is the regulation of the poor. Welfare assistance is not intended to equalize societal opportunity, to redistribute wealth, or to facilitate upward mobility. Rather, it functions to stigmatize out-groups, especially racial minorities,[60] to serve the macroeconomic needs of capital (smoothing out conflict in times of economic contraction, and forcing more individuals into the market in good times).

All egalitarian intellectuals seek a welfare system whose main purpose is the alleviation of need rather than the enforcement of moral norms. They see discussion of "dependency" as a tactic for attributing an individual cause to a social phenomenon. Nancy Fraser and Linda Gordon argue, with one eye on the culture of poverty theorists, that "with economic dependency now a synonym of poverty, and with moral/psychological dependency now a personality disorder, talk of dependency as a social relation of subordination has become increasingly rare. Power and domination tend to disappear."[61]

For egalitarians, generous, "non-punitive, universal income grant program[s],"[62] which are considered the ideal way of helping the poor, are almost always preferable to programs that push the poor into the labor market. Their rationale is that

> income security programs reduce unemployment and temper desperation. They remove millions of people from the labor market and protect millions of others from the ravages of unemployment. The consequence is to tighten labor markets and reduce fear among those still in the market, and thus to strengthen workers in bargaining with employers over wages and working conditions.[63]

Welfare is not an isolated program, unrelated to the larger economic and political structures of society. Current American welfare programs have the effect of reinforcing capitalist growth; egalitarians want them to work against this dynamic and strengthen the power of labor in its competition against capital. If working persons could be made to see that their interest is not in pushing those on welfare into the workforce but in keeping them out, more generous welfare could be an essential part of the reconstruction of a left-wing, class-based party of the oppressed.

Short of a broad-based income guarantee, egalitarians can only accept welfare reform that increases the power of the poor to bargain in a capitalist economy. Egalitarians argue against advocates of workfare, saying that "significant improvement in self-sufficiency cannot occur without dramatic increases in the numbers and favorable locations of available job opportunities for the marginally prepared worker—all else is simply reordering the queue."[64] Coercive welfare reform only has the effect of shoving poor people into a crowded, low-skill economy, which is made even less attractive by the added wage competition that they themselves create. Only completely voluntary education and training programs, which give the poor skills that are not already in high supply, are considered acceptable to egalitarians.

Egalitarian intellectuals are hostile to efforts to use the welfare system to enforce desirable sexual and marital behavior. Egalitarians accept the claim from the right that welfare has the effect of increasing the formation of single-parent households. In fact, egalitarians consider this effect desirable. June Axinn and Amy Hirsch argue,

The current furor over "family disintegration" is a protest against the increased choices women have made in the past several decades. For women in abusive relationships, AFDC has offered hope and choice by supporting women and children outside marriage. Welfare reform that attacks women for having children outside marriage represents a backlash against women's life options outside the traditional family structure.[65]

Welfare has a similar effect on the gender market as it has on the labor market. It gives women more power to negotiate because it gives them the ability to survive without the assistance of a man (just as welfare gives them the ability to survive without the assistance of an employer). The more generous welfare is, the more it empowers women in the home and in the marketplace. Conversely, the more regulative and punitive it becomes, the less power all women possess.

CONCLUSIONS

American elites and the American public at large think in very different ways. Elites emphasize ideological thinking; the public is attracted to approaches that integrate ideas that ideologues see as contradictory. Furthermore, the cultural split within America's elites reproduces itself, in slightly different ways, in a number of contexts. Among professional elites as a whole, the elite conflict can best be described as a battle between traditional and insurgent elites. At the level of charitable foundations that are involved with public policy, the conflict is ideological, while at the level of think tanks and intellectual movements, the division is cultural.

Because America's cultural, political, and intellectual elites use a cognitive approach to public issues that differs greatly from the one the public uses, there is a profound influence on the policies the political system produces. A conjunction of public and elite, which is one definition of a healthy society, would suggest a relatively conflict-free politics; a disjunction suggests that the politics will be unstable and volatile. As the balance of this book suggests, this disjunction has characterized welfare politics since the 1960s.

5

The Failure of Comprehensive Reform

Opposition to AFDC has been strong since the early 1970s, in part as a result of the failure of the new welfare consensus to be translated into public policy. This chapter investigates why that new consensus has failed to lead to a transformation of AFDC.

Two pivotal events in the debate on poverty and welfare in the mid- to late 1960s encapsulate the problems of transforming AFDC in a dissensual political context: the controversy surrounding the document that became known as the Moynihan report and the failed effort to enact the Nixon administration's Family Assistance Plan (FAP). Both the Moynihan report and FAP represented consensus approaches to poverty and welfare in that they were based on a culturally integrative mode of political reasoning. Each attempted to reconcile the various elements of America's cultural heritage by supporting the traditional values of work, family, and self-reliance through an expansion of the government's role in income support and employment. Both the Moynihan report and FAP were attacked most virulently not by those who opposed their call for expanded government but from those on the left who claimed to speak for the less advantaged.

In this chapter I analyze the Moynihan report in depth for two reasons. First, it is important to establish that the report was a progressive response to what was then the very new problem of welfare dependency and to establish Moynihan's reasoning as the consensual road not taken in poverty policy. Second, against that background, the attacks on the report can be seen for what they were: the manifestation of a new kind of left politics in America. That new politics was aggressively monocultural, rejecting any attempt to integrate humanitarian instincts into the other elements of the public's consciousness. That new politics saw America as fundamentally flawed, incapable of responding to the needs of the poor by any but surreptitious means. The attack on the Moynihan report stunted the possibility of a consensus approach to welfare and poverty and set the stage for the divisive politics that have characterized AFDC since the mid-1960s.

Against the background of the attack on the Moynihan report, the defeat of FAP becomes much clearer. FAP was, in retrospect, the last opportunity the nation had to address AFDC in a culturally integrative fashion. The campaign against FAP utilized much of the rhetoric that had been used against the Moynihan report and was based upon a similar political strategy: all or nothing. All of the characteristic elements of dissensus politics emerged in the debate over FAP and led to the defeat of a proposal that would have meant, for millions of the nation's poor, greater income and integration into the American social mainstream. Why such a proposal was defeated by those who claimed to speak for people who would have been helped most by its passage is the primary question I will answer.

THE THEORY OF DISSENSUS AND COMPREHENSIVE POLICY CHANGE

Dissensus is characterized by a structure of opinion in which there are large or intellectually powerful elites at the extremes of the ideological spectrum who possess roughly equal power and in which there is an insufficiently large or intellectually independent element in the center to act without support from parts of both sides. Almost by definition, to be at an ideological extreme is to see evil either in intent or effect in those at the other extreme. Thus, to enter into agreement with the other side is immediately suspect: There must be something wrong with a proposal if the other side is willing to accept it. Jane Mansbridge describes a similar psychopolitical dynamic in her book *Why We Lost the ERA:*

> Like nationalism and some forms of religious conversion, some kinds of political activity engender a transformation of self that requires reconfiguring the world into camps of enemies and friends. Running for office or campaigning for social legislation is likely to have this effect. Other kinds of political activity, like holding political office, require people to break down such boundaries, or at least make them subtle.[1]

This opinion structure leads to a constant ratcheting up of demands. If the other extreme can accept it, then it must not be sufficiently pure. This process leads each side to increasingly purify its position.[2] Every time those in the center think they have created a sufficiently broad agreement to enact a proposal, at least one side will see in it capitulation to evil and will push for more. Dissensus politics is intrinsically Sisyphean, at least from the point of view of those at the center. Every attempt to push the rock of legislation up the hill of sufficient agreement is met with a push back down. The center is attempting to create a consensus that the extremes will by definition be unwilling to accept.

Another aspect of dissensus politics is that it can be created by an intellectual, rather than arithmetic, insufficiency of the political center. In dissensus politics, there may be many individuals who see themselves as moderate liberals or moderate conservatives. The group may, in fact, be large enough to enact comprehensive legislation. In this form of dissensus politics, however, the centrism exists without an intellectually confident alternative to the ideological positions put forth by the extremes. Centrists of this sort see themselves as similar to the radicals but somewhat less strident or insistent on getting everything immediately. They draw their fundamental ideas, however, from those on the extremes.

This structure might work if the views of the extremes are posed in such a way that they involve things that can be subtracted from or added to. This scheme presupposes that the central good in question is agreed upon, and the only differences concern amounts. For example, if a centrist liberal sees himself as a "30 percent-er," meaning that he agrees with those on his left but is willing to take 30 percent less than what they demand, it is possible that consensus can arise if there is a large enough pool of centrists on the other side who are willing to cut a similar percentage off their side's demands, creating an area of overlap. Say, for example, that the liberal extreme has decided that the rich should be taxed at a rate of 50 percent. A 30-percent liberal would say, "I would like to get it up that high, but I am willing to accept anything as low as 35 percent." On the other side, the conservatives have concluded that a 30-percent tax rate is the proper contribution from the rich. A conservative 30-percenter would respond, "I would like to get it that low, but I am willing to accept anything as high as 39 percent." That leaves a range in which the center, while not creating an ideological structure of its own, can come to a consensus because each is willing to negotiate in the range of 35 to 39 percent.

In dissensus politics, however, the positions of the extremes are put in a less easily moderated form because politics is not a matter of negotiations concerning an agreed-upon good. For example, radical egalitarians will say that requiring the poor to do any work for their benefits is racist. Can moderates respond that this is all well and good, but they are willing to be slightly racist in order to get a bill? Conversely, hierarchists might say that not requiring the poor to work off their entire benefit check makes a mockery of the work ethic, and individualists might suggest that welfare as a whole threatens to ruin our capitalist system. Can moderates say that they are willing to ruin 30 percent of the work ethic or the capitalist system to get a bill?

This problem is compounded by the structure of comprehensive reform. By definition, comprehensive reform involves a shift in the existing fundamental expectations, institutions, and patterns of social interaction. It involves scrapping a preexisting system, whose functioning may be obscure and intent difficult to divine, for a new system. Comprehensive reform, in the absence of a true crisis situation (such as the collapse not of the program but of the society in which it operates), demands clarity. The longer the debate on comprehensive change occurs, the more parties to the change will demand that the new standard be made clear. Debate will then occur not just on the change (which might be acceptable on its own) but on the justification (which might be unacceptable, even if used to justify something acceptable). When comprehensive change is attempted, standards of justification must be made clear, but by doing so a new area for conflict is opened up. If the debate is carried on at the level of justification, rather than effect, an ideologically polarized situation will yield no change.

Dissensus and consensus politics are created by, and produce, differing interest group structures. I note that interest groups that are typical of consensus politics have an experience orientation; those that are typical of dissensus politics have an advocacy orientation. Interest groups with an experience orientation gain support by delivering tangible benefits, defined as improvements in the status quo, to those they represent (usually by some sort of membership structure). This sort of group is judged not by the quality of its arguments or the evil of its opposition but by the change in the conditions experienced by those represented. If change does not happen, the group itself, and not its opponent, will be in for a large share of blame. Typical of this organizational pattern are labor unions and most business lobbying groups.

The second type, the advocacy interest group, is not held responsible for changes in the conditions that its followers experience. Instead, the group is given support in exchange for coherently and courageously defending its legitimacy and for presenting its claim of justice in the most unvarnished manner possible. If conditions change for the worse, the blame is rarely placed on the group itself. Instead, blame is placed on its enemy because a deterioration of conditions is not evidence of the incompetence of your advocate but of the illegitimate strength of your opposition. These groups have a mix of members, some of whom belong to the population being advocated for; but in sharp distinction to experience groups, these groups also contain a large number who are not in the affected population but who support the population's interests. These groups have a tendency to be maximalist in their demands because, by accepting anything short of justice, they tarnish their claim to represent not only a population but rectitude itself. In short, experience groups attract support by changing the conditions of the population they represent while advocacy groups are nourished by preserving a standard of rectitude.

The theory of dissensus politics suggests that a dissensus situation contains the following elements: either a numerically small center or a large center split between moderate liberals and moderate conservatives; demands by the ideological extremes that cannot be moderated in such a way as to preserve any of their content; a situation in which more information leads to a hardening of positions rather than suggestions of how those differences can be narrowed; and an advocacy interest group structure. Against this theoretical background, the ordeal of comprehensive change in the AFDC program should be significantly easier to understand and certain key elements of the history will stand out.

THE MOYNIHAN REPORT

The Moynihan report may seem a strange place to begin an analysis of the failure to enact radical reform of the AFDC program because the report did not constitute a formal legislative proposal and did not have AFDC as its principal focus. Still, the Moynihan report does represent the first prominent suggestion that the nation's welfare programs were inadequate to the task of maintaining families and that they should be replaced by encompassing (nontargeted) institutions and policies. The Moynihan report was a call for a radical expansion of the American welfare state. Ten years earlier it would have been seen as such. By 1965, however, it was widely characterized as a message of social regression and an expression of racial animus. How was a call for dramatic liberal change interpreted and denounced as a racist slur?

The most important point to bear in mind when discussing the Moynihan report is that it was not written by Daniel Patrick Moynihan alone. What we know as the Moynihan report, *The Negro Family: The Case for National Action,* was published as a collaborative effort by members of the Department of Labor (DOL) Office of Policy Planning and Evaluation; Moynihan's name never appeared anywhere on the report. These points are not semantic.

The report was only one of a number of such studies done by the office (which Moynihan headed). The studies were a key part of the strategy of the secretary of Commerce and Labor, W. Willard Wirtz, to convince President Lyndon B. Johnson to propose, and Congress to enact, a wide-ranging jobs program to be administered by the Department of Labor. Moynihan had already collaborated on the publication of *One-Third of the Nation,* a study of the rejection rate of those eligible for the draft. That study argued that the high rejection rate was a signal of profound weaknesses in the education, health, and overall fitness of American youth, which if not repaired (by broad-based government programs) would threaten the nation's economic and military security. At the same time, Moynihan's office was also studying the viability of a system of family allowances, along the lines of European pronatal policies. *The Negro Family* was written with much the same intent as *One-Third of the Nation.* These studies attempted to use social science data to support an employment and income strategy for the alleviation of poverty. This agenda was formulated by the secretary of Labor;[3] Moynihan saw his job as providing evidence to support that agenda and, thus, along with his staff, produced *The Negro Family* as a Department of Labor document.

By 1964, the Department of Labor had been virtually locked out of the major programs of the nascent War on Poverty. In place of the jobs and income strategy of the DOL, the White House had thrown its weight behind a strategy of "community action," the intellectual foundations of which were laid by Richard Cloward and Lloyd Ohlin in their work *Delinquency and Opportunity* (which will be discussed in more detail later in this chapter). Proponents of community action saw the problem of black poverty as one of dysfunctional communities. Poor neighborhoods were minimally organized and thus did not possess enough political power to bring social opportunities into their communities. Weak organization failed to create opportunities, the lack of which led youths to seek illegitimate sources of income, and ultimately cut away at the rest of the social infrastructure of poor communities. Community action advocates surmised that if poor communities could be organized, they could extract resources from government, business, and the charitable sector, creating opportunity and reducing deviant behavior.

When this new explanation of poverty and the set of programs were embraced by President Johnson at the expense of the income and jobs strategy of the DOL, Wirtz and Moynihan despaired. How could they get the president behind their program? Moynihan thought that *One-Third of the Nation* would provide a dramatic foundation for such a proposal, but the White House was not as interested as he had hoped. In late 1964 Moynihan noticed an odd trend in unemployment and AFDC enrollment. The two trends had previously run parallel, but they had just started to run in opposite directions. Unemployment was falling, but welfare dependency was increasing. Suspecting that something important was behind these numbers, Moynihan put his office to work.

What the Office of Policy Planning and Evaluation discovered was published in the now-famous work entitled *The Negro Family: The Case for National Action.* The report represented a new type of policy and political strategy. It argued that the major goals of the New Deal—economic stabilization; providing for the aged, blind, disabled, and unemployed; reining in corporate power—had been or were nearly met. The social problems that the New Deal aimed to fix had been essentially caused by a disequilibrium of power. Big business had power, the mass of people did not, and corporations used their power to keep wages low and social provision meager. The New Deal had partially solved this disequilibrium but had left a number of problems that were not willed, not directly attributable to, anyone. The New Deal pitted group against group, but the report suggested that more recent social problems were not caused by the dominance of one group over another. Most of these social problems were caused by inaction, by the fact that no single group was either aware of the problem or was sufficiently motivated to push for action. A new kind of social policy would emerge from the observations of a new class of social scientists, who would discover dangerous social trends and point to means for averting or reversing their growth.

Moynihan presumed that the liberal nature of this enterprise would be obvious. In the older politics of the New Deal and before, the discussion by a member of one group of the problems of another was a means of preserving a disequilibrium of power; for example, whites in the South would point to blacks' perceived inability to control their sexual appetites or taste for violence as a means of protecting the status quo. Moynihan was pointing to similar behavioral dysfunctions but with a very different agenda, which was signaled by the report's subtitle, *The Case for National Action*. Moynihan had observed a similar pattern among early Irish immigrants in *Beyond the Melting Pot*,[4] which pointed out the loss of cultural subtlety and self-control that had accompanied the transition from rural Ireland to urban New York. After a period of time, however, the community righted itself and began its collective rise up the socioeconomic scale. In *The Negro Family*, Moynihan described a similar pattern, with one terrible exception. Black Americans were experiencing the same behavioral problems as the Irish but did not show signs of cultural correction and ascent. Instead, blacks were headed in the direction of retrogression and descent.

What explains the difference? "The fundamental, overwhelming fact is that Negro unemployment, with the exception of a few years during World War II and the Korean War, had continued at disaster levels for 35 years."[5] The unemployment of the male head of the household led to a transference of power to the female because it was through her that relief could be obtained. For the most part, AFDC at this time was only available to unattached women (the AFDC-UP program had been enacted just two years earlier), and thus the only aid available to poor families was provided to women, largely through female social workers. With his role in the family shattered, the black male either deserted or became estranged from his family. Only work could remedy this cycle and bring the male back into the family, but "work is precisely the one thing the Negro family head in such circumstances has not received over the last generation."[6] Adding to the problem was the generally low income that black men could generate for their families even if they could get jobs, which created strains in the family and led to breakdown.

Those years of crisis unemployment, combined with a cultural weakness caused by the experience of slavery and the movement from the rural south to the urban north, created a situation in which welfare and unemployment had become uncoupled, which resulted in a cultural shift. To this phenomenon, Moynihan applied the term "tangle of pathology." By pathology, Moynihan did not intend to insult the black community or to argue that the problems of black Americans were of their own creation. Instead, he argued that the tangle of pathology "is not the least vicious aspect of the world that white America has made for the Negro."[7] Racial segregation and slavery had created a problem significantly more severe than polite opinion had previously accepted. A rational reading of the report would lead one to conclude that Moynihan was simply pointing out the results of 300 years of slavery, segregation, racism, and economic discrimination and suggesting that the removal of those factors would not be sufficient to compensate for their effects. Things had gone too far for society to get out the door through which it had come in.

Those writing about the Moynihan report often fail to mention the other articles that he published at the same time. In an article in the Catholic magazine *America*, Moynihan suggested, "The United States is very possibly on the verge of adopting a national policy directed to the quality and stability of American family life. It would mean an extraordinary break with the past. This could be the central event of our new era of social legislation."[8] What was so new about "family policy?" Prior to the "new era," which he predicted, "American social policy . . . has been directed toward the individual. The individual—and the various circumstances relating to him—have been our primary unit of measurement: men, women and children all lumped together."[9] Only one program of the national government aided families, AFDC, and it did so only for families that had begun to (or had already) come apart. He found that "what the AFDC program has amounted to for most of its history is a family allowance program for broken families."[10] At the same time, however, there was no program or institution within our government aimed at preventing the dissolution of families.

Moynihan chose the black family as the opening wedge in developing a national family policy. It was with the black family that the enormity of the government's failure was clearest, the gravity of its responsibility was largest, and the impact of increased employment and income support would be the most profound. Moynihan pointed out that "as society, in the form of government, more and more acknowledges its responsibilities to the poor and disadvantaged, it follows that it must be concerned with family patterns that help or hinder efforts to bring people out of poverty and into the mainstream of American life."[11]

In essence, what Moynihan proposed was that the irrational provision of aid to broken but not intact families be eliminated by pulling all families into a system of children's allowances. This aid would eliminate the incentive for a family to split up in order to receive aid, and (of more importance) it would prevent family income from dropping precipitously—a crisis that could damage the family's stability. Combined with the massive jobs and training programs that the Department of Labor was pushing, a national family policy would amount to a system of social insurance for all families. It would stabilize the poor black families described in *The Negro Family* by the same method that it would aid all American families, a strategy that social scientists would later call "targeting within universalism." This strategy would provide the foundation for virtually every future effort to transform the nation's welfare programs.

To put it mildly, Moynihan's strategy failed. What happened next is the subject of some controversy. There are those on the right who remember the Moynihan report controversy as the collapse of the moral center of liberalism, and to some degree they are right. Glenn Loury, for example, remembers that "those committed to the silencing of Moynihan, and to the banishment of the topic of behavioral pathology in the ghetto from public discussion, managed to have their way."[12] For conservatives, the outcome of the controversy was that blacks' role in remedying their own condition, and the need for independent social uplift on their part, was banished from the discussion of poverty. This account ignores the fact that a debate on pathology in the black community was not what Moynihan was trying to spark. Conservatives fall prey to the same misperception that liberals at the time did. The only difference was that conservatives found some merit in focusing on deviance at the level of the individual whereas liberals at the time called it "blaming the victim." Moynihan was trying to use the plight of the black family as evidence of the nation's failure to anticipate and use the resources of the national government to remedy a range of major social problems.

The crux of the conflict over the Moynihan report had to do with race, but not all black leaders were on one side and all whites on the other. In fact, the most virulent attacks on Moynihan's racial motivations came from whites, and some of his most important supporters, at least in the beginning, were blacks. The split occurred not on what were the clear ramifications of Moynihan's analysis: more employment for black men, income support for poor families, better education, and so on. Rather, the conflict occurred at the level of justification. Moynihan justified this increase in government effort on the basis of family dysfunction. Those who could accept that there was a problem with the state of black families supported Moynihan and stressed the role that employment and income support would play. Those who could not accept that there was a problem condemned Moynihan and ignored his call for such policies, usually because of their belief that such an emphasis meant deemphasizing further efforts against discrimination.

In the first group were many of the most important black civil rights leaders. Before President Johnson made his famous speech at Howard University, which was written by Moynihan and embodied most of the arguments in *The Negro Family*, the address was cleared by Martin Luther King of the Southern Christian Leadership Conference (SCLC) and Bayard Rustin of the National Association for the Advancement of Colored People (NA ACP), which at the time were the largest civil rights groups in the nation. Both supported the speech wholeheartedly. King echoed the report's spirit perfectly.

> A recent study offers the alarming conclusion that the Negro family in the urban ghettos is crumbling and disintegrating. It suggests that the progress in civil rights can be negated by the dissolving of family structure and therefore social justice and tranquility can be delayed for generations. . . . As public awareness increases there will be dangers and opportunities. The opportunity will be to deal fully rather than haphazardly with the problem as a whole—to see it as a social catastrophe and meet it as other disasters are met—with an adequacy of resources. The danger will be that the problems will be attributed to innate Negro weaknesses and used to justify neglect and rationalize oppression.[13]

King understood very well that the issue of the black family could cut two ways. He made a judgment that the problem was severe enough, and the goodwill created by the civil rights movement strong enough, that it could be made to cut the right way. Therefore, he supported the report and continued to discuss the problem in the few years he had left.

By 1965, however, Martin Luther King was not the only, or necessarily even the strongest, voice for black America. James Farmer of the Congress on Racial Equality (CORE) supported an opposing interpretation of Moynihan's report, suggesting that the report represented a more sophisticated form of the same rhetoric blacks had heard from Southern segregationists. "By laying the blame for present-day inequalities on the pathological condition of the Negro family and community, Moynihan has provided a massive academic cop-out for the white conscience and clearly implied that Negroes in this nation will never secure a substantial measure of freedom until we learn to behave ourselves and stop buying Cadillacs instead of bread."[14] Farmer represented a mind-set that had not yet recognized that all issues affecting blacks were not necessarily framed in terms of insult or compliment to the race. Moynihan's study was not intended as either, although it certainly did put a great deal of blame on one group: whites. Farmer's decision to frame the report in terms of symbolic politics—"who is a greater friend of black people"—prevented him from seeing the obvious conclusions of the report, as King did. This reaction explains Farmer's error in stating that "nowhere does Moynihan suggest that the proper answer to a shattered family is an open job market where this 'frustrated' male Negro can get an honest day's work."[15] If anything Moynihan went further than Farmer, suggesting that even a nondiscriminatory job market was insufficient to the challenge of providing job opportunities for blacks. Like King, Moynihan was beginning to think beyond an antidiscrimination framework for civil rights. He and King saw that the future development of black-white equality would be accomplished by aiding blacks within the context of programs for everyone. This vision required a level of even-headedness that, at the time, Farmer was incapable of. "I say all this because I'm angry," Farmer wrote, "really angry and I intend to spell out this anger in just one more effort to convince somebody, anybody, down in the places of power that the cocktail hour on the 'Negro Question' is over and that we are sick unto death of being analyzed, mesmerized, bought, sold and slobbered over while the same evils that are the ingredients of our oppression go unattended."[16]

As it happens, parts of the Moynihan report have stood the test of time, while others have not. Moynihan's argument that there were weaknesses in black family structure inherited from slavery, an argument he lifted virtually unedited from E. Franklin Frazier (the sociologist and first black president of the American Sociological Association), has been called into question by a number of social scientists. The most important study of the subject, Herbert Gutman's *The Black Family in Slavery and Freedom*, which was an explicit attempt to test this side of the Moynihan thesis,[17] concluded that blacks had maintained family and kin relations throughout slavery and that family dissolution in the black community was the result of influences that were felt after the great black migration to the cities. This point, however, does not damage Moynihan's central intent for the report, which was to alert the policy-making community to the effects of high levels of unemployment on black family structure. If anything, arguing that things were better before the onset of high levels of unemployment makes his basic point all the more compelling because unemployment must have been an even more dev-astating factor if it could erode fundamentally strong black families. This aspect of the Moynihan report has been powerfully supported by William Julius Wilson's research, including *The Truly Disadvantaged,* a work that can be seen as an attempt to resurrect Moynihan's employment-based argument.[18] Unfortunately, many critics of the Moynihan report substituted invective for analysis, attacking Moynihan for his hidden racist or sexist motivations and ignoring the progressive policy implications of his argument. This reaction helped make the Moynihan report a document remembered more fondly by conservatives, who recall only the argument about the effects of illegitimacy, than by liberals, who until recently have ignored the strong public employment implications of his argument.

By the time Farmer's columns were published on the subject, the issue was no longer the Moynihan report as such but the phantom issue of black versus white blame. What was lost was that Moynihan had clearly intended the report as the first shot in an effort to pull centrist Americans into the struggle for black equality. The debate never got back to Moynihan's fundamental concern: Family structure and economic opportunity were linked. Thereafter, the debate settled into who sided with the former or the latter as the main cause of black problems. Moynihan presented a framework in which both could be seen as relevant simul-taneously: the epitome of consensus politics. Once the debate stopped being about the report itself, as it did almost from day one, that consensual mode broke down and along with it any chance that the nation could enact sweeping reform in its support for families. The debate never progressed to the point at which AFDC was addressed specifically, as it would have had to be, given the thrust of Moynihan's analysis. Welfare reform was killed before it got off the ground. Welfare dependency continued to rise, setting the stage for the next major attempt at changing the American welfare system.

THE RISE OF THE WELFARE RIGHTS MOVEMENT

Most accounts of the collapse of Richard Nixon's Family Assistance Plan present the welfare rights movement as a late entrant into the politics of its rejection. In this reading, the National Welfare Rights Organization entered the fray at the very end, using its vigorous efforts to reject FAP as a strategy to increase the group's strength by forcing the establishment to deal with them as the welfare recipients' true representative. This type of account ignores the important role that the welfare rights movement played in setting the stage for the creation of FAP, by forcing a series of changes in law and administration that made change of some sort inevitable. Even in Daniel Patrick Moynihan's book on the subject, *The Politics of a Guaranteed Income,* NWRO's role in creating the welfare explosion that led to FAP is ignored. We have to put the welfare rights movement at the center of our account of the FAP debacle if we are to see not only why it lost but why it became an issue at all.

The rise of NWRO and its role in the rejection of the Family Assistance Plan are crucial to an understanding of why comprehensive reform of AFDC is impossible in a dissensual political climate. Although NWRO claimed to represent the interests of welfare mothers, it was in fact not organized in a representative fashion. It never claimed more than a small percentage of the AFDC population as members and only in the high-benefit states. It was always oriented toward highly symbolic victories, rejected real improvements in the condition of those on welfare in favor of impossibly optimistic alternatives, and failed to ever connect the needs of the poor with the values of mainstream America. Although seemingly more radical than its historical predecessor, the mothers' pension movement, NWRO was ultimately less successful. The difference between the two movements, which in many ways pursued similar goals, is the difference between consensus and dissensus politics.

The crisis in welfare did not just happen. It was the result of a well thought through strategy by a number of groups that stylized themselves as advocates for the poor. The strategy was the practical expression of a particular theory of the politics and ethics of social welfare. To adequately understand how the crisis occurred, we must see why those who created it did so.

One of the little-read (at least today) classics of social welfare studies is Richard Cloward's and Lloyd Ohlin's *Delinquency and Opportunity*. Published in 1960, it presented a theory of poverty and delinquency that was to have important effects on poverty politics in the 1960s and beyond. Cloward and Ohlin differed with previous analysts of delinquency, who envisioned the deviant youth as somehow developmentally handicapped and thus in need of the rehabilitative intervention of a social worker trained in modern professional methods. The analysis of *Delinquency and Opportunity* pointed in the opposite direction. Delinquent youth were not inadequately socialized. Indeed, they responded to their environment in a manner that had all the hallmarks of rationality. "Adolescents who form delinquent subcultures, we suggest, have internalized an emphasis on conventional goals. Faced with limitations on legitimate avenues of access to these goals, and unable to revise their aspirations downward, they experience intense frustrations; the exploration of nonconforming alternatives may be the result."[19] Cloward and Ohlin suggested that to understand the problems of deviancy, attention should be focused on the institutions surrounding the ghetto youth, not the youth himself.

Why was opportunity blocked for ghetto youth? The core of the institutional problem is the dysfunctional nature (for the poor) of the ghetto community. The dysfunction is manifested in the disorganized nature of those communities, which "cannot provide the resources and opportunities that are required if the young are to move upward in the social order."[20] Cloward and Ohlin derived this connection by reference to a classic pluralist explanation of differential group power. When a community is organized it can wield power vis-à-vis other interests and receive its share of the social pie. This explains why Cloward and Ohlin concluded their study by finding that "the major effort of those who wish to eliminate delinquency should be directed to the reorganization of slum communities."[21]

The first part of this strategy was community action. Lloyd Ohlin was brought into the Kennedy administration as the director of the Office of Juvenile Delinquency in the Department of Health, Education and Welfare and was subsequently appointed executive director of the President's Commission on Juvenile Delinquency. Ohlin used this position to push the War on Poverty toward an emphasis on community action, a strategy that sought to eliminate poverty by providing support for local organizations that would both deliver services and bargain against other groups that had resources necessary to their community's welfare.[22]

Cloward and Ohlin presented a theory at odds with then-contemporary understandings of the nature of poverty. Whereas most in the Kennedy-Johnson administration saw poverty as an aberration in America, *Delinquency and Opportunity* suggested that it might be functional for society's institutions. The argument was put succinctly a few years later by Herbert Gans, who concluded his famous article, "The Positive Functions of Poverty," by stating:

> To wit: social phenomena which are functional for affluent groups and dysfunctional for the poor ones persist; that when the elimination of such phenomena through functional alternatives generates dysfunctions for the affluent, they will continue to persist; and that phenomena like poverty can be eliminated only when they . . . become sufficiently dysfunctional to change the system of social stratification.[23]

The difference between viewing poverty as functional or aberrant is not insignificant. If poverty is aberrant, it makes sense to assume no malevolent intent on the part of the existing political system and to work with that system to eliminate it. If, however, you view poverty as functional, meaning that the political system has an interest in perpetuating poverty, you are likely to view that system as your enemy and to view any suboptimal change as an effort to buy off the poor. The political strategy that emerged from this theory was the latter, and it led to a frontal assault on the stability of the American welfare system.

Richard Cloward went on to work with Frances Fox Piven to develop a movement based on these principles. In "A Strategy to End Poverty," published in the *Nation* in 1966, they laid out a strategy for realizing a guaranteed annual income. The first wave would work within the current policy and institutional structure of the American system but would involve hijacking those institutions, turning their own laws against them. AFDC, the largest public relief program, was administered so as to keep the poor off the rolls. Piven and Cloward's first strategy was to make AFDC politically unstable by implementing a "massive drive to recruit the poor onto the welfare rolls."[24] They estimated that over half of those eligible for assistance under the AFDC program were not receiving aid. "Until now," Piven and Cloward observed, "they have been inhibited from asserting claims by self-protecting devices within the welfare system: its capacity to limit information, to intimidate applicants, to demoralize recipients and arbitrarily to deny lawful claims."[25] Through a "massive educational campaign" the administrators of aid would be stripped of their power over AFDC recipients and would thus be flooded with applications for assistance. If no further reaction occurred, great strides would be made in the interests of the poor, both by getting them the aid to which they were legally entitled and by the organization that would be the result of the campaign.

Piven and Cloward gave a name to the kind of politics they were pursuing: dissensus.[26] The idea was to continue to attack the stability of the system until it completely broke down. Since the objective was total victory rather than gradual improvement, the strategy rejected out of hand conciliation, compromise, or coalition-building: all the hallmarks of consensus politics. This approach had a further function. Piven and Cloward, unlike "technocratic" poverty intellectuals, thought in terms of creating a movement. Creating and maintaining a movement requires two basic elements: selective incentives and high levels of moral fervor. The selective incentives of Piven and Cloward's movement for a guaranteed annual income were provided by the AFDC benefits, which welfare rights groups helped poor people receive. Joining the group would have immediate tangible financial benefits, which would lead to continuing fidelity to the movement. This fidelity would be reinforced by the no-compromise strategy. Keeping pressure on the welfare system until it broke meant that the movement would be continually hit with setbacks. For an experience group this process would be devastating, but for an advocacy group it is of the essence. Defeat would only prove the moral worthiness of the poor and the cravenness of the establishment. This strategy would be of critical importance when the Family Assistance Plan was debated in the Senate.

The effort at additional enrollment took two forms. The first was a litigation strategy, which sought to increase the welfare rolls by eliminating the various obstacles to assistance that states had used, such as morality tests and residency requirements. The second form was direct organization of the poor by local organizations, most of which were associated with the National Welfare Rights Organization. NWRO was organized as a grass-roots group driven by welfare recipients—albeit a group funded and conceived by upper middle-class social reformers. Supported by charitable contributions, federal government community action funds, the small contributions of welfare mothers, and other funds squeezed out of sympathetic groups, NWRO grew steadily. NWRO provided assistance to people in getting on the welfare rolls, avoiding work requirements, obtaining special needs grants (which at the time could be quite substantial), and fighting attempts to push recipients off the rolls. NWRO did not center its efforts on lobbying legislative officials. Rather, it attacked high-benefit states at the level of the local welfare office, exploiting AFDC's weakest spot—its own rules. As noted in Chapter 2, the welfare rights movement was, in the short term, quite successful. Participation rates shot up, the total welfare population increased, and the funds committed to the poor skyrocketed.

However, such cost increases demanded a governmental response. One need not take a doctrinaire state-centered approach to realize why rapidly increasing budget items that are uncontrollable within an administrative context are priorities for a political system. A priority of all governments is control over the costs incurred by its programs. When the government loses control, that is, when costs increase without a collective decision to bring about those increases, a fundamental aspect of sovereignty is brought into question. Certain programs are designed to increase and decrease counter-cyclically, such as unemployment insurance. These fluctuations do not present challenges to political sovereignty, at least in the short run. AFDC is a different case altogether. Increased AFDC costs were a function of changing social patterns, hostile litigation, and low-level organization, factors over which the political system had little or no control. Welfare reform in such a situation is mandatory because without it the authority of the political system, its ability to set its own agenda, and pick its own financial priorities is undermined. This kind of situation was, of course, just what the welfare rights movement had in mind.

In what would prove to be a prescient comment, Piven and Cloward noted in 1968 that "a dissensual political strategy is risky for another reason. The poor who generate disruption have little control over the responses to it."[27] Piven and Cloward developed a very precarious strategy, one dependent upon a particular set of establishment responses at each stage. By 1968, the first steps had succeeded gloriously. The AFDC system was well on the way to being transformed from a highly discretionary grant-in-aid program to a near-entitlement (as measured by participation rates), and this transformation had wreaked havoc on the finances of state and national governments. The political system had two alternatives: an effort to somehow push the new recipients off the rolls or cut their benefits, or the federalization of the program and its transformation into a broad-based income maintenance program. Piven and Cloward predicted the latter, since the litigation and organization of the earlier stages would make a "repressive" strategy unworkable. As it happened, a guaranteed annual income was proposed by Richard Nixon in 1969 (with the encouragement of Pat Moynihan, who by this point was assistant to the president for urban affairs). In the end the income maintenance option failed and the "repression" option succeeded. How did this happen?

FAILURE OF THE FAMILY ASSISTANCE PLAN

In large measure, the income maintenance strategy failed because of the actions of the welfare rights movement itself. There is insufficient room in this chapter to discuss all the details of how FAP came to be proposed and ultimately rejected, but some background is useful. In the campaign of 1968, Richard Nixon stated a guarded, but ultimately negative view on the idea of a guaranteed annual income. During that campaign however, he had given support for the equalization of benefits across the nation[28] and had suggested that a central defect of the present system was the absence of a strong work incentive. Although campaign statements suggest that he was not thinking about moving toward a radical change in the welfare system, the upshot of the comments he did make was in a direction consistent with such a shift. At the same time, forces within the Republican party, such as the Ripon Society, had specified a negative income tax as the best way to achieve Nixon's two objectives.[29] Furthermore, Nixon appointed an assistant for urban affairs (Daniel Patrick Moynihan) who had strongly supported an income strategy against poverty (albeit one based on a family allowance, rather than a negative income tax [NIT]).[30]

The process that led Nixon to propose an NIT was best described by Vincent and Vee Burke, who called it a "conspiracy for the poor."[31] The NIT idea had been bouncing around the poverty-fighting community, and especially within HEW, for a number of years and was the subject of what may be the largest planned social experiment in world history: the federal negative income tax experiment. Nixon's transition committee on welfare, headed by Richard Nathan, had decided that the administration would push for a floor on welfare payments, to be paid for by the federal government.[32] This floor would have the effect of increasing payments in low-benefit states dramatically while also providing substantial fiscal relief to state and local governments, a major administration priority. The Nathan committee's recommendation soon evolved into a full-blown NIT, with a work incentive (benefits would only be reduced by half of earned income) and a provision that states whose benefits were above the floor (set at $450 per adult and $300 per child[33]) would be required to maintain their current levels.

There was substantial opposition within Nixon's cabinet—notably from Arthur Burns and Martin Anderson, who likened the proposal to the Speenhamland program of 1795,[34] but Nixon (with the strong encouragement of his HEW Secretary Robert Finch and Moynihan) decided that FAP would be his program, the center of a Nixon strategy against poverty. In typical consensus politics form, Nixon decided to co-opt the program of his opponents. He would agree with them on the need for a guaranteed annual income and then make it his achievement, sold under his own rhetoric (supporting the dignity of work). Because it was their idea in the first place, liberals would have to accept it. Who on the left would oppose more than quadrupling the welfare benefits of a Mississippi child? The substance would be the same, but the symbolic victory would be for the value of work, not the insufficiency of the capitalist system.[35]

The fight over FAP was delayed somewhat and those supporting it were caught off guard later by the honorable and professional treatment it received in the House of Representatives.[36] The political structure of the House at the time was such that great deference existed toward the Ways and Means Committee.

"Where so many political institutions are skewed in one direction or another, and much taken up with the advancement of particular positions or causes, much concerned with the symbols of politics," Moynihan has written, "Ways and Means was almost wholly taken up with its substance."[37] This orientation to "substance" was respected by the House as a whole, which led to the tradition of treating committee legislation under a closed rule "on the theory that tax bills were too complex and important for uninformed outsiders to tamper with."[38] This special role meant that a consensus style of politics, governed by a norm of professionalism, was institutionalized in the treatment of subjects under the committee's jurisdiction.

This norm of professionalism, supported by a high quality staff, meant that the committee had the capacity to rewrite suggested legislation on its own or with the assistance of the executive branch bureaucracy. The absence of such a capacity, and a professional norm, was an important cause of the ideological circus that FAP became when it was taken up by the Senate Finance Committee. The first difference with the Senate Finance Committee was that Ways and Means understood that the program could only be discussed in comparison with the system that already existed. Given that the inadequacy of AFDC was no longer in question and that a Republican president had suggested improving it by moving in a more compassionate direction (in distinction to the 1967 Social Security amendments), the only question left for a Democratic committee was: Will the proposed legislation operate as advertised?

Because the committee had the capacity to rewrite the legislation itself, it could make the incremental changes necessary to satisfy itself that the program would lead to genuine improvement. It added somewhat to the fiscal relief for high-benefit states, provided a greater incentive to federal takeover of administration, and established full federal funding for child care projects.[39] Ways and Means reported the bill out of committee on a vote of 21 to 3. It passed the full House by 243 to 155, with roughly equal numbers of Democrats and Republicans supporting the bill. In the end, the primary opposition to the bill came from Republican conservatives and Southern Democrats, a typical voting pattern of the time.

As I mentioned before, nothing in the political pattern in the House prepared the bill's supporters for the incredible political alignment that occurred in the Senate. In the House, opposition to the bill was on the right-wing side of the ideological spectrum, and centrist support was cemented by Ways and Means' role in the legislation; in contrast, the Senate saw an utterly new ideological structure: both extremes against the middle.

The conservative opposition to FAP was predictable. After all, it established the quintessentially liberal principle of a guaranteed annual income. The Nixon administration hoped that many conservatives could be swayed by FAP's antibureaucratic administrative structure and by its work provisions. Many in the House were so swayed, and on the Ways and Means Committee a forceful conservative argument against FAP was all but absent. One could have predicted that this conservative support would dissipate once the real facts about FAP became clearer. This dissipation was inevitable given that the program's work provisions, at least on paper, were weaker than those currently in place (under the Work Incentive Program).

What was less easily predicted was liberal opposition to the program, opposition that was the key ingredient in FAP's collapse. To understand why FAP failed, it is necessary to go to the end of the story first. FAP was voted down in the Finance Committee by a margin of 10 to 6. Included in the opposition were Senators Fred Harris, Eugene McCarthy, and Albert Gore, Sr., all of whom were among the most liberal members of the Senate. Had these senators supported FAP, the margin would have been 9 to 7 in favor of reporting the bill out of committee, and the bill would almost assuredly have been approved by the full Senate.

At this juncture we return to the National Welfare Rights Organization and the welfare crisis strategy of that organization and others in its movement. If we set aside the money aspect of the program, we note that FAP would have established an institutional structure significantly more favorable to generous welfare payments than the AFDC structure. As Paul Peterson and Mark Rom argue in *Welfare Magnets*, under a national standard benefits are more likely to increase than decrease. This is not true simply because a national floor (which FAP would have established) would have raised the payments in the lowest-benefit states, such as Mississippi, but also because it would reduce the incentive for high-paying states to lower their benefits. Peterson and Rom explain it:

> Government officials in states with high benefit levels perceive that poor people are migrating into their state, apparently in response to their relatively high welfare benefits. The more the state does for its needy, the more needy people it attracts from throughout the country, and the higher the percentage of poverty the state suffers.[40]

The welfare rights organizations did not anticipate the pressure on benefit levels in states like New York and California that was caused by those states being perceived as welfare magnets. FAP, by reducing the gap between high- and low-benefit states, would have limited the political incentives for lowering benefits in the states where NWRO was most highly organized.

Furthermore, FAP would have transferred a great deal of authority over benefit levels to the national government, whereas in the AFDC system benefit levels are set solely by the states. By folding together the working and nonworking poor in a system with a 50-percent tax on earnings, moreover, politicians translated their desires to raise the benefit level of low-earning workers into higher benefits for the nonworking (NWRO's constituency). FAP would have centralized financial decision-making for welfare and would have created a more politically sound foundation for future increases in benefits. Institutionally, then, FAP would have been a dramatic improvement over AFDC.

NWRO and its controversial chairman George Wiley did not concentrate on the institutional aspects of FAP but on its immediate financial consequences. The institutional argument for FAP was complicated, and Wiley was in charge of a movement, not the Syracuse Chemistry Department (where he once taught). The gap between the $1,600 FAP promised ($2,400 when food stamps were folded in) and the amounts paid in the high-benefit states was dramatic, and even when the administration added a provision that no state's benefit levels would go down as a consequence of FAP, most of NWRO's constituency wound up with nothing more, at least in the short run.

The decision was not difficult: a new system, which at best promised no improvement for the organization's constituency, or the old system, which NWRO had become very adept at exploiting (flooding the system with requests for special needs, such as furniture and winter clothing). NWRO responded to the proposal by calling it repressive, which in a certain sense was accurate. FAP was designed to eliminate AFDC's discretionary character, which had become the central means by which NWRO increased its membership rolls (by trading help with administrators for membership and payment of dues to the organization). With this discretion eliminated, the organizational basis of the movement Wiley was trying to create, which went far beyond welfare, would have been destroyed. This explains why "NWRO . . . sabotaged an effort by Common Cause, a citizens lobby, to marshal a coalition behind a compromise."[41] NWRO's role in the process was not to support the concept of the bill while attempting to make it more generous[42] (as was the case with Senator Abraham Ribicoff of Connecticut) but to assault the motives underlying the bill and thus to eat away at the political foundations of those who might support it.

This was certainly the effect on the three liberal senators who voted with the conservative majority in the Senate Finance Committee. Wiley's rhetoric of repression and impugning of motives infected their thinking and made it impossible for them to support any bill that a majority of the Senate could accept. Senator Fred Harris originally supported the FAP concept while also claiming (mistakenly) that its proposed levels would "mean for many a sad plunge into the lower depths of even greater poverty"[43] and thus counterproposed a negative income tax beginning at $2,520 and reaching the poverty line of $3,740 in three years.[44] Senator McCarthy accepted NWRO's proposal of $5,500 a year, but this support was more symbolic than real.[45] Gore never offered a counterproposal and at various times attacked the proposal from both the right and the left (appropriate given that he was a liberal senator from a basically conservative state).

All three senators were insensitive to the precarious political compromises that went into the administration's FAP proposal and did not comprehend that the real alternative to FAP was not something better for poor people but something much worse. These senators did not recognize that the politics of welfare in

1969 and 1970 was such that something would be done. The political pressure, both from state officials and the general public, was in the direction of reducing the rolls. The brilliance of the FAP strategy (from the liberal point of view) was that it harnessed the public's desire to reduce the rolls by actually increasing them. NWRO and the liberals who supported it did not realize that the movement's strategy of creating a crisis in order to get a guaranteed annual income was very precarious and could lead to a real crackdown as easily as it could to the end they desired. They did not realize that FAP went as far, perhaps farther, in the liberal direction as the politics of the situation would permit. They may have thought that if they forced the system into greater resistance, as with the SCLC's strategy in the South, it would reach a point where it could no longer resist and would have to capitulate. If so, they were very wrong.

FAP, at least in its manner of presentation if not in the substance of the proposal, was an attempt to fuse egalitarian and hierarchical cultural principles: egalitarian because it proposed to dramatically expand the federal government's direct spending on the poor as well as equalize funding geographically (between the North and the South); hierarchical because (at least in its rhetoric) it directed this redistribution through the principle of work. In this, it greatly resembled the cultural pattern of the Moynihan report, with its plea for greater federal aid to the poor supported by the hierarchical principle of family stability. Both FAP and the Moynihan report were repudiated because egalitarians had rejected making coalitions with hierarchists (as they were willing to do during the New Deal) and had swung their attention over to cultural individualists and their rights-orientation. This coalition was able to defeat arguments like the Moynihan report or programs like FAP but would prove highly ineffective at generating popular or congressional support for egalitarian alternatives.

Congress was already weakening as the focus for the poverty warriors' attention. With its horse-trading and changes on the margin, Congress was an inhospitable place for the welfare rights movement. By the late 1960s, the welfare rights movement had found a place it could call home: the Supreme Court.[46]

THE ALTERNATIVE TO FAP: THE WORK INCENTIVE PROGRAM (WIN)

Although the members of the welfare rights movement and its allies were successful in blocking comprehensive reform that was less sweeping and generous than they would have liked, they were not able to quench the public's desire for welfare reform. The crucial assumption of the Piven and Cloward approach was that a guaranteed income was the only solution to the welfare problem and that, even if this was not possible, the flood of new recipients constituted progress in and of itself. Regression in the nation's welfare system was not a live option in their strategy, but that was what happened.

Warning signs were visible years before the debate over FAP. The clearest one was the passage of the 1967 amendments to the Social Security Act, in particular the Work Incentive program (WIN). The principal elements of the 1967 amendments were a requirement that every state establish a work program for those on welfare, with sanctions (including the elimination of the welfare grant entirely) for noncompliance; a financial incentive for work, known as the "30 and 1/3 rule," which exempted the first $30 of wages and one-third of any additional wage; day care for those required to work; a cap on the number of persons under 18 who could receive welfare payments (which was never implemented); and a requirement that states provide family planning services for those on welfare.[47]

Both the Senate Finance and the House Ways and Means committees had come to the conclusion that the 1962 amendments had not succeeded and that the issue was becoming politically charged. The House report observed: "Your committee is very deeply concerned that such a large number of families have not achieved independence and self-support, and is very greatly concerned over the rapidly increasing cost to the taxpayers. Moreover, your committee is aware that the growth in this program has received increasingly critical public attention."[48] There could have been no clearer signal as to the alternative to FAP than the committee's clear words just three years before the FAP debate. First, the committee expressed a concern for dependency and, particularly, with the large numbers of persons on the welfare rolls. Second, it suggested that Congress was aware that the "increasing cost to the taxpayers" was making AFDC an important political issue. Taken together, these two points suggest that FAP went far beyond what Congress might otherwise accept. Even at the $1,600 level the program was far more progressive than what Congress had already enacted just three years earlier. Furthermore, the WIN approach was all that was left after FAP was defeated, and although it was never implemented with any degree of seriousness, WIN did require a substantial amount of hassle and inconvenience for those on the rolls and did prepare the way for the more stringent work requirements of the 1980s. At the least, WIN set the stage for WIN II, which eliminated many of the exemptions that WIN had provided for mandatory work and training.

FAP pushed the political system as far left as it was then willing to go. By the time the program was better understood, especially in regard to its primarily cosmetic work requirements, many hierarchists (Southerners in the Democratic party and Westerners in the Republican party) went from suspicion to outright opposition. A number of writers, especially Lawrence Mead have, for this reason, identified the weakness of the work requirements in FAP as the cause of its defeat.[49] This interpretation is valid in relation to the defeat of President Jimmy Carter's Program for Better Jobs and Income (PBJI).[50] However, the fact remains that FAP would have passed had the three liberal senators voted it out of the Finance Committee. They did not because of the angry, extremist arguments coming from the far left. The influence of this same ideological tendency prevented, as Mead rightly points out, the imposition of strong work requirements in later reform plans. Only the recent weakening of this tendency in American politics has allowed reform to move to the center. As we shall see in Chapter 8, however, the rise of an equally vigilant right wing in the 1990s may have the same influence that the NWRO had in the 1970s. Knocking reform off balance and making comprehensive, culturally integrative change impossible.

CONCLUSIONS

FAP was defeated in part because of the unexpected intransigence of the left and the predictable opposition of the right but also because of the political and intellectual weakness of the center. The three senators who were responsible for the defeat of FAP in the Senate Finance Committee were drawn in by the extremism of the left largely because there was no powerful ideological force drawing them to the center. This situation demonstrates one of the key components of dissensus politics. The most confident ideologists exist at the extremes, making it difficult to hold together a centrist proposal. A thesis can be generalized to other efforts to comprehensively reform welfare: All such attempts will be faced with opposition on the extremes, but the key determinant of their success will be the presence of a strong, culturally integrative ideological center. Dissensus politics will exist where that type of center is absent and will be overcome where it is present.

Dissensus politics also makes transformative change difficult by poisoning the atmosphere within which discussion occurs. The substance of the Moynihan report and FAP was lost in a whirlwind of accusation, blame, and raised voices. In the highly emotional atmosphere of dissensus politics, debate over the content of proposals for change can easily be sidetracked into symbolic arguments unrelated to reality. Part of what makes agreement possible in any context is a framework within which arguments can be made without fear of an attack on motivations or accusations of prejudice. It is difficult to develop agreement in a dissensual context because this baseline expectation of comity is stripped away. So long as motivations rather than facts and arguments are at the forefront of debate, real change will be elusive.

Dissensus politics cannot be overcome by political pragmatism or a centrist politics that attempts to split the difference between the two extremes. On issues such as welfare, split-the-difference moderation will not be possible. The center must devise its own ideological position that can resist, and even ignore, the extremes of left and right. The Moynihan report and FAP were both, in their own ways, efforts to establish a culturally integrative alternative to the existing welfare system. They failed because the political incentives were in the direction of extremist ideology and political tactics. I have focused much of my attention on NWRO because it was the only group that claimed to speak for those actually affected by welfare and because its advocacy approach was such a key element in the failure of comprehensive welfare reform. NWRO's orientation toward symbolic victories, at the cost of regression in the nation's welfare programs, is another characteristic element of dissensus politics. A second thesis is suggested by this experience: Reform will be unlikely if welfare politics is dominated by groups with an advocacy rather than a representative orientation.

One of the reasons that NWRO and its allies were so intransigent was that they had won early victories in the Supreme Court. Many members of this coalition pegged their hopes on using the Supreme Court to establish a "right to live," a right that would lead to a much higher guaranteed income than Congress was willing to consider. The next chapter investigates this litigation strategy and determines how it fits into the pattern of dissensus politics.

6

The Role of the Supreme Court in AFDC

Elite dissensus on welfare had blocked all major efforts to reform AFDC since the early 1970s until the mid-1980s. But gridlock in Congress was not the final word on the AFDC story. When laws are not passed, elite demands for change do not dissipate but disperse. This chapter shows how the individualist-egalitarian elites abandoned the legislative process and directed their efforts to transform AFDC through the courts.

When agreement is stymied at the center, that is, in Congress, action spreads to the periphery. Politics, when forced out of its natural, legislature-centered stream, takes on a different character. It becomes more ideological, more absolute, and more confrontational. In addition, by drawing energy out of Congress, elite dissensus tends to weaken the legislative capacity to deal with major, contentious issues. Actors who have become accustomed to life at the periphery are less likely to engage in the give-and-take and compromise that are the essence of the normal legislative process. The government is thus unable to effectively respond to a particular issue, and its overall legitimacy and larger ability to govern are also impaired.[1]

Why did elite dissensus result in such a substantial role for the courts in regard to AFDC? As we have already said, elite dissensus led to gridlock in Congress. At that point, egalitarian-individualist elites turned to the courts, where they had had some early successes; they were then less likely to accept congressional changes in the program that were short of their goal. Court intervention weakened the legislative process, which led to pressure for additional court intervention. The courts' willingness to act weakened Congress and also attracted more activity to that arena.

The courts are an especially attractive forum for cultural conflict because litigation permits substantially more absolutist political claims than can be presented in a legislative context. The incentives are usually in the direction of comity and civility, the necessary elements of institutional order. Comity requires a certain restraint in demands, which is an indication of seriousness and which has the effect of preserving the possibility of compromise. In litigation strategy, the incentives are all in the other direction. Only rarely do competing litigants have an ongoing relationship that they desire to protect. Thus, they are likely to present their arguments in the most challenging, passionate, and confrontational manner. The politics of cultural conflict is, therefore, consistent with the process of litigation.

The nature of Supreme Court intervention is also consistent with the non-popular nature of elite cultural conflict. More so than most other forums in the American system, the Supreme Court is insulated from public opinion. Although the Court does have some awareness of public opinion and does act to protect itself when its legitimacy is endangered,[2] it has no mechanism for investigating or discovering the views of the public. The Court hears only those who come before it. Legislative politics is structured by the tension between elites and the public; the politics of litigation has no such tension. Thus, the process of Supreme Court rule is primarily one of choosing between elites. In the late 1960s and early 1970s, the Court chose radical egalitarian elites. The cases we will look at are the consequence of that choice.

Had the Supreme Court even wished to follow a consensus approach to changing AFDC, it would have been incapable of doing so. The Court had to work within the structure and language of the program as it existed on the books. It could not have set up a public jobs program, even if it had wanted to. It could not have required training or education as a qualification of assistance. For the most part, all the Court could do was stop ongoing action or change the interpretation of existing law. Within these parameters, the Court did quite a bit. It was incapable, however, of balancing what it did do with other measures that would assure the public and Congress that the program embodied their priorities. Nixon's FAP, for instance, would have achieved all that the major judicial decisions did, and more. As we shall see, a resort to the courts cannot be a substitute for congressional action.

Elites may actually prefer pursuing change through the courts for another reason. The language of the law can permit the kind of abstract argument and novel ethical principles that popular language cannot. The kind of argument that Charles Reich used to justify intervention in AFDC, and that the Supreme Court accepted, would seem strange and foreign to most Americans and to many representatives for that matter. Pursuing an issue in a popular forum demands that one's arguments draw on popularly accepted principles of justification. The argument that the idea of rights had application to welfare is outside the standard norms of American politics and thus very difficult to make in a popular setting.[3]

Claims of rights are not likely to be welcome in other, less popular settings, either, such as in administrative and legislative contexts. Administrators are likely to favor arguments based on efficiency, and most legislators tend toward claims of interest. The stock in trade of courts, however, is rights, which makes them especially attractive to advocates in a dissensus politics situation. Courts and advocates exist on a parallel rhetorical plane, whereas administrators will find themselves uncomfortable because budgeting and implementation form the core of their way of thinking about public policy.[4] Administrators do not have a rights claim to present against the advocates, which can put them at an acute disadvantage, especially because courts will not have to raise the taxes or administer the changes the advocates demand. Courts think in terms of rights; advocates think in terms of rights; the government, however, usually thinks in terms of consequences. This difference in view creates a rhetorical incongruity that advocates are likely to take advantage of.

Finally, it became much easier to approach the courts in the years leading up to the AFDC cases. The creation of the Legal Services Corporation in the mid-1960s provided money, institutional legitimacy, and the capacity for strategic direction. With more lax rules of standing and a loosening of previously accepted legal principles (such as the rights-privilege distinction), the way was opened for advocates to bring arguments to the courts that would previously have been thought inappropriate. Finally, the Supreme Court had placed itself on the side of racial minorities and others who were seen as victims of governmental authority and discretion. This positioning of the Court sent a signal to advocates that an attack on governmental discretion in relation to AFDC would be treated generously and that they would not have to face the compromise and debate that pushing through changes in the law would require. AFDC could be the next *Brown v. Board of Education, Miranda v. Arizona,* or *Reynolds v. Sims* and could draw on the same revolution in jurisprudence that made them possible.

THE CAMPAIGN FOR COURT INVOLVEMENT IN AFDC: INTELLECTUAL SOURCES

Until 1962, Aid to Dependent Children granted assistance only to unmarried women. Many states interpreted this rule in a broad fashion, forbidding assistance not only to families with legal male guardians of the household's children but also to those with "substitute parents." South Carolina was the first state to place such a rule into law, declaring that "though not staying in the home regularly, [if he] visits frequently for the purpose of living with the applicant, the two shall be considered as living in common-law relationship. Where there is a pattern of the mother having a series of relationships, resulting in children or not, this is considered the same as if she has a continuous common-law relationship with the same man."[5] As noted in Chapter 2, a number of other states adopted similar policies under the moniker of "suitable home" provisions. The administrative consequence of such policies was that some instrument of government would have to determine whether a woman receiving assistance was being frequented by a man or whether other aspects of her conduct rendered her family unsuitable. This need for information led to the creation of investigative units in public assistance offices.

One of the primary tools of these investigative units was the midnight welfare search, in which agents of the welfare office would arrive unexpectedly at a recipient's home and attempt to conduct a "routine" search, presumably to determine whether the recipient child was being cared for properly. The real purpose of these searches was to determine if there was a man present or regularly living with the recipient. Administrators argued that because they were not conducting a criminal investigation, ADC recipients were not coerced into cooperating with such searches. The requests were not fully voluntary, of course, because denying such a request was grounds for the termination of assistance.

One obvious purpose for the rules regarding a woman's "relationships" was to prevent or reverse the expansion of the welfare rolls and thus reduce the costs of the program. Another, less obvious purpose was to ensure that welfare assistance reached only the "right sort of people." The concern for the moral quality of welfare recipients goes back as far as the creation of mothers' pensions. In 1931, only four states had programs that provided assistance to those who had never married.[6] These programs further reduced the eligible population by determining that assistance could only go to applicants if "they were personally 'worthy'—for example, not drunkards, not living with male partners out of wedlock, not neglecting their children."[7] The rolls needed to be protected from the unworthy because the political claim of assistance was based on the unvarnished innocence of the assisted: They were good mothers in a bad situation. Mixing persons who created lesser degrees of visceral sympathy, such as blacks, immigrants, and unmarried mothers, along with those who did, primarily white, native, and widowed, would reduce the political appeal of the program as a whole. Political stability was maintained by keeping the rolls small.

This is not to say that the only purpose of moral tests for those who received ADC/AFDC was program maintenance: far from it. The moral tests only made political sense if they represented an ethical consensus in the larger society, one that mixed concern for the social effects of "improper" sexual behavior with a faith-based abhorrence for illegitimacy. Whether the advocates for mothers' aid accepted this societal standard or merely acceded to it for reasons of program maintenance is a more complicated question.

Midnight welfare searches were an integral part of the moral tests. They were a public declaration that the welfare department was willing to act affirmatively to prevent the unworthy from infecting the welfare rolls; taxpayers were thus reassured that their money was not going to the wrong sort of person. To those on the right, such searches were a positive sign of the authority of the state, but to those on the left they symbolized unfettered, arbitrary state power. The image of a social worker pushing her way into a black woman's home late at night symbolized a range of intrusive practices, and thus it should come as no surprise that these searches were the opening wedge in the attack on AFDC.

The primary obstacles in the way of national government intervention in such matters were the federal nature of the ADC program and the clear intention of the congressional framers of the Social Security Act (but not necessarily those in the executive branch) that such policies were permissible. The 1935 Senate report on the act states, "This program does not represent an attempt to dictate to the States how they shall care for families of this character, but is recognition of the fact that many States need aid to carry out the policy which they have already adopted."[8] Both House and Senate reports contained language that explicitly recognized that a state could "impose such other eligibility requirements—as to means, moral character, etc.—as it sees fit."[9]

A case against such moral tests would thus have to be made against a very difficult historical background. The main intellectual foundation for this case was made by Charles Reich, who, in a number of articles in the *Yale Law Journal,* laid out a legal strategy that would ground virtually all the major AFDC litigation of the late 1960s and early 1970s. If Piven and Cloward were the Machiavellis of the welfare rights movement, devising crafty strategies for an attack on the welfare system, then Reich was the Copernicus, turning previous intellectual understandings on their head, forcing the legal system to see the welfare state in an entirely new way.

The beginning of Reich's attack on morality tests was at the level of administration. Reich observed that the primary claim in favor of a state's right to conduct a search of a welfare recipient's home was consent; the argument held that such a search was part of the package the recipient had accepted when she went on welfare. Reich observed that in a nation where virtually all classes and characters of persons were receiving some form of public assistance,[10] such a claim could mean the gradual erosion of all constitutional rights: "The official demand for entrance is sufficient to render any apparent consent involuntary and the threat of loss of public assistance underscores the coercive nature of the demand for entry."[11] The decentralized nature of the nation's welfare programs made protection of constitutional rights more problematic because the agent of coercion was a subnational government. Given the potential for subnational agents to divest recipients of their rights, the national government had a responsibility to oversee those agents much more carefully.

> Thus if the Secretary [of HEW] permits federal funds to be dispensed to states which use administrative methods that violate the Constitution, he permits the "power, property and prestige" of the federal government to support such practices—practices which cannot effectively be contested by the unfortunate victims. In such circumstances, the Secretary's duty to exercise

his power by prohibiting the unconstitutional practices seems both plain and unavoidable. Here, as in the case of racial discrimination, there is evidence of the increasing need for government to intervene affirmatively if rights guaranteed by the Constitution are to be secured in fact.[12]

In this article, Reich was dealing not so much with the right to welfare as with the rights of welfare recipients. His later work would make clear that his framework for the nation's welfare state included the former as well as the latter idea of rights.

In his seminal article, "The New Property," which may be one of a handful of the most important law review articles ever published in the United States, Reich broadened his view. America was developing an entire system of property rights that were unlike those in existence at the time of the nation's founding. At the founding, property was principally tangible, inhering in things such as land and other physical resources. The economy of the mid-twentieth century, however, was based on a number of claims that did not directly inhere in any physical thing but in such government-created properties as grazing and motor carrier permits, occupational licenses, franchises, subsidies, and the right to use public resources.[13] These types of law-created or -sanctioned properties were at the center of the American economic system, but the American judicial system had not yet created a coherent system of rules to protect them as it had physical property. Although the courts had taken steps to protect the new property of the wealthy, they had failed to extend that protection to the new property of the poor. The law had previously recognized a "rights-privilege distinction," the former protected by the courts, the latter at the discretion of administrative agencies. The new property of the rich was in the process of being translated into a right, while that of the poor languished in the category of privilege. A large part of Reich's analysis was focused on extending rights protection to all new property, with special attention to entitlement benefits, the provision of which he saw as spotty at best in the case of the poor.

Reich's fear was similar to that of John Stuart Mill in "On Liberty."[14] The old regime of small government had collapsed: "There can be no retreat from the public interest state. It is the inevitable outgrowth of an interdependent world. An effort to return to an earlier economic order would merely transfer power to giant private governments which would rule not in the public interest, but in their own interest."[15] Instead, a new law of the public interest state would have to be created, the cardinal principle of which would be: "Government must have no power to 'buy up' rights guaranteed by the Constitution. It should not be able to impose any condition on largess that would be invalid if imposed on something other than a 'gratuity.' "[16]

More dramatically, Reich observed that the public interest state would have to put certain kinds of assistance in a new legal framework; this is where AFDC enters the picture. In Reich's view, income generated and distributed through the state is as central to the operations of a modern industrial economy as other forms of new property and deserves to be treated as such.

> The concept of right is urgently needed with respect to benefits like unemployment compensation, public assistance, and old age insurance. These benefits are based upon a recognition that misfortune and deprivation are often caused by forces far beyond the control of the individual. . . . The aim of these benefits is to preserve the self-sufficiency of the individual, to rehabilitate him where necessary, and to allow him to be a valuable member of a family and a community; in theory they represent part of the individual's rightful share of the commonwealth. Only by making such benefits into rights can the welfare state share in the goal of providing a secure minimum basis for well-being and dignity in a society where each man cannot be wholly the master of his own destiny.[17]

What is interesting, for our purposes, in Reich's analysis is the manner in which he embraces part of the ideal of the welfare state while ignoring another element. A welfare state encompasses a number of different ideas. First, it suggests that the primary end of society is an idea of welfare. Welfare itself is a complex and somewhat ambiguous idea, but it can reasonably be said to include two different components: the provision for need and the support of an idea of the good life. A welfare state, as opposed to a pure redistributive state, is concerned not so much with equality as with sufficiency for some dignified manner of living. A welfare state must concern itself therefore both with the goods to be distributed and with the impact that such a distribution will have on the conduct of life in a particular society. Although Reich gestures toward the idea of "self-sufficiency," he ignores wholly the impact that various means and modes of redistribution will have on that end. Apparently, any redistribution will enhance self-sufficiency, a point that is far from obvious.

The second aspect of a welfare state is that it is a state. In the most minimal (Weberian) definition of a state, it is a monopoly over the legitimate use of force in a particular area. Within this idea is the concept of legitimation: In a state, authority is granted to a particular agent for the support of societally sanctioned ends. A state legitimizes the use of coercive force by granting authority to selective agents, even as it constrains that legitimate force within certain constitutional boundaries.[18] The central thrust of Reich's analysis, however, is an attempt to delegitimize the authority of the state. He desires a welfare state that removes authority from private actors and places it in the hands of public actors. Having made the transformation, however, he goes on to remove authority from the public sphere as well. For Reich, the end of creating a state is to remove relationships of authority altogether from social interactions. The state cannot embody any particular idea of the good in this framework because it is prevented from exercising its power in such a way as to support this idea. This concept is the central conundrum of contemporary liberalism and thus of the modern welfare state.[19] The Court's acceptance of Reich's strategy, and the delegitimation of public authority that accompanies it, was the central problem of the Court's AFDC cases and the core element that would later cause them to be slowly reversed.

THE LAST LINK: THE FEDERAL GOVERNMENT PAYS TO SUE ITSELF

Cloward and Ohlin's opportunity theory, Cloward and Piven's crisis strategy, and Reich's new property thesis would not have amounted to much had the federal government not provided funds to defend indigent clients. Two actions—the Kennedy administration's multimillion-dollar grant to the Mobilization for Youth (MFY) and the creation during the Johnson administration of the Legal Services Program—provided the necessary political resources to challenge the national and state administration of AFDC.

In May 1962, the Kennedy administration approved a $2.1-million grant to the Mobilization for Youth, which when combined with $11 million from the Ford Foundation, the National Institute on Mental Health, New York City, and the Columbia School of Social Work[20] instantly made MFY a social service powerhouse in the city of New York. The organization had powerful friends, not the least of whom was Lloyd Ohlin, who not only helped design the MFY proposal but also served as research director for the President's Commission on Juvenile Delinquency, which approved the MFY grant. Furthermore, Ohlin, Cloward, and Piven were all associated with the Columbia School of Social Work, which put up money and provided intellectual firepower and cachet for the organization.

MFY had a number of purposes, all of which were more or less directly connected to the "opportunity theory," but its most important operation, for the purposes of this work, was the MFY Legal Unit, created a year after the group was founded. The Legal Unit was initially conceived of as being a largely service-driven organization, helping the poor settle everyday legal disputes that they had neither the experience nor the money to competently handle. Quite early in the organization's history, there evolved another function of legal services for the poor. The man who developed that new vision was a former communist and labor union lawyer, Ed Sparer.

Other poverty lawyers looked at the degradation and exploitation of the poor by those who knew the law and the way around it and concluded that what was needed was widespread access to lawyers to help settle individual cases. Sparer conceived of the poor as a class, linked by their common position in American life and the common legal regime under which they suffered. Because they were a class, the problems poor people experienced could only be dealt with collectively, through a legal strategy that sought to remedy not only the individual poor person's claim but, ultimately, the system of law that permitted a cavalier approach to their rights.

Basic to Sparer's vision, then, was the priority of centralized legal strategy: not hundreds of lawyers across the country pursuing separate agendas, but a few highly skilled and intellectually disciplined lawyers linked to a grassroots welfare rights movement pursuing a common goal. That goal was a guaranteed adequate minimum income for all Americans, regardless of age or perceived moral worth. Sparer accepted the "crisis theory" but was perhaps more enamored with an approach that did not merely flood the welfare system with clients and cause Congress to enact an NIT, but that handled the entire operation through the courts. This was indeed the ultimate goal of the MFY Legal Services Unit and its close collaborator, the Columbia University Center on Law and Social Policy: a national right to live grounded in the Constitution and established by the Supreme Court.

The MFY strategy was, therefore, not based on providing legal services to the poor (although the organization thought such services were important) as much as it was founded on legal strategy for the poor. The "test case," the selection of a particular litigant who would allow the Court to establish what "the law is," was the primary tool of Sparer's organization. The model for the MFY Legal Services Unit's operations was the NAACP Legal Defense Fund, which was small in numbers of lawyers but powerful in that it had the support of an organization with a wide membership and a legal strategy that could conserve and focus resources on the most fruitful cases.

The strategy that the Legal Services Unit and its allies pursued was put forth by Sparer in a 1965 article for the *UCLA Law Review*.[21] In that article, Sparer identified the four basic aims of "militant advocates" for the poor in the welfare process. Those were: "the right to privacy and protection from illegal searches";[22] "freedom of movement and choice of residence"; freedom from the "imposition of standards of morality"; and prevention of "illegitimate punishment on 'work relief' projects." Sparer shrewdly recognized that his "right to live" would be too large a step for the courts to take at once. The courts had to be familiarized with the plight of the poor over a number of years and a number of cases. Moreover, the courts could more easily take the big step if they had a foundation of smaller steps to claim as precedent. The goal of the welfare rights movement in the courts was to legalize welfare; the first step would firmly establish that assistance to the poor was a legitimate arena for judicial action.

Much as the early civil rights lawyers searched for a few highly sympathetic clients, the first task of the welfare rights attorneys was to find the right person, in the right place, suffering from the right kind of mistreatment, to get their claims on the Supreme Court's docket. The genesis of the first case the Supreme Court heard was a memo by a first-year law student at the Center on Law and Social Policy, Robert Cover. Cover made two arguments that had substantial consequences for the center's strategy. First, the best region for an early test case was the South, where welfare abuses were most severe and where federal courts were already familiar with the problems of blacks and the poor through their handling of civil rights.[23] Second, the best strategy for effecting client's rights was statutory construction and enforcement of the Social Security Act, concentrating on HHS's inability to enforce the uniformity that the act's language demanded.[24]

The center found its sympathetic client in the person of Sylvester Smith of Alabama. Smith had been taken off the Alabama AFDC rolls because her caseworker ruled that she violated the state's "substitute father" rule, despite the fact that her occasional lover had a wife and did not perform any of the functions one would ordinarily associate with a parent. Furthermore, Smith was black, and Alabama's administration of the substitute father provision had an unmistakable racial bias. In virtually every case the center could track down the recipients who were removed from the rolls were black.[25] Although it was doubtful that the courts would directly address the racial disparity in the administration of the rule,[26] the fact that the rule was used in such a discriminatory manner would certainly make Alabama a much less sympathetic defendant. The welfare rights lawyers had found their client and their claim. Because of the creation of the Legal Services Program, they had a network of poverty lawyers searching for cases. In the person of Ed Sparer, they had a strategist to help guide a national effort. What was impossible at the beginning of the 1960s, because of the lack of a disciplined and adequately funded movement, was possible by mid-decade. The only question was whether the Supreme Court would accept the movement's arguments. In the main, it did.

THE SUPREME COURT TRANSFORMS AFDC

Prior to 1968, the Supreme Court had never accepted an AFDC case. A few lower courts had and were unsympathetic to those challenging the program's administration. In a 1966 case, *Smith v. Board of Commissioners of District of Columbia,* the U.S. District Court for the District of Columbia was faced with a challenge to midnight welfare searches.[27] The district court rejected the plaintiff's complaint on three grounds. Two are important for our purposes. First, "it [the court] has no jurisdiction over the internal administration of this agency or any other government agency."[28] Second, the court argued that "the administration of relief involves discretion on the part of the agency entrusted with that duty. Payments of relief funds are grants and gratuities. Their disbursement does not constitute payment of legal obligations that the government owes. Being absolutely discretionary, there is no judicial review of the manner in which the discretion is exercised."[29] The overall tone of the court's decision was dismissive, as if the idea of judicial review for AFDC was ridiculous.

Two years later, in *King v. Smith,* the U.S. Supreme Court handed down a decision in its first AFDC case. The challenged provision in the case was an Alabama regulation that denied AFDC payments to families that included a "substitute father," that is, an individual cohabiting with the mother of the eligible child, taking the role of parent and thus nullifying the mother's claim to aid. The Supreme Court found that the man "co-habiting" with Mrs. Smith was the father of nine of his own children, was not a guardian to Mrs. Smith's children under Alabama law, and "is not willing or able to support the Smith children, and does not in fact support them."[30]

Although the plaintiffs sought relief under the Social Security Act and the 14th Amendment, the Court based its case purely on statutory grounds. The Court found that "there is no question that States have considerable latitude in allocating their AFDC resources, since each State is free to set its own standard of need and to determine the level of benefits by the amount of funds it devotes to the program."[31] Furthermore, the Court claimed that "the AFDC program is based on a scheme of cooperative federalism," which it defined as a division of power whereby the states had unquestionable control over benefit levels but eligibility was to be principally determined by the national government. Central to the Court's argument is the claim that "provisions of the Act clearly require participating States to furnish aid to families with dependent children who have a parent absent from the home, if such families are in other respects eligible."[32] Eligibility is a function of need, and the purpose of the act is to alleviate that need.

Alabama countered that it supported the substitute father regulation in order to prevent immoral sexual relations and illegitimate births. The Court responded:

> Alabama's argument based on its interest in discouraging immorality and illegitimacy would have been quite relevant at one time in the history of the AFDC program. However, subsequent developments clearly establish that these state interests are not presently justifications for AFDC disqualification. Insofar as this or any similar regulation is based on the State's asserted interest in discouraging illicit sexual behavior and illegitimacy, it plainly conflicts with federal law and policy.[33]

The Court discovered this change in circumstances in the promulgation of the Flemming rule and the enactment of the 1961 and 1962 Social Security amendments.[34] It found that

> The most recent congressional amendments to the Social Security Act further corroborate that federal public welfare policy now rests on a basis considerably more sophisticated and enlightened than the "worthy person" concepts of earlier times. . . . In sum, Congress has determined that immorality and illegitimacy should be dealt with through rehabilitative measures rather than measures that punish dependent children, and that protection is the paramount goal of AFDC.[35]

For obvious reasons, the Court ignored the ambiguity in the statute and its history, finding that "the pattern of this legislation could not be clearer" and that "in denying AFDC assistance to appellees on the basis of this invalid regulation,

Alabama has breached its federally imposed obligation to furnish aid to families with dependent children ... with reasonable promptness to all eligible individuals."[36] In so doing, the Court was not without a coherent view of the federal nature of the program. In its view, the state's interest is the preservation of its fiscal integrity and sovereignty. By unambiguously limiting the scope of its decision— "its [the state's] undisputed power to set the level of benefits and standard of need"[37]—the Court headed off the second main goal of the welfare rights movement: to use the Court to expand the level of aid granted by the program.

The Court went furthest in nationalizing AFDC and establishing a right to welfare in *Shapiro v. Thompson* and *Goldberg v. Kelly*. In *Shapiro*, the Court struck down the Connecticut Welfare Department's one-year residency requirement for AFDC assistance, despite the fact that the Social Security Act explicitly provides for just such a requirement.[38] The Court judged the requirement suspect on equal protection grounds because it established two classes of individuals (those who entered the state within one year and those who had not), a division that threatened to impede the constitutionally protected right of travel. The Court shrugged off the state's defense that it was acting within the Social Security Act: "On its face, the statute does not approve, much less prescribe, a one-year requirement. It merely directs the Secretary ... not to disapprove plans submitted by States because they include such a requirement."[39] Even if Connecticut's interpretation of the act was correct, "Congress may not authorize the States to violate the Equal Protection Clause."[40]

Equal protection claims, of course, are activated only when an important constitutional right is at stake. In *Shapiro*, as mentioned before, the Supreme Court based its argument on an extratextual constitutional right to travel. It is of some interest that the Court used as its most prominent precedents the Passenger Cases of 1849, *United States v. Guest,* and *United States v. Jackson,*[41] when in fact the case most closely paralleling that in *Shapiro* was *Edwards v. California*. At issue in *Edwards* was a California law that made it illegal to assist in the transportation of an indigent individual into the state. Arguing for the Court, Justice James Byrnes stated that "Article I, subsection 8 of the Constitution delegates to the Congress the authority to regulate interstate commerce. And it is settled beyond question that the transportation of persons is 'commerce' within the meaning of that provision."[42] The state's claim for the constitutionality of the law, the Court claimed, thus rested solely on the distinction between "paupers" and "non-paupers," which was made legitimate by the states' right to make laws in relation to the poor. Previous Supreme Court cases upheld the legitimacy of such a distinction, but the Court in *Edwards* clearly stated that it could no longer accept it.

> Whether an able-bodied but unemployed person like Duncan is a "pauper" within the historical meaning of the term is open to considerable doubt.... But assuming that the term is applicable to him and to persons similarly situated, we do not consider ourselves bound by the language referred to.

Whatever may have been the notion then prevailing, we do not think that it will now be seriously contended that because a person is without employment and without funds he constitutes a "moral pestilence." Poverty and immorality are not synonymous.[43]

Given the commerce clause foundation of the case, the debunking of the standard of "pauper" can only be seen as an attempt to make all persons equal as regards their contribution to interstate commerce.

Those concurring in the decision found this argument discomfiting. Justice Robert H. Jackson contended that "the migrations of a human being, of whom it is charged that he possesses nothing that can be sold and has no wherewithal to buy, do not fit easily into my notions of commerce. To hold that the measure of his rights is the commerce clause is likely to result eventually either in distorting the commercial law or in denaturing human rights."[44] He then went on to state an argument that would later be the crux of *Shapiro:* "This Court should, however, hold squarely that it is a privilege of citizenship of the United States, protected from state abridgement, to enter any state of the Union, either for temporary sojourn or for the establishment of permanent residence therein and for gaining resultant citizenship thereof. If national citizenship means less than this, it means nothing."[45] The *Shapiro* Court used the dissenters' argument but failed to acknowledge it. To admit the real source of their argument would require that they state why they picked the argument of the concurrence rather than that of the majority. They did not because the commerce clause argument was insufficiently broad to permit the kind of activism they were attempting.

Unlike *King v. Smith,* which was decided by a unanimous Court, *Shapiro* was controversial. Chief Justice Earl Warren and Justice Hugo Black dissented on federalism grounds they claimed were supported by the argument in *King v. Smith.* The dissenters began their argument with an invocation of King's concept of "cooperative federalism" and argued that the residency requirement was a conscious and necessary part of the AFDC program.

Faced with the competing claims of States which feared that abolition of residence requirements would result in an influx of persons seeking higher welfare payments and of organizations which stressed the unfairness of such requirements to transient workers forced by the economic dislocation of the depression to seek work far from their homes, Congress chose a middle course. It required those States seeking federal grants for categorical assistance to reduce their existing residence requirements to what Congress viewed as an acceptable minimum. However, Congress accommodated state fears by allowing the States to retain minimal residence requirements.[46]

Given that Justice Black was once Senator Black of the Finance Committee that helped draft the Social Security Act, one would have thought his position would have carried more weight.

Warren and Black argued that residence requirements were essential to the furtherance of the act's purposes: "One fact which does emerge with clarity from the legislative history is Congress' belief that a program of cooperative federalism combining federal aid with enhanced state participation would result in an increase in the scope of welfare programs and benefits."[47] In the dissenters' view, the presence of residency requirements did not simply further the interests of decentralization but was an important guarantor for the states that more generous benefits (which were an interest of the act) would not lead to massive influxes of the destitute from other states.

The dissenters saw "cooperative federalism" as a framework within which the federal government would provide the resources necessary for a larger welfare state. They viewed the majority opinion as reducing the concept of cooperative federalism to the idea that the states should cooperate with the national government. The unanimous *King* Court was beginning to unravel.

The apex of the court's confusion was reached in *Goldberg v. Kelly*. Ironically the issue in the case was quite small. The Social Security Act required all states to furnish hearings for those who wished to challenge AFDC eligibility decisions. The matter in *Goldberg* was whether the hearing had to occur before aid could be withdrawn; the Court ruled that such a hearing did have to occur. Although the facts suggested a minor case, the symbolic aspect was significant. The Court grounded its claim on welfare as a form of property, which requires the same due process rights accorded to other forms of property:

> Appellant does not contend that procedural due process is not applicable to the termination of welfare benefits. Such benefits are a matter of statutory entitlement for persons qualified to receive them. Their termination involves state action that adjudicates important rights. The constitutional challenge cannot be answered by an argument that public assistance benefits are a "privilege" and not a "right." . . . Relevant constitutional restraints apply as much to the withdrawal of public assistance benefits as to disqualification for unemployment compensation, . . . or to denial of a tax exemption, . . . or to discharge from public employment.[48]

The first fallacy in the Court's argument is its conflation of various forms of government assistance. One can reasonably conceive of unemployment compensation as a form of property in the traditional sense because it is funded by employee contributions and is considered by most Americans to be a form of insurance. AFDC, unlike the old-age assistance or unemployment programs contained in the Social Security Act, is not constructed as an insurance program and thus is, at the least, not property to the same degree as the others.

Having swept away the very concerns that led to the necessity for a federal welfare system, Justice William J. Brennan, Jr., gave an unconvincing nod to federalism: "We wish to add that we, no less than the dissenters, recognize the importance of not imposing upon the States or the Federal Government in this developing field of law any procedural requirements beyond those demanded by rudimentary due process."[49] Once again in dissent, Justice Black rejected the Court's claims to benevolence and the short shrift it gave to decentralization. First, he found that

> The Court apparently feels their decision will benefit the needy. In my judgment the eventual result will be just the opposite. . . . Since this process [administrative hearing prior to removal] will usually entail a delay of several years, the inevitable result of such a constitutionally imposed burden will be that the government will not put a claimant on the rolls initially until it has made an exhaustive investigation to determine his eligibility. While this Court will perhaps have insured that no needy person will be taken off the rolls without a full "due process" hearing, it will also have insured that many will never get on the rolls, or at least that they will remain destitute during the lengthy proceedings followed to determine eligibility.[50]

Black's argument works within a framework, alien to the majority opinion, where actions taken for benevolent purposes often have perverse effects. The Court, even when it acts in arguably legislative manner, is incapable of asking legislative questions. Indeed, the most important legislative question that might be asked in the field of social welfare ("Does this help the people it is designed for?") is outside the competence of the Court. The Court had taken away just enough authority from the states to create difficulties but insufficient authority to grapple with the problems created by its intervention. That is, it still held to the idea that states should have administrative control of determinations of eligibility, creating the problem that forms the crux of Black's critique.

Black further addressed the complexity problem created by judicial determinations in this area: "The operation of a welfare state is a new experiment for our Nation. For this reason, among others, I feel that new experiments in carrying out a welfare program should not be frozen into our constitutional structure. They should be left, as are other legislative determinations, to the Congress and the legislatures that the people elect to make our laws."[51]

Although Black's invocation of the benefits of decentralization and judicial restraint is meritorious, he fails to do anything with it. In fact, it comes only at the end of the dissent, as a kind of rhetorical flourish after the foundations of his argument have been produced. One reason for the justices' circumspect use of decentralization might be that they are unsure just what place it should take in AFDC jurisprudence. Is it a "compelling state interest"? They do not explicitly state it as such. In fact, the dissenters' arguments for decentralization are somewhat undercut by the fact that they joined the unanimous decision in *King*. Once everything but control of the treasury has been withdrawn from the states, the ability to experiment disappears. If states cannot vary eligibility conditions (the basic holding of *King*), the *Goldberg* claim that AFDC benefits are like property, and thus deserve constitutional treatment, becomes plausible. Without a means of jurisprudence substantially apart from the *King* approach, one with decentralization at the center, the dissenters' arguments collapse for lack of a foundation. Neither side could develop a decision rule to render coherent the relevant laws, administrative history, and larger policy goals of welfare. Without such a foundation, the cases that follow from these fundamentals go off in a number of inconsistent directions.

Briefly, the subsequent Court cases on AFDC can be divided into those with a pro-state and those with a pro-national effect. In order to emphasize the inconsistency over time I will discuss them chronologically. Further, I will not discuss all important AFDC cases but only those in which the main controversy is over the federal nature of the AFDC program (and not, as was the case in *Rosado v. Wyman,* where the issue is the legitimacy of judicial versus administrative oversight).

In *Dandridge v. Williams,* the Court upheld Maryland's "maximum grant" provision, which provided funds for AFDC recipients only up to $240 a month ($250 in Baltimore County), a provision that served as a de facto family cap. The provision was challenged on equal protection as well as statutory grounds, both of which the Court found unsatisfactory.

The Court denied that AFDC assistance could be seen as, primarily, assistance to individual children. Writing for the Court, Justice Potter Stewart found that "it is no more accurate to say that the last child's grant is wholly taken away than to say that the grant of the first child is totally rescinded. In fact, it is the family's grant that is affected. ... Given Maryland's finite resources, its choice is either to support some families adequately and others less adequately, or not to give sufficient support to any family."[52] Rejecting a comprehensive role for the Court in welfare adjudication, Stewart argued:

> The intractable economic, social, and even philosophical problems presented by public welfare assistance programs are not the business of this Court. The Constitution may impose certain procedural safeguards on welfare administration. ... But the Constitution does not empower this Court to second-guess state officials charged with the difficult responsibility of allocating limited public welfare funds among the myriad of potential recipients.[53]

The Court divided possible challenges to AFDC administration into "substantive" questions (those that touch the "economic, social and even philosophical problems" of welfare) and "procedural" ones (concerned with "safeguards" on administration). The question the Court did not address is whether there is an interaction between these two factors and whether the existence of procedural safeguards enforced by the Court can change the substantive aspects of the program. If so, could the Court be held responsible for considering such effects? In *Dandridge,* the Court takes a slight step back from the expansive interpretation of AFDC in previous cases but does not reject the one foot in, one foot out approach of those cases.

In *Townsend v. Swank,* the Court cemented the statutory interpretation of eligibility for AFDC established in *King.* At issue was whether Illinois's practice of granting assistance to 18- to 20-year-old children who were attending high school or vocational training—but not college—is valid under the Social Security Act. The Court found that

> *King v. Smith* establishes that, at least in the absence of congressional au-
> thorization for the exclusion clearly evidenced from the Social Security Act
> or its legislative history, a state eligibility standard that excludes persons eli-
> gible for assistance under federal AFDC standards violates the Social Secu-
> rity Act and is therefore invalid under the Supremacy Clause.[54]

In *King,* in fact, the Court had not quite so clearly established the principle that it had surely hinted at: the Social Security Act's description of individuals eligible for federal assistance was in fact a requirement that states aid such indi-viduals. *Townsend* leaves no question that, henceforth, AFDC assistance would be a statutory entitlement for those eligible under federal standards and that the transformation of the program was complete. It is interesting that the Court was unanimous in this case, even though in *Dandridge* the Court had found that "the starting point of the statutory analysis must be a recognition that the federal law gives each State great latitude in dispensing its available funds."[55] Given the Court's completion of the *King* principle in *Townsend,* one wonders whether it could conceive of any area for latitude or, at the very least, give an argument for why such latitude should be granted in one area and not another.

King had set up a system in which eligibility was to be determined by the national government and level of benefit by the states. However, in subsequent cases, the Court could not even maintain this standard. For example, in *New York State Department of Social Services v. Dublino,* the Court approved a state re-quirement that individuals accept employment as a condition of receiving AFDC assistance, despite the fact that it was a state standard that made the eligible population smaller than the group who would qualify under national standards. The national government had a work program in effect for AFDC, the Work In-centive program, to which the state Work Rules served as a supplement. The Court accepted the Work Rules on the argument that:

> To the extent that the Work Rules embody New York's attempt to promote
> self-reliance and civic responsibility, to assure that limited state welfare
> funds be spent on behalf of those genuinely incapacitated and most in need,
> and to cope with the fiscal hardships enveloping many state and local govern-
> ments, this Court should not lightly interfere. The problems confronting our
> society in these areas are severe, and state governments, in cooperation with
> the Federal Government, must be allowed considerable latitude in attempt-
> ing their resolution.[56]

This argument directly contradicts the finding in *King,* in which the Court de-clared that states could only control access to their treasury by varying benefit levels, not by adding additional standards of eligibility. In fact, the Court did not even acknowledge that *King* was the relevant precedent in the case and thus did not state explicitly that it was overturning that precedent (an oversight noted by Justices Marshall and Brennan in dissent). The Court treated the issue as one of federal preemption because opponents of the Work Rules argued that the WIN program would preempt similar state programs, when in fact the real issue was eligibility; failure to comply would result in loss of assistance. By denying the existence of *King,* the Court avoided the need to put in place a new standard, and thus the lack of clarity of previous decisions became even worse.

Regardless of the Court's inconsistency in argument, the results of its decisions possessed a consistency in effect. If the purpose of the *King* Court was to ensure that eligible individuals would receive assistance, the justices' efforts can be judged a success. As discussed in Chapter 2, the rate at which eligible individuals were granted assistance in the AFDC program was thoroughly transformed in the years after the *King* decision. The Supreme Court successfully undercut the states' legal foundations for program discretion: Along with the efforts of the welfare rights movement to reduce the stigma of welfare and changes in the methods of social workers, the Court's actions effected a major change in the nation's welfare programs.

Although legal aid attorneys thought that this change would lead to the breakdown of the AFDC system and its replacement by a negative income tax, the result was the opposite: an effort to reduce costs by making it harder to get on the rolls (through additional income and asset reporting requirements) and the gradual reduction in the real value of AFDC benefits. By 1977, participation rates had already begun to slide, partially as a result of the federal government's program of "quality control," which sought to reduce the provision of assistance to ineligible individuals. At the same time, the value of AFDC benefits, which reached their peak of $9,000 (on average, combined with Food Stamps) in 1972, were beginning their steep downward drop.[57] As discussed in the previous chapter, the negative income tax, which was the ultimate program goal of the welfare rights movement, was defeated in no small part because of the opposition of the social service and legal aid professionals. By the end of the 1970s, the entire strategy of the left in regard to AFDC was unraveling. With the election of Ronald Reagan in 1980, the program was about to undergo another sharp shift in direction.

The early 1980s were a disaster for the welfare rights litigation strategy, as Congress—at the urging of the president—partially or completely overturned much of the Court's statutory interpretation of the act. The heart of most of these changes was in the area of eligibility and determinations of available income, changes that were made primarily for fiscal reasons. Although *Goldberg* and *Shapiro* could not be overturned by Congress, a number of the precedents drawing on the *King* foundation did fall.[58] These changes were made without great fanfare, for the most part buried in omnibus budget bills. Still, they took much of the air out of the welfare rights movement's sails, destroying what little momentum still remained.

Not only did Congress shift gears but so did the Supreme Court. The Court heard two important AFDC cases in the 1980s (although certainly of less moment than those of the late 1960s to early 1970s), and a number of minor ones, all of which were decided in favor of the government. In *Heckler v. Turner,* the Court ruled that mandatory tax withholdings could legitimately be regarded as part of income for purposes of calculating AFDC payments. In *Bowen v. Gilliard,* the Court found constitutional a 1984 federal law requiring that children living in the same home be considered as part of the same filing unit, effectively forbidding a child of the recipient from shielding child support income from determinations of family eligibility. The Court struck a significantly more nonintrusive line in these cases, no longer reaching out to the principles underlying the Social Security Act but indicating significant deference to the administrative agencies and their interpretation. Both cases led with Justice Warren's finding in *King* that AFDC is "based on a scheme of cooperative federalism" but used it in virtually the opposite direction that the Court had intended in *King:* as a means of justifying state and administrative agency action rather than a means for supervising it. The language of *King* was still in use but the substance had evaporated, leaving only a bare, infinitely malleable phrase in its place.

The nation's elected political actors did not choose to transform AFDC in the direction that the legal services lawyers desired, and they did not ultimately ratify the changes that the Supreme Court dictated. In fact, the truth is almost directly the opposite. Important members of Congress were initially hostile to the Court's actions, and that hostility, if anything, increased over time. A 1970 report of the Senate Committee on Finance stated, in direct contradiction to the Court's finding in *King v. Smith,* that "it should be remembered that welfare is a statutory right, and like other statutory rights, is subject to the establishment by Congress of specific conditions and limitations which may be altered or repealed by subsequent Congressional actions." Senator Russell Long, the chairman of the committee, took every opportunity offered him to attach amendments to legislation coming out of his committee that would overturn the Court's statutory interpretations. Although this effort failed in the 1970s, virtually all of the changes he desired were implemented in the early 1980s. Although "man in the house" and "substitute parent" rules are still a thing of the past, the vogue in state welfare reform is now toward making the program more contingent upon various recipient behaviors (such as getting children immunized, participating in work activities, reporting paternity).

CONCLUSIONS

The litigation strategy failed to move public opinion or legislative action on the right to welfare—just the opposite of the school desegregation decisions[59] but quite similar to that of abortion rights.[60] The nation was probably moving toward a consensus on welfare at the end of the 1960s and early 1970s, in the form of a negative income tax. The opinion of public officials liberalized somewhat, only to be hardened by the debate in the Supreme Court over whether assistance was a right or a privilege. The Court ratified an understanding of public assistance out of step with public and governmental opinion and thus helped put that under-standing, rather than the mix of financial generosity and behavioral stringency that conformed with public norms, at the center of the welfare debate.

The Court played a part in the dissensual politics of welfare by diverting at-tention and resources from the legislative arena to the judicial sphere, thus sup-porting what became an elite cadre of poverty professionals rather than the broad-based political mobilization that would have been necessary for legislative change. It made those who supported a more humane poverty program even more absolute in their demands than they otherwise might have been and less likely to seek compromise than they might have if the legislative option had been open. This danger exists in any kind of judicial activism and in many cases it is an acceptable cost to bear for substantial change. However, it is clear that the Court was unwilling to take the most important step necessary for a real transformation of the welfare system: an attack on the fiscal sovereignty of the national and state governments in the area of welfare. State governments reacted to the Supreme Court's actions by simply lowering benefits, an option that the Court was unwill-ing to forbid.

Why, in the end, were the courts so influential in the evolution of AFDC?

- The Courts were more accessible to intellectuals than Congress, and they were less dependent upon ability to mobilize public opinion or muster interest-group strength. Instead of doing the arduous work of changing popular opin-ion, intellectuals could change policy by convincing five men insulated from popular control.
- Change through the courts was consistent with the preservation of radicalism. In order to mobilize a congressional majority, demands must usually be mod-erated, and one must come to some kind of agreement with one's opponents. The litigation process has no institutional mechanism to facilitate or reward this kind of consensus-building. What is rewarded are clear, compelling argu-ments for justice. Deeply engaging the legislative process tends to weaken ideological and cultural purity, while engaging the litigation process strength-ens it.
- The Courts were seen, at this time, as the ultimate protector of the weak and the vindicator of rights. Because the purpose of the welfare rights elites was the transformation of AFDC in an egalitarian, rights-oriented direction, the courts were especially attractive. Change in AFDC was seen as the extension of previous battles in civil rights, criminal rights, and voting rights, all of which regularized and legalized previously traditional, discretion-oriented programs.
- AFDC was seen by the public interest law movement as a symbol of the ulti-mate evolution of this previous work. Free speech, protection against search

and seizure, and so on were all important, but they were limited. They were quintessentially individualistic but did not satisfy the egalitarian side of the culture conflict. Egalitarians wanted to ensure that the welfare state did not permit violation of these rights as a condition of assistance and wanted to ensure a decent income for everyone, which they conceived of as a precondition for adequately exercising one's rights in American society. AFDC was, therefore, vested with enormous symbolic significance.

- Substantial resources were available for this work that were not available for lobbying and movement-building. Although NWRO was strong enough to block action through flamboyant displays, it was not a mass movement capable of effecting massive change. Furthermore, welfare mothers were poor and unable to mount an effective challenge. However, real resources were available for legal challenge, through the federally sponsored Legal Services Corporation. What is more, the most important work, that involved developing compelling intellectual and legal justifications for action, could be done by professors on their own (or, more accurately, their university's) time.

- The legal process promised change through a few, well-planned interventions. Strategy, rather than mobilization, could effect the change. Selecting the right series of challenges, directed at the right judges, and presented in the right way could quickly move policy. One would not have to wait for the president to come around to one's issue and would not have to put one's faith in the executive's desire to act. Litigation would put egalitarian lawyers in a more pro-active place.

Chapter 7 will show that this attempt to circumvent popular political forms failed. Eventually, most of the gains of the welfare rights movement were rolled back—in small ways by congressional action and in large and important ways by executive authority in the form of waivers.

7

The Persistence of AFDC's Federal Form

What are the consequences of America's ideological dissensus on the federal character of AFDC? I believe that in a dissensual political structure, the tendency will be for fewer important moral and political decisions to be made at the center and more made at the state and local level. Although power may drift temporarily to the center as the result, for example, of Supreme Court intervention, the forces of ideological dissensus will constantly push the issue down to the state and local level. Although substantial change in welfare is impossible in Washington because of the ideological alignment of national politics, it may be possible in the states, where such sharp lines have not been drawn. In this chapter, I will examine the use of AFDC waivers—a striking example of how change in welfare under dissensus is possible only through extraordinary political means, in this case the dramatic expansion of a minor provision of law.

Federalism is a term whose meaning is not clear and obvious. If we were simply to say that the United States has a federal system because elements of governmental authority are manifested both at the national and the state level and that this division has its origins in the constitutional makeup of the nation, it would be a true statement but not a particularly useful one. The statement is not useful because it fails to tell us how power is divided or whether the relationship is static or dynamic. I understand federalism to be the relationship between a political center and its periphery, between a single power source that represents the entire nation-state and the various other political power sources that exist at the substate level. We should not ask: Is the governmental structure federal? (In virtually all nations some power exists at the subnational level.) We should ask instead: What is the degree and character of decentralization in the system? To what degree is power at the center contingent upon agreement at the periphery (or vice versa), and in which cases does this relationship differ across issues?

A second and vitally important question for our investigation is, Once the particular federal make-up of an issue area is revealed, what political or social factors cause a particular issue area to either conform or deviate from a more general national pattern (if one exists at all)? Most analyses properly utilize a functional mode, assuming that a certain form exists because it fulfills some particular need or interest. Economists argue that federalism exists because it allows a more efficient allocation of resources. Because preferences and conditions are not uniformly distributed across the nation, allowing subnational political units to determine policy allows for a "fit" that will maximize utility more than a uniform policy would. Other analyses emphasize federalism's political impact. This line of argument finds that federalism, by allowing local majorities to work their will, increases interest and participation in politics, preventing the alienation that a distant and uniform political structure would create.[1]

I accept some points of these two conceptual frameworks, but I find that a more skeptical argument fits the facts of AFDC. I argue that federalism is functional, not for the people as a whole but for those who govern. Recent students of Congress, using a rational choice model, found that, for example, separation of powers permits both blame-shifting and credit-claiming.[2] Members of Congress can enact vague laws and claim credit for taking action against a particular problem; at the same time they can place blame for the poor implementation of the policy on administrative agencies. Lawmakers can sidestep serious issues and enact laws even if no majority exists on how the world should change. A process such as this does not so much create change as shift the institutional venue.

Federalism creates the possibility for a similar dynamic by permitting politicians to claim credit for action and to avoid blame for the failure of policy. In a federal system, politicians at the center can claim, for example, that welfare rolls continue to go up because of "local foot-dragging," in the same way that separation of powers allows them to blame "bureaucratic inaction." In many cases, the venue may be so completely shifted that the public does not believe the center has any responsibility for the welfare system; politicians can thus avoid taking action that harms some group.[3] Local officials, who have to make the decisions on the ground (decisions that actually alter material reality), are politically advantaged by this system as well because they can blame any unpopular decisions on "federal government tight-fistedness," "unfunded mandates," or "restrictive national rules." With the institutional landscape fogged up, voters have a difficult time identifying who is to blame for the results of the welfare system; they will thus direct their anger in a diffuse way—in complaints about the "system" rather than the element of the system that is to blame. In addition, when successful social intervention occurs at the state level in a political system where responsibility is shared between the national and state governments, federalism permits national officials to claim credit for the success, even if they had little to do with the program at issue. Dissensus politics is, therefore, characterized by a decentralized, center-periphery institutional alignment because that alignment allows for credit-taking and blame-shifting in the absence of definitive decision-making.

What would be the federal structure of a consensual issue area? In part, a degree of institutional confusion would also be present because federalism's political effects would continue even when a strong majority in favor of a particular change could be created. Even if a majority knows what it wants, it still serves the interests of governmental agents to avoid blame if the results of change are not what they anticipate. Self-interest exists in any opinion structure. Even so, the content of that self-interest may change. A strong political majority for a certain change may wish to have its results clearly identified with its actions. The majority will want the enhanced credit-claiming ability that results not simply from the perception of action but from the reality of changed experience. In this case, a more centralized locus of decision (but not necessarily a centralized locus of administration) may be politically advantageous. The more the political system at the center moves toward a consensus model, the more likely we are to see the locus of decision move definitively to the center. Important value judgments will be made explicitly by policy-makers at the center, and actors at the periphery will be assigned a larger role in implementation and a smaller one in critical decision-making. Even if those at the center decide to shift decision-making outward, they will do so because concrete changes will come about as a result.

My effort in this chapter, then, will be to relate facts to this theory, which posits that fewer critical value judgments will be made from the center when the opinion structure is more dissensual and more when it is more consensual. I will describe changes in the federal nature of the program and attempt to distinguish those that are a result of blame-shifting and credit-claiming from those that are the result of definitive value decisions at the center. The case of AFDC waivers, which developed between the mid-1980s and the mid-1990s into the primary avenue for state discretion in welfare policy, will be used to demonstrate the validity of this theory. Waivers are a particularly apt case of dissensus because they facilitate change in the absence of legislative action but still allow the complex system of blame-shifting and credit-claiming to occur.

WAIVERS: A CASE STUDY OF FEDERALISM IN A DISSENSUAL ENVIRONMENT

As we have seen, the dynamic in national-state relations, almost from the genesis of the ADC program, has been in the direction of greater national uniformity and reduced state discretion. National legal standards, but of greater importance, executive oversight, have gradually stripped states of their freedom to determine important aspects of the welfare programs for which they share costs and which they administer. Except in areas where the states' freedom of action is clearly provided for (e.g., the level of benefits), the states have gradually become little more than the administrators of programs, the basic contours of which are determined in Washington, D.C. Even so, AFDC has resisted the level of centralization that is characteristic of other parts of the nation's social welfare state, a primary indication of a dissensual issue structure.

Since the late 1980s, however, this national-state dynamic has been reversed, at first in small steps but more recently in a dramatic and clearly stated way. This change has occurred through the federal waiver provisions that were created by the 1962 Social Security Act and which were used in a sparing and highly discretionary manner until the mid-1980s. Through the use of the waiver authority, under which HHS may "waive," or fail to require the application of certain rules and regulations, the executive branch of the federal government has permitted a range of state AFDC policies that, prior to 1986, would have been unthinkable.

Federal waiver authority was the crucial instrument of the Reagan administration's program for reforming welfare. When its legislative proposal for expanding that authority was ignored by Congress, the administration implemented it by purely executive action and by centralizing the decision-making process for approving waivers in a White House working group. The creation of that group, the Low-Income Opportunity Advisory Board (LIOAB), along with the publication of a report suggesting directions for reform, sent a strong signal to the states to propose major changes in their welfare programs, including behavioral requirements and eligibility standards that had previously been the object of federal suspicion. The board quickly dropped the programmatic aspect of its report but managed to achieve much the same ends through an institutional (state discretion) strategy. The creation of a centralized institution within the federal government, located in the White House, expedited the process of approving waivers, and the general attitude of the board, which emphasized its fundamental agnosticism to the substance of state reforms, created an incentive for widespread state action.

The Reagan administration's reform program, with waivers as its central aspect, was a dramatic success. By the time the reins of power were handed to the Bush administration, almost half the states were conducting some sort of experiment that involved the waiving of certain elements of federal law or regulations. Considerable variation in state AFDC programs was the result, consistent with the administration's intentions and without any express consent by Congress. In fact, Congress has had nothing to do with the expansion of waiver authority that occurred since the mid-1980s, despite the fact that the changes it has wrought are, arguably, more important than the welfare reform legislation that Congress passed, in the form of the Family Support Act (FSA).

This reform by executive fiat and Congress's lack of involvement are institutional and political consequences, as well as examples, of AFDC's dissensual political structure. Since the mid-1970s, Congress has tried and failed to make meaningful, dramatic changes in the AFDC program. Every attempt was blocked by a conflict of political ideologies, resulting in stasis and the conservation of much of the AFDC system. And yet the need for change in the AFDC system has only grown, and the realization of that need has been especially palpable among those with the most direct responsibility for welfare programs: the state governors. The ideological gridlock has been unbreakable at the national level, but in many cases it has been broken at the state level, where organized ideological groups have less direct influence.[4] Reform has only been possible by circumventing the national political structure entirely and pushing action down to the states. That the reform could be accomplished only by stretching statutory authority beyond its breaking point is a clear indication of the ideologically charged, and, thus, inert dissensual political system that has developed around welfare policy in the United States.

Waivers, despite their temporary political attractiveness, were not a solution to the welfare dissensus. The underlying law is in substantial tension with the policy of stretching waivers past the point of experimentation and using them as an instrument for facilitating substantial state discretion. The wrangling over, and eventual withdrawal of, Massachussetts's waiver request, along with the recent successful legal challenges to the waiver process, are indications that it has reached its breaking point. Congress can no longer pass the buck on welfare reform by permitting the executive branch's elastic interpretation of the law, and the taste for discretion that the process has whetted in the mouths of state governors will not permit the process to go backward. If Congress passes welfare reform, the primary effect of which is to give virtually unquestioned authority to the states, it will largely be the result of the situation created by the politics of federal waivers, as well as the limits inherent in that politics.

WHAT IS A WAIVER?

The 1962 Social Security amendments, which I argued in Chapter 2 were the beginning of the modern era of welfare reform, included a number of provisions for delivering services to welfare mothers as a way of encouraging them to join the workforce and to get off the welfare rolls. In addition, the amendments included a provision for demonstration projects, "which, in the judgment of the Secretary, is [sic] likely to assist in promoting the objectives of Title I, X, XIV, XVI, or XIX, or Part A or D of Title IV, in a State or State."[5] The provision gave the secretary wide discretion to decide whether the state proposal was consistent with the objectives of the statutes, which included AFDC. There was no provision for congressional approval of the experiments.

The standards that the amendments established for waiver requests were generally minimal, although we shall see that even those standards were ignored when waiver authority came to be widely used in the late 1980s and 1990s. Those standards were:

1. Cost-neutrality to the federal government
2. No more than one state-wide experiment
3. Observance of health and safety standards

4. No displacement of employed workers
5. Compensation at the prevailing wage
6. Workman's compensation for participants
7. All participation is voluntary.[6]

The provisions that could be waived were those pertaining to statewide operation, administration by a single state agency, disregard of earned income, and,
later, the work incentive program. At various times, the amounts of money involved and the dates in the law have changed, but the basic standards have remained constant.

The language of the law has been virtually irrelevant with respect to how the
waiver authority has been used—most of its provisions have been ignored. The
courts have only recently intervened in the waiver process to declare that an experiment was inconsistent with its enabling legislation.[7] Congress has not acted
to reverse any waiver request, although in a few cases it has instructed the secretary of HHS to approve a few specific state programs, and it has not changed the
underlying statute. For the most part, the waiver process has remained a matter
between the executive branch of the federal government and the states.

With this background, I will examine how this fairly nondescript provision
of the Social Security Act became the foundation of a major shift in the federal
nature of the AFDC program. Ironically, the geographic decentralization was
only realized by centralizing power within the national government, taking it out
of the hands of Congress and the administrative agencies, and putting it into
those of the White House.

THE ROOTS OF A REFORM

The genesis of the waiver strategy for welfare reform can be found in the 1986
State of the Union address. In that address, President Ronald Reagan declared:

> Tonight I am charging the White House Domestic Policy Council to present
> [to] me by December 1, 1986, an evaluation of programs and a strategy for
> immediate action to meet the financial, educational, social and safety con-
> cerns of poor families. I am talking about real and lasting emancipation, be-
> cause the success of welfare should be judged by how many of its recipients
> become independent of welfare.[8]

On schedule, in December 1986, the White House Domestic Policy Council delivered to the president its report, entitled *Up From Dependency.*

The report did not constitute a specific, programmatic agenda for congressional approval. In fact, for the most part it completely eschewed such an approach. It stated, "We have recommended that the federal government undertake
a process of reform rather than propose any single program of reform."[9] That

process was, in essence, one of shifting authority previously vested in the federal government to the states. This process was viable because

> In welfare policy today, dozens of states have demonstrated that they are eager to pursue new ideas and fresh strategies. A number have already used the limited independence they now have to improve their welfare systems. This state and local energy, so important to our success as a nation but so ignored in recent decades, is waiting to be tapped by any welfare reform effort.[10]

The report discussed experiments that the states were already conducting but noted that "current federal laws limit what can be attempted. State leaders told the Working Group that they would be willing to propose and implement more comprehensive experiments, *if only federal laws allowed them to do so* (emphasis added). They want the freedom to do better than they are doing with the current system; the Working Group's proposed legislation to allow experiments would give them that freedom."[11]

The core of the administration's reform strategy, then, was to "create the proper climate for innovation by giving states the broadest latitude to design and implement experiments in welfare policy."[12] As the administration's actions would later prove ironic, the report emphasized the need for legislative change if the agenda were to be enacted.

> To foster state and local experiments that truly are imaginative, federal enabling legislation is required. The limited waiver authorities currently available to the federal Departments of Labor, Agriculture, and Health and Human Services do not go far enough and typically apply only to individual welfare programs. A general and system-wide waiver authority is required so that state demonstrations may differ in whole or in large part from established rules and procedures. . . . The only absolute requirements are that these proposals be consistent with the policy reform goals listed in this report and that they satisfy federal civil rights and due process standards.[13]

As Professor Michael Wiseman of the Institute for Research on Poverty and the University of Wisconsin has noted, "A review of the "Up from Dependency" policy goals indicates that they are so general as to impose little significant constraint on waiver option. At no point were the general principles contained in "Up from Dependency" translated into an agenda sufficiently specific to be used as the basis for a consistency standard for waiver evaluation."[14]

The administration quickly abandoned its effort to get increased waiver authority written into the law. Chuck Hobbs, who as assistant to the president in the Reagan administration and the head of the Low Income Opportunity Advisory Board was the single most important figure in shaping welfare policy for the executive branch during this period, describes the situation: "We threw in, almost immediately after that January 1986 announcement of Reagan's, [a proposal] that would have greatly expanded the waiver authority of the executive branch . . . and the Democrats just yawned."[15] A senior House Republican staff member noted that even though some Democrats supported increased discretion, most balked: "[Representative Thomas] Downey finally agreed to write a letter to the other committees, in which he said, would you be willing to allow some change in the statutes . . . so that we could have demonstration projects? . . . And the answers came back from the Democrats, and they ranged from no to hell no."

The administration's proposed legislation, the Low-Income Opportunity Improvement Act of 1987, was submitted to the Congress on February 26, 1987. The first title of the proposal concerned state demonstrations and stated that "in order to conduct a demonstration in accordance with the provisions of this title, a State shall submit a filing . . . to the Interagency Low-Income Opportunity Board established pursuant to title II of this Act."[16] The demonstrations that the board would consider, as specified in Sec. 102 of the proposed legislation, were those included in the "Up from Dependency" report and focused on increasing the poverty programs' efficiency and their capacity for encouraging work. Despite the capacious nature of these goals, it is difficult to see how if the administration's proposal had become law, the demonstrations that were later conducted on family composition could have been justified under the law. Ironically, if Congress had acted on the Reagan administration's proposal, the likely consequence would have been a narrower range of demonstrations because those demonstrations would have to conform with those specified in the law.

Facing a Congress that was at best indifferent and at worst hostile, Hobbs followed an alternative course, acting on the changes the administration desired without adjustments to the law—in fact, as if those changes had already occurred. "So I went to Reagan and said, what we need to do is to put together some kind of administration task force that's going to look at these waivers, because the secretaries are reluctant about granting waivers because their own bureaucracies are telling them, 'you don't want to let a state do that.' "

The organization that Hobbs set up to circumvent the departmental bureaucracies was the Low Income Opportunity Advisory Board, chaired by himself and with representation from most of the agencies with an interest in policies for poor people: three representatives from HHS (the assistant secretary for Planning and Evaluation, the administrator of the Family Support Administration, and the administrator of the Health Care Financing Administration); the assistant secretary for Food and Consumer Services in United States Department of Agriculture (USDA); the associate director for Human Resources, Veterans and Labor at the Office of Management and Budget (OMB); staffers for the White House Office for Policy Development; and other representatives as their input was required.[17] The function of the board was to act as the gateway for waiver processing. Previously, when a state wanted to operate a demonstration under a waiver, it would have to send its waiver package to each agency whose programs would be affected by the project, creating bureaucratic complexity and interminable delays in processing the requests. Back in the states, few governors could be sure if their proposals would receive an objective review from these agencies, and even if they could be sure, the institutional structure meant that they would have to wait many months if not years to get their proposals accepted. Furthermore, there was a strong partisan flavor to the decision in Washington whether to accept a waiver request. Hobbs describes the surprise that one Democratic governor expressed to him after receiving waiver approval from the administration:

> I remember, six to nine months later [after receiving waiver approval], I ran into [Dick] Celeste [governor of Ohio] at the National Governor's conference in Cincinnati, and he was just effusive. He said, "Chuck, I never thought Ronald Reagan would grant waivers to me." And it was just that blunt. He thought, he was a Democrat, he was always opposing Reagan, and therefore the waivers wouldn't be granted. So what the governors' understanding of that process had been all along was, if you're a Republican you might get waivers if there's a Republican president. If you're a Democrat, forget it.

Even when the president was a Republican and the governor was a Republican, however, a waiver request was not automatically granted. Hobbs remembers that he was chief deputy director of Social Welfare in California under Reagan in 1971 when the first major waiver request was made.

> There were a passel of federal waivers attached to that. It took a year and one-half to get them out of the Nixon administration. In fact, the Nixon administration said, "No, we're not going to grant them to you, it's too big a change. You don't know what you're doing out there: Dumb Actor." And so, there was a meeting in San Clemente between Reagan and Nixon. Nixon said, "I'll give you your waivers if you support FAP." And Reagan said, "nope," and so Reagan came back and testified against FAP and Nixon gave Reagan his waivers and that's how it worked out. The political pressures built enormously, not just in California but in Washington too, to allow welfare reform to go on. Those waivers were all granted, but they took 18 months.

Centralizing authority in the White House facilitated the subsequent explosion in waiver activity in three significant ways. First and most obvious, it simplified the administrative process of approving waivers. Second, it centralized, in the governors' mind, the relevant actors and motivations that they had to take into account. Third, it permitted the White House to take over the waiver process and use it as a means for pursuing long-term political goals, such as restructuring the federal nature of the program and encouraging welfare reform, and it convinced the governors that more petty, partisan motivations were no longer active considerations in the waiver process. Finally, because of the constraints the administration placed on waiver proposals, in particular cost neutrality, it virtually guaranteed that the movement for welfare reform would take a conservative direction.[18]

Where did the impetus for the new policy on waivers come? Were the states pushing against the federal government for freedom of action, and did the White House's creation of a special board simply remove the impediments to their pre-existing desires? It seems as if the Low-Income Opportunity Advisory Board did some soliciting of interest, but, in the main, many of the basic contours of welfare reform were already bubbling around in the states as a result of their experiences with the Community Work Experience Program (CWEP). When Hobbs was in the process of putting the board together, he began a series of discussions with the nation's governors. Most of the important White House players, with the exception of Ed Meese, were not interested in Hobbs's welfare reform plans and predicted that the governors would smile and pretend to listen and then do nothing. Hobbs describes the point at which he felt he was on to something important:

> The first one I went to was Dick Thornburgh of Pennsylvania, and I was really leery about sitting down with him. I had never met the guy and he was the governor of a big state. . . . After an hour or so, he said, "Chuck, not only am I interested in doing something about this, but you'll find forty-nine other governors who are enthusiastic." That really got my spirits up, and by a three-year period I had gone to forty of the governors' offices around the country and getting [sic] almost universally that response.

Not all of the interest was latent, however. One of the board's first actions was to approve two waivers—for New Jersey and Wisconsin—for which rejection letters had already been written and signed by HHS Secretary Otis Bowen. The board pulled back the rejections and approved both waivers within 90 days. This dramatic action was a clear signal to the states.

The board's intervention in the waiver process did not remove the involvement of the executive departments completely. What it did was transform their role. A senior HHS official involved in the waiver process told me,

> Prior to late in the Reagan administration, you had to view the way we used it as truly a discretionary authority. We exercised discretion as to whether we approved the waivers, [discretion defined] as what we'd like, as what policies we'd like to see tested. A state could propose something, but if we weren't interested from a policy stand-point or for other concerns we would say no, we won't approve those kinds of waivers.[19]

The LIOAB removed the discretionary authority that functionally existed at HHS and transferred it to the White House. By doing this, it removed the policy preferences of HHS from the equation; one administrator in HHS told me, "Prior to LIOAB, there were enough states that weren't sure what the federal government would approve or wouldn't approve and there wasn't a guarantee that we would be reasonable in their eyes." By moving the functional authority to the White House and transforming the role of HHS into research and advice, the LIOAB further simplified the process and made it more transparent to the outside world.

The structure of the LIOAB also encouraged a positive attitude toward experimentation and an eschewing of a policy-discretionary role. Because approval of a proposal was now in the hands of a group that represented a cross section of the domestic policy departments, the structure of relevant interests was expanded and made more encompassing. When the executive departments had authority over waiver requests, the department saw the states as performing a service for them and thus the relevant interests were those of the departments rather than some overriding national interest. The board created a structure of interests that brought the national values of decentralization and experimentation for their own sake into the mix. Chuck Hobbs describes the change:

> And generally on the assistant secretary level, once they committed themselves [prior to LIOAB], the secretary wasn't going to change. . . . Now, what it [LIOAB] did, instead of just having one honcho over there who took the work of his staff, we had a round-table discussion of these things that went on and a bunch of people who were interested in seeing the states actually do some innovative things.

The board created a dynamic in which more senior officials, who were less likely to be affected by the received wisdom of the department, wrested control from the individual bureaucracies.

> HHS would always show up with a couple of appointed people who made sense, and a bunch of bureaucrats who sometimes made sense and sometimes were obstreperous. But since they are sitting in the back of the room, and the debate was going on among appointees, we began to get much more of an influence on the policy end of the thing.

Even so, the federal government did not give up all of its discretionary authority during this period. Instead, it shifted its locus. One of the first actions taken by the board was to establish two key criteria for judging state welfare waiver requests. The first standard was cost neutrality to the federal government, which in the early years of the board was calculated on an annual basis[20] and was later changed to neutrality over the length of the experiment (additional costs at the beginning could be offset by lower costs at the end). The second standard was a rigorous evaluation (the meaning of which will be discussed below). In addition, there was a third standard—consistency with priorities established in "Up with Dependency"—which, in interviews with those involved in the process, was revealed to have been largely ignored. The federal government was giving up its discretion as to the goals of the experiments but was highly concerned with ensuring budgetary discipline and a research design competent enough to render defensible results.

The board was not shy in enforcing these standards. Of the 26 waiver requests filed in the first (pre-1992) phase of the process, only 7 utilized a random assignment method for evaluating their demonstration projects; most preferred a pre-post method.[21] States preferred this evaluation technique because it was relatively simple and did not demand that any of the recipient pool be exempted from the experiment. However, there are serious limitations to this method. The first is that in the absence of a randomly assigned control group, it is difficult to distinguish between the changes in outcomes that are the result of the treatment and those that occurred for other, unrelated reasons (such as varying levels of economic growth). Second, a pre-post method makes it difficult to implement a cost-neutrality standard. If there is a control group, it is easy to assess the costs that the federal government would have incurred in the absence of the experiment; if a pre-post test is used, such an analysis is inevitably more speculative and based on controversial assumptions and statistical methods. Thus, the board convinced all but one state, West Virginia, to use a method other than pre-post test. All but a handful of the states either withdrew their waiver requests or switched to some form of random assignment.[22]

Despite the board's fundamental agnosticism toward the policy objectives of the state demonstrations, the experiments generally fit within a fairly narrow range. According to Wiseman, most of the first-wave experiments involved one or more of six basic programs.

(1) Demonstrations featuring program integration; (2) demonstrations emphasizing manipulation of the so-called "100-hours" rule in AFDC-UP; (3) welfare-to-work demonstrations emphasizing job search and training assistance for recipients; (4) demonstrations supporting efforts to move recipients to self-support through private business; (5) demonstrations emphasizing services and/or requirements for teenage recipients; and (6) a general category covering a variety of special projects [many of which involved administrative aspects of AFDC, a few concerned with incentive approaches or child support].[23]

Most of the demonstrations, then, did not involve high levels of coercion or intervention in highly sensitive aspects of recipient functioning (such as family structure). Only the third category, concerning job search and training, could be said to add significant obligations to the receipt of public assistance. This relatively narrow scope for reform distinguished the first wave from those that would come after President George Bush's State of the Union address.

BUSH'S STATE OF THE UNION ADDRESS AND THE SECOND WAVE OF WAIVER REQUESTS

Despite the great success the Reagan administration had using the waiver policy as the primary instrument of welfare reform, in the first year of the Bush administration the flow of waiver requests virtually dried up. There are three plausible explanations for this change. First, in 1989 all of the states were working strenuously to set up their programs under the Job Opportunity and Basic Skills Training program (JOBS) provision of the Family Support Act; this activity was taking up most of their time, energy, and capacity for innovation. Second, half of the states were already in the waiver business, leaving a much smaller pool of states to engage in experimentation. Third, and perhaps most important, during the first three years of the Bush administration, the LIOAB had been allowed to wither, primarily because of the Bush administration's cooler ideological temper. According to Hobbs, "Whether Bush had any interest, the people he put into domestic policy did not have the interest in the stuff we had. . . . The whole thing shifted back to the departments."

It would be fair, albeit partisan, to observe that prior to 1992, President Bush was almost completely uninterested in welfare policy. In the first three years of his administration, the subject of welfare appears in his public papers only twice. President Bush introduced no legislation on the matter, did not discuss it in public, and issued no important executive orders on the subject. Furthermore, welfare was not an issue that he had made a priority while he was vice president. The only evidence I could uncover of his involvement in welfare in his entire public career was his support of the Nixon administration's FAP proposal,[24] support that, like many other things in his career, was completely reversed upon his ascendancy to executive power.

Nineteen-ninety-two was not, however, a normal year in the politics of welfare. One of the front-runners for the Democratic nomination for president, Bill Clinton, had made "ending welfare as we know it" one of the most important parts of his platform, a critical distinction from the other Democratic candidates for president.[25] Furthermore, Bush found that he could no longer run on his foreign policy record because the Gulf War was slipping from its prior importance in national politics and a prolonged recession was pulling the public's attention to domestic affairs.

This set of unusual circumstances provides the context for the president's unexpected injection of the welfare issue into his public agenda on January 28, 1992, in his State of the Union address. The president reached the subject near the end of his speech, as his last substantive policy proposal. He began by repeating, as President Reagan had before him, Franklin Roosevelt's description of welfare as a "narcotic" and a "subtle destroyer" of the spirit.[26] He called on the American people, and their representatives in Congress, to "replace the assumptions of the welfare state and help reform the welfare system."

Of particular interest is the strategy for reform that he proposed: increased state autonomy in the welfare system. He observed:

> States throughout this country are beginning to operate with new assumptions that when able-bodied people receive Government assistance, they have responsibilities to the taxpayer: A responsibility to seek work, education, or job training; a responsibility to get their lives in order; a responsibility to refrain from having children out of wedlock; and a responsibility to obey the law.[27]

The president did not announce, however, that he agreed with what the states were doing and was prepared to make it national policy. Rather, he proclaimed, "we are going to help this movement. Often, State reform requires waiving certain Federal regulations. I will act to make that process easier and quicker for every State that asks for our help."[28]

That the president had no serious commitment to the subject and that his proposals were completely driven by politics (i.e., his fear of being upstaged by Clinton) became quite clear in a press conference later in the year (April). Asked by a reporter, "If you are so concerned with this issue, why haven't you been closely involved with it for the last 3 years?" the president responded,

> Well, that was a good question. And I think the politics drives some things. I think we've tried to move forward in terms of helping people in these cities. I don't think we've done absolutely nothing. . . . Well, I think a lot of the issues we're talking about—some were asking about the environment, some were asking about these other issues. They get much more clearly in focus every 4 years, and then you go ahead and try to follow through and do something about them.[29]

Regardless of his motives, the president began to make welfare reform a higher priority in his public speeches and presidential pronouncements; the subject of welfare appears in his public papers 37 times in 1992. Typical of Bush's approach was a question-and-answer session in Paducah, where he was asked a question about the welfare problem. He noted, "This isn't just the Federal Government, ma'am. The way we do it, you give States waivers. Wisconsin's taken a lead, New Jersey's taken a lead. All of these States are trying different formulas for working and learning."[30] The administration had come late to the welfare reform issue; in fact, it brought Chuck Hobbs to the White House for discussions on the subject only two weeks before the president made his address to Congress. They were playing catch-up, did not have time to create a full-fledged welfare reform proposal, and thus reached out to the easiest and most timely strategy they could find: granting new authority to the states.

More liberal use of executive authority to grant AFDC waivers became the Bush administration's welfare policy primarily by default. There does not appear to have been a vigorous debate on welfare policy within the Bush administration and little momentum for nonprocess changes beyond what had been achieved earlier in the administration. Bush administration officials concluded that in 1992, Congress would not pass any welfare reform the administration would recommend. Furthermore, the administration did not want anything much beyond what it could do through administrative action.[31] Seeing that changes in the law were impossible, given the increasingly ideological environment, the Bush administration chose process over substance.

Although Bush's strategy of welfare reform by waiver was not a smashing success electorally, it was a success in spurring greater state action. The president put the encouragement of state waiver proposals into his FY 1993 budget proposal, but it is interesting that none of the criteria that he announced differed from the two standards that had already been put in place. The main difference was that Bush announced his interest in the subject and communicated that he would do something to ensure that state proposals would get a serious review. Chuck Hobbs observes,

> Most of the states that came under that last year under Bush already had stuff they wanted to do, but didn't figure it was worth coming forward because there was no interest back here. . . . So, there had been interest generated, and I think, frankly, pressure put on the White House before they called me up, because obviously they were responding to pressure out there . . . from people like Tommy Thompson [governor of Wisconsin] and Carroll Campbell [governor of South Carolina].

On April 10, the president convened a major, televised news conference to announce that he was approving Wisconsin's waiver request. Exhibiting his usual artfulness, Bush began: "Photo opportunity here on welfare reform."[32] The president stated that he thought, "it'll be a good example for the rest of the country. We can all learn from that, all the States can learn from it."[33] He was then asked, "[whether] you expect to have a Federal plan?" The president responded, "Well, I think the main thing here which we're doing at this juncture is to facilitate innovation by the States. In a sense, they're laboratories, but they're also on the firing line. . . . These States aren't all the same. Welfare problems in Milwaukee are quite different than those in Juneau, Alaska, for example, or in California someplace."[34] The president was clearly confused as to the purpose of his waiver strategy. At first he announced that the Wisconsin waiver proposal would be something other states could learn from, suggesting an experimentation strategy. Then, he observed that every state was different, suggesting that the applicability of experiments in one state to another was limited. He closed with his final, and probably most honest, justification for approving Wisconsin's waiver proposal:

> I'm very interested in the innovation of the Wisconsin plan. I want to see how it works. The Governor can defend or criticize any aspect of his own plan he wants. The Federal role is to encourage these Governors to do exactly what this Governor has done. . . . I'm not going into it point by point. I'm sure I have great confidence in him. If he thinks it's smart, that would be very persuasive with me. I can't say I know every detail of his plan.[35]

Despite the lack of any consistent justification for the waiver strategy, there were a number of changes made that helped encourage more state waiver proposals. An official at HHS summarizes what happened: "Everything changed after '92. In '92, basically, we articulated that we were going to be policy-neutral. . . . Rigorous evaluation, cost neutrality, we'd learn something from it, go with it. That's essentially the message we sent out. Then, they came in like gangbusters."[36]

The other significant change was a shift in the cost-neutrality standard. In

1992, the cost-neutrality standard was changed to neutrality over the course of the entire demonstration. This change had a substantial effect not only on the number of waiver requests but the type as well.

> If you think of these as investments . . . there are some front-end costs to doing reforms, and states wouldn't eat that. . . . "If we have to eat the costs, we're going to pull back our proposal. We can't come in with these." So we said, alright, we'll give you some slack on the front-end. The basic structure of our cost-neutrality is, you can have some front-end costs and we'll front you the money, if they're not excessive.[37]

By communicating a policy-neutral stance, the federal government was letting the states know that it would approve any policy the states wanted; this was the neutrality aspect. However, by shifting the cost-neutrality standard the federal government was actually encouraging the states to make their waiver proposals more ambitious. For example, if a state decided to require all recipients to enter a job training program, the costs would be up front, but the returns in lower welfare expenditures would be years into the project. Under year-by-year neutrality, a state would have to swallow the up-front costs of training without being able to receive additional funds when programs started reaping benefits. By agreeing to forward some funds to the states in the early years, the federal government encouraged the states to achieve neutrality by means other than, for example, cutting benefits. These two changes had a substantial effect on the number and character of the waiver proposals the states developed over the next two years, continuing into the Clinton administration.

The Bush administration spurred change not so much through the particular adjustments it made in the regulations governing AFDC waivers. The most important change was in tone. The administration let the states know that if they sent in a waiver request, the White House would provide its support, its energy in smoothing out interagency conflicts, and its ability to track frequently complex waiver requests through the bureaucracy.[38] The White House's involvement moved welfare waivers to the top of the relevant agency's priorities. Although the waivers might have previously been approved, the White House's interest reassured policy-makers in the states that the approval process would be relatively smooth. The interest on the part of a number of governors and the popular demand for change in welfare programs were all that was necessary.

CLINTON'S CONUNDRUM: WAIVERS OR NATIONAL POLICY?

Only weeks after entering the White House, President Bill Clinton faced the issue of AFDC waivers. The issue, although less pressing than the budget or health care, had symbolic import, one of the first indications of the new president's approach to governance. The politics of waivers was much different for Clinton than it had been for Bush. Bush sought to substitute the process of waivers for any substantive policy prescriptions, but Clinton campaigned on and repeatedly declared his intention to "end welfare as we know it," a cant phrase made substantial by his specific promise to put a two-year limit on welfare.

Furthermore, Clinton put major figures in the welfare reform movement in critical positions in his administration: Mary Jo Bane and David Ellwood at HHS; Isabel Sawhill at OMB; Bruce Reed and William Galston in the White House Domestic Policy Office. Mary Jo Bane had been the administrator of welfare programs in New York, where she supervised the administration of a major welfare demonstration, the Child Assistance Program (CAP). Finally, Clinton was aware of the welfare experimentation in the states, had gone through the waiver process himself as governor, and had been one of the key figures in the 1988 Family Support Act negotiations. Unlike Bush, Clinton knew the substance of the welfare issue, including the issue of waivers, and was fully confident in his ability to handle the substance of the issue himself.

The administration had all the elements in place to mount a full-scale effort to reform the national welfare system: knowledgeable appointees, a well-established ideological structure (Clinton had appropriated Ellwood's solutions in *Poor Support* for the book issued during his campaign, *Putting People First*), and a president who was one of the most informed persons in the country on the issue. Welfare reform that combined additional services with strict expectations was a critical aspect of his effort to groom himself as a "New Democrat," one willing to balance opportunities with responsibilities and establish authoritative values that would guide policy.[39] However, the New Democrat label meant something else as well. It also suggested a discomfort with overbearing national mandates and controls on the states, and a progressive appreciation of the need for experimentation and state flexibility (another of Clinton's advisers was David Osborne, author of *Laboratories of Democracy,* a celebration of the role of state governors, Clinton in particular, in pushing important new ideas and approaches[40]). The decentralization aspects of his approach suggested the perpetuation and extension of the waiver approach, but his tough, value-based stance suggested an attempt to craft a national solution.

Clinton made his first public statement on the subject at the National Governor's Association meeting on February 2, 1993. He declared, "I think the Governors have exemplified for the last dozen years the bold, persistent experimentation that President Roosevelt called for at the beginning of the Great Depression when he took office."[41] He then observed that despite the good intentions that went into its creation, the Family Support Act had not been fully administered and was not close to a solution to the nation's welfare problems. However, change had occurred, mainly as a result of the actions of state governors. "In spite of that," Clinton argued, "I think it would be a great mistake to conclude that that act was of no significance or that nothing good has occurred. Bipartisan efforts in State after State, from New Jersey to Georgia, to Wisconsin, and many others all across the country, have resulted in innovative approaches to help move people off welfare rolls and onto paychecks."[42]

Clinton announced that he would create a working group on welfare reform that would craft a plan for transforming welfare based on enhanced child support, a two-year limit, improved child care, and a substantial work program. Finally, Clinton got around to the issue of waivers and state discretion. He said:

> I do not want the Federal Government, in pushing welfare reforms based on these general principles, to rob you of the ability to do more, to do different things. . . . My view is that we ought to give you more elbow room to experiment. . . . So I will encourage all of us to work together to try things that are different. . . . If we say, okay, we're going to have more waivers and you're going to be able to experiment in projects that use Federal dollars, let's measure the experiment, let's be honest about it. And if it works, let's tell everybody it works so we can all do it. And if it doesn't, let's have the courage to quit and admit it didn't.[43]

Although the effect of Clinton's statement, at least in the short term, was to signal to the states that the previous administration's policy on waivers was still in effect and the federal government would not exercise policy discretion, the justification for waivers was clear and somewhat different.

Clinton did not understand waiver policy to be the totality of the administration's welfare reform proposals. In fact, it did not appear as even the most important part. Waivers were not a way to adapt federal policy to local standards. Finally, waivers were not given out of deference to the states' superior knowledge of the subject. By suggesting that some of the projects would succeed and some would fail, and those that failed should be terminated and those that succeed should become national policy, Clinton was suggesting a new structure. That structure had one foot in the old approach, which used waiver authority to pursue the goals of the national AFDC program (and which would logically culminate in a change in national policy, not the perpetuation of state differences) and one foot in the new, which allowed states full discretion in determining what, if any, experiments they thought were desirable. Unlike the Bush and Reagan policy, Clinton's policy seemed to envision an AFDC structure where eventually all of the successful experiments would be incorporated into a uniform, national policy; state experiments would drive national policy rather than national policy consisting of state experiments.

Apart from the change in justification, which seems to have vanished as a result of political pressure, there have been two major changes in waiver policy in the first year and one-half of the Clinton administration: the elimination of LIOAB (and the return of the primacy of HHS in overseeing waivers) and the integration of state discretion into an actual policy program—the proposed Work and Responsibility Act of 1994, which was released in June 1994. The primary function of LIOAB was to create a single institution to process and approve waiver requests, and LIOAB's place in the White House was indicative of a lack of trust of the ability of HHS to fairly decide the merits of state experiments (which in the Reagan and Bush administrations meant keeping policy preferences out of the decision). The Clinton administration pushed the waiver process out of the White House and opted instead to make HHS the "lead agency" on state demonstrations. Thus, HHS was given the responsibility for receiving requests, negotiating with the states, and coordinating proposals with other relevant agencies.

There is little evidence that this shift to HHS resulted in a tightened review process. During the Clinton administration (through July 1994), 41 applications from 29 states have been received, of which 9 from 7 states were left pending from the Bush administration.[44] Of these, 14 applications from 14 states have been approved, 2 from 2 states have been denied, 5 from 3 states have been withdrawn or the review has been terminated, and 20 from 16 states are still pending. The 2 rejected proposals, the Relocation to Illinois Project and the Wyoming Relocation Grant, both involved interstate movement (Illinois's proposal, for example, would have paid recipients from other states at the level of the state they migrated from), the constitutionality of which is highly questionable, since it seems to run afoul of the Supreme Court's decision in *Shapiro v. Thompson* and a recent California court's rejection of a similar proposal in that state. The accepted proposals include a number of very controversial approaches (the substance of which will be discussed in the following section), in particular Georgia's Project Fulton, which would "cap AFDC and Food Stamp benefits at the point of entry into the project," and which would have the effect of denying additional benefits to recipients who have children while on the rolls.[45] In contrast to the Clinton record, the Bush administration received 33 applications from 19 states, of which 23 from 13 states were approved, 1 was denied, and 10 from 7 states were pending on the last day of the administration. The true test of Clinton's administration, despite the highly controversial proposals it has already accepted, will be how it treats the even more inflammatory and questionable experiments it has yet to pass judgment on, an issue that will be addressed later in this chapter.

The now-irrelevant Clinton welfare reform plan would have turned the entire waiver policy upside down. The Clinton proposal's explicit changes in waiver authority were fairly small and basically permitted child support savings to be used in determining the cost neutrality of waiver proposals. The proposal allowed states to experiment with innovations in the administration's program but strictly circumscribed the number of demonstrations that could occur (no more than 5 waivers for experiments involving time limits other than 24 months). Although it is true that as the administration claimed, "this plan gives States unprecedented flexibility to innovate and learn from new approaches[, much] of what once required waivers will become available to States as State options,"[46] there is no question that the proposal would have substantially eclipsed the significance of state welfare demonstrations.

This "transformation" of waivers to options would have occurred for four reasons. First, the proposal incorporated many of the items that the states had been requesting waivers for, in particular the two-year limit.[47] Second, by increasing the number of state options, the proposal made many waiver requests superfluous; state flexibility would become part of the legal structure of the program rather than an addition on its rump. Third, the program substantially increased the number of demonstration projects that HHS would solicit, thereby tying up state energies in experiments that were federal priorities.

The final reason that the Clinton proposal would have taken the wind out of the sails of the waiver process is that it would have put into action much of what the public had demanded. Waivers became such a pressing issue because there had been an impression that the program at the federal level was a failure and did not incorporate the public's key values into the operation of welfare policy. The states had been highly involved in this issue because no publicly accepted action had come from Washington. If such action had transpired, and the public accepted that action as real reform, there would have been much less pressure on state legislators and governors to get involved.

THE SUBSTANCE: WHAT THE STATES HAVE DONE, HOW THEY HAVE CHANGED WELFARE, AND WHY WE SHOULD CARE

Ultimately, it is the substance of the state experiments that is the true test of the decentralizing significance of increased waiver authority. Had the states been merely experimenting with increasing the administrative efficiency of the program or had they been conducting experiments solely in areas in which the federal government had already sent a clear signal of interest, it would be difficult to say that there had been a clear decentralizing trend. As we shall see, neither of these two possibilities have occurred; experiments have been conducted in areas that involve the core assumptions of welfare programs, and they have increasingly moved away from clearly stated federal priorities. The states have been permitted to determine the basic values implicit in the welfare system and have been more daring and have taken more authority as time has gone on. We are quickly approaching a critical period in the history of the AFDC program when we shall be asked whether the nation will have a relatively uniform national program of assistance to the nonworking poor or whether the states shall, within quite broad limits, be able to determine the ways and means for serving this population.

We can roughly divide the substantive history of state waiver proposals into three periods. In the first period, which continued through Bush's State of the Union address, state waiver programs were primarily concerned with the same issues that the Omnibus Budget Reconciliation Act (OBRA) demonstrations were: increasing the work, training, and education effort of those on welfare. During the second era, which extended almost to 1994, waiver proposals involved more controversial matters, including family composition and structure, and became much more severe in nature. The third era, which began in 1992, was signaled by a few highly questionable waiver requests, such as those of Massachusetts and Wisconsin, which threaten to cut off assistance after a relatively short period.

The programs of the first era were characterized by an effort to move recipients on AFDC off welfare and into the world of work. Some were actually conducted under the 1982 OBRA law, and others came later but had essentially the same purpose. The first two proposals passed by the LIOAB involved intensive case management (New Jersey) and financial incentives for school attendance (Wisconsin). Other programs added expanded job training assistance and child and health care, but all followed the basic strategy of enhancing human capital. This strategy was the basis of both the WIN program and the 1982 OBRA changes, and we can therefore conclude that the states were operating on the assumptions the national government had established for approaches to welfare experimentation. Few of the programs were punitive in nature, even those that had some mandatory component.

Although elements of this approach continued to mark most of the state welfare experiments, the programs that came out of the states in the second period (beginning after the 1992 State of the Union address) contained a new component for which there was little history of federal interest or acceptance: family structure. The first two programs of this sort were those of New Jersey and Wisconsin. Wisconsin (which submitted its proposal in March 1992) proposed a pilot test, conducted in Milwaukee, which paid one-half the usual increase for a second child and no additional increase for subsequent children, and which required unmarried minors to live in the home of their parents or guardians in order to qualify for assistance. New Jersey, which submitted its proposal three months later, was bolder in that it applied its "family cap" to all recipients of AFDC while also providing assistance to married families in which the husband is not the father of the children. The two provisions, when combined, were expected to reduce birthrates and encourage marriage.

Other states followed Wisconsin and New Jersey's lead. Vermont's Family Independence Project (FIP) included the requirement that minor parents live with their parents or guardians. Arkansas and Georgia both included family cap provisions in their welfare reform proposals. It appears that once HHS approves a particularly controversial welfare reform idea, other states are made aware that the proposal is acceptable to the federal government. This pattern has also emerged in the case of family cap programs. The acceptance and spread of family-centered programs indicates that the states, during this second period, recognized that they could act on their own initiative and not simply look to prior federal government action for clues as to what they should experiment with.

To understand why the experiments in this second period were such a sharp break from the previous assumptions of the AFDC program, it is instructive to remember what the Supreme Court had done in the welfare cases. In *New York State Department of Social Services v. Dublino,* the Court approved a New York State law that imposed work requirements in excess of those provided for in WIN. The Court stated:

> To the extent that the Work Rules embody New York's attempt to promote self-reliance and civic responsibility, to assure that limited state welfare funds be spent on behalf of those genuinely incapacitated and most in need, and to cope with the fiscal hardships enveloping many state and local governments, this Court should not lightly interfere.[48]

This attitude differed markedly from the one the Court showed in *King v. Smith,* where it declared that "insofar as this or any similar regulation is based on the State's asserted interest in discouraging illicit sexual behavior and illegitimacy, it plainly conflicts with federal law and policy." The Court sharply distinguished between attitudes toward work, which it considered malleable and thus within the bounds of acceptable state regulation, and sexual behavior, which it treated as innate (and private) and thus beyond the realm of state jurisdiction.

The Supreme Court's action in these two cases reminds us why the second period of welfare waivers was so remarkable and the first was rather unexceptional. The Court had engaged in a sweeping act of centralization and standardization in *King,* in the area of sexual matters, that it had chosen not to extend to the area of employment-related issues. In the first era of welfare waivers the states were not really recovering authority that had been previously removed from them. In the second era they were. The Court had stripped them of the authority to regulate sexual behavior in *King;* with the New Jersey and Wisconsin experiments, the states were retrieving their lost authority. We can thus say that it was during the second period that the truly significant trend of decentralizing the moral components of welfare began.

It may not be useful to define a third period in the history of welfare waivers, but there are indications that a new kind of experiment is becoming popular in the states. This new type of experiment involves strict time limits on welfare. Previous waiver experiments have required certain types of behavior after certain time periods, such as job training or supervised job search, but none have simply cut off assistance after a certain date. The first states to propose a hard time limit were Wisconsin and Florida. Florida's program, which was approved in 1994, limited eligibility for AFDC benefits to 24 months in any 60-month period. A similar, and much more dramatic, experiment is being planned in Wisconsin, which has proposed to do away with cash assistance altogether, substituting bridge loans, private and community jobs, and child care.[49]

These programs are radical in that they do not simply create financial incentives for particular behaviors, but actually create new standards of eligibility that are nowhere in the Social Security Act or any other legislation. These programs create a new class of the current welfare population for which there is a new, major condition of eligibility: previous acceptance of assistance. Earlier value-based programs cut off only the caretaker's part of the grant, thus avoiding, if only rhetorically, the claim that they were taking food out of the mouths of children. The new programs remove the entire grant, including the children's portion.

The award for most radical welfare proposal (passed in Spring 1995) must go to Governor William Weld of Massachusetts for his state's Employment Support Program, which would limit cash assistance to nonexempt cases to no more than 60 days, during which the head of household is expected to look for work.[50] During that period, the family would receive the equivalent of three months of benefits. All those who did hit the 60-day cap would then be required to perform 25 hours of community service and at least 15 hours of continued job search. In what could be considered either righteous anger or a political stunt, Governor Weld ultimately pulled the waiver request from HHS consideration in the summer of 1995, citing excessive and unreasonable departmental demands.[51]

REFORM THROUGH THE BACK DOOR: THE CASE OF THE MISSING CONGRESS

The rise of the waiver strategy in the late 1980s was the result of four institutional responses: state action; White House support for state experimentation; court inaction; and congressional inaction. The absence of any one of these four factors could have blocked the expansion of waivers and prevented reform from taking place. The first two factors have already been discussed. The last two, congressional and court inaction, are still to be explained.

Depending upon how one defines congressional action or inaction, my observation that Congress has not influenced waiver policy could be questioned. For my purpose, congressional action means an explicit decision by the body as a whole to call upon or forbid movement by other governments or private institutions. No such action has materialized on the subject of waivers. Legislation has been proposed (but not passed) to further expand waiver authority, but no similar proposals have attempted to restrict it. In general, the left and its public interest groups have failed to restrict waiver authority, even though many of the experiments conducted under it conflict strongly with their fundamental principles. The left was strong enough to veto certain policies in a legislative context that it has been unable to stop when pursued through the waiver process.

Congressional involvement, however, has been almost completely in the other direction. Although Congress has not acted as a body on the subject of waivers, it has been involved on a delegation-by-delegation basis. There are two principal modes of congressional influence on the issue. The first, and most direct, has been in the relatively few cases where Congress has, in legislation, directed the secretary of HHS to approve certain waiver proposals, the most prominent being New York's CAP, which was explicitly provided for in the 1988 Family Support Act. Cases such as this are few and far between, however.

The more common form of congressional involvement is for a state delegation to act in concert to put pressure on the executive branch to expedite the processing of a waiver proposal.[52] I have not been able to find any evidence that a congressional delegation has been able to cajole HHS into approving a waiver that it would not have approved otherwise, but delegations have exercised substantial influence in cutting down the time it takes for a state to get its proposal approved.

HHS almost never rejects a waiver request outright because the process is usually more of a negotiation than a confrontation. Typically, a state submits its request and HHS sends the state an initial analysis (including a list of concerns and matters that need to be addressed if the waiver is to be approved). Most of the concerns, which are about evaluation technique, are negotiated. Obviously, because HHS can, in most cases, negotiate indefinitely, the incentive is for the state to accept most of the reasonable demands. However, if a state's congressional delegation leans on HHS to speed up its approval of its state's waiver request, the compressed schedule can cause federal officials to be somewhat less strict than they would be in the absence of such involvement.

Rallying the state delegation is, in fact, one of the crucial parts of a push for HHS approval. Chuck Hobbs, who has advised a number of states on their waiver requests, describes the mode of congressional involvement.

> Generally, the most direct way is the governor calls them all [members of the state's congressional delegation] up and says, "We've got a waiver package coming, we'd really like to do this, the state legislature's passed this thing." Of course, to the congressional delegation, the state legislature's an important body, they came from there for the most part. Then, you get congressional staffers who actually get into the process of talking and calling the department, saying, "How's it coming along . . ." You get a congressional staff leader who will call a meeting and get the parties together and say, "What's going on here and how soon are you going to get the waivers out?" . . . It's a quasi-legislative process.

The process is quasi-legislative, then, because influence is exercised informally, by members of Congress rather than by Congress. Members of Congress generally function in the waiver process as their state's advocate in Washington, protecting and advocating their state's interest much as they would in the case of a defense contract or toxic waste clean-up grant. Although the state's interest may not be as clear-cut as in those cases, and the issue may have been controversial when it was winding its way through the maze of state politics, by the time the proposal gets to Washington, most representatives understand their task as deference to their state's officially expressed will.

This atmosphere may explain why Congress has never acted to second-guess the approval by HHS of any state waiver request. Because waivers are in many ways akin to pork-barrel politics and have the added advantage of lacking any zero-sum component, questioning the wisdom of a state proposal would be seen as mean-spirited meddling in another state delegation's affairs. Despite the occasional complaints of liberal interest groups, waiver politics in Congress is almost completely parochial. Because of the way the process was constructed, there is also little impetus for consideration of the policy's wisdom as a whole.

WAIVERS IN THE COURTS

Liberal public-interest lawyers have attempted to interest the courts in the waiver process, with mixed results. As of July 1995, the high point of these efforts was *Beno v. Shalala,* which was decided in July 1994 by the Ninth Circuit Court of Appeals.[53] The plaintiffs in *Beno* argued that California's work-incentive "experiment," which was little more than an across-the-board benefit cut, was an exercise in illegitimate discretion, violated the Social Security Act, and was approved without the appropriate administrative procedures. This case is interesting not only for the decision the court rendered but for the arguments that HHS made in its defense.

The law granting the secretary of HHS waiver authority states that the decision to grant a waiver should be based on the secretary's judgments of what is in the interests of improving the program. Amazingly, in defense of her decision to approve California's waiver, Secretary Donna Shalala admitted that the arguments of those who opposed the waiver "raise serious concerns about California's undertaking, including consequences stemming from the loss of income, the failure to limit the study to those unable to work, and the statewide scope of the project" and "concedes that these matters deserve careful attention."[54] The *Beno* court observed, however, that the secretary was of the opinion that "she is not required to give them such attention. We cannot agree." The court observed that "Congress intended that the Secretary would 'selectively approve' state projects."[55] The rest of the case laid out a series of criteria that the law authorizing AFDC waivers requires. First, it would have to be shown that the secretary had considered not just the experimental design but the substance of the experiment: that is, whether any useful information could be derived from it. Second, the experiments would have to serve the purposes of the AFDC program as laid out in the Social Security Act. Finally, the project could not be for a period of time or cover more recipients than was necessary for experimental purposes.[56]

The core of the difference between the *Beno* court and the secretary of HHS concerns the validity of the entire new waiver process under the law. The two criteria HHS has been working under, cost neutrality and a rigorous evaluation, would fall far short of the criterion the *Beno* court would require. If standards that derive from the law were used, many of the waiver requests, and almost all of the ones that have been applied statewide, would not be approved.

The logic of the *Beno* court was that the secretary's discretion in the case of welfare waivers derived from their experimental nature. Policies that strayed from experimentation, then, were outside of her statutory authority. For example, antiwaiver advocates have been critical of HHS decisions to grant waivers for experiments that were already being attempted in other states. That is, the fact that a policy was duplicative should have made it pass a higher hurdle than one that had not yet been tried. However, as Gail Wilensky, former deputy domestic policy adviser in the Bush administration told me, "The fact that it [a waiver request] was duplicative meant that it should have been easier to get through."[57] Although experimentation was a secondary purpose of the waiver strategy, none of the individuals involved in creating the policy would question that increased state discretion was primary. Experimentation, however, was the thin reed on which this extralegal power was exercised.

This new wave of welfare litigation rests on a much firmer legal basis than did *King v. Smith* and its progeny. In the latter cases, public interest lawyers demanded of the courts that they expand the meaning of the law in a manner that was, at the minimum, in tension with its language and intent. In the waiver cases, however, the plaintiffs are asking the courts to recognize that the secretary of HHS is acting in a manner at variance with the clear meaning of the law.

One subsequent case that addressed a similar issue came to the opposite conclusion of the *Beno* court. In *C.K. v. Shalala,* the New Jersey district court approved the state's family cap waiver. In *C.K.,* the court treated the issue as one of procedure, dismissing the plaintiff's arguments with the observation that "the record need not be a trail emblazoned every few yards with signposts detailing every minute fact that went into the Secretary's decisional process."[58] However, the finding in *Beno* was not primarily about the need for an HHS paper trail. Rather, the court's argument was that the law required the secretary to take into account certain substantial criteria and that the HHS process was ignoring them. HHS had transformed AFDC into a program with much more state discretion than the law provides for, by using the ruse of experimentation as a fig leaf.

The legal debate over the legitimacy of waivers suggests an irony about welfare politics. Before 1968, AFDC was administered in a manner more or less consistent with the language and intent of the law. Starting with *King* and running through *Goldberg,* the ordinary legislative process was circumvented and state discretion substantially reduced. Partially in response to this strategy, welfare waivers were used to once again circumvent the legislative process, this time to reverse the restriction of state discretion. The two strategies have, more or less, canceled each other out. Thus, we see the partial and temporal nature of dissensus politics, which rests on going around, rather than through, the legislative process.

CONCLUSIONS: POLICY VERSUS PROCESS, DECENTRALIZATION VERSUS NATIONAL SOLUTIONS

Waiver politics and the decentralization of reform in AFDC are consequences of a dissensual opinion structure on the national level combined with the desire of the states and the public for reform. The courts, and in some cases the HHS bureaucracy, have made strides toward creating a more uniform national welfare policy, but those efforts have met with resistance from a polity unwilling to accept uniformity if it means that its basic values are not incorporated into national policy. Although there are reasons to think that the public would desire uniformity if it meant the authoritative enforcement of generally agreed-upon values, such a policy has not been enacted. Waivers and additional state discretion are the result.

This "solution" to the welfare problem is questionable on a number of counts. The most important point is that only a very circumscribed range of reforms is possible given the constraints of the waiver process. The cost-neutrality provision, which is at the center of the waiver process, determines that state demonstrations cannot incorporate solutions that require the expenditures of additional funds. Thus, although the states can address the authoritative side of the public's mind they are incapable of doing very much in the direction of expanding opportunity. When new training or jobs programs are created, the programs can only involve a small percentage of the welfare population or must be accompanied by cuts in benefits or other punitive measures. Almost all serious programs for comprehensive reform involve increasing welfare expenditures; but this kind of solution is impossible within the waiver structure.

A second and equally problematic aspect of the waiver process is that it is conducted under the guise of experimentation, despite the argument by many involved that it is the welfare solution. Radical decentralization might be one sort of solution (one that, for reasons I will discuss in the conclusion, is ultimately unsatisfactory), but the waiver process cannot succeed. Thus, the governors of many states have been pushing for block grants and have come to see the waiver process as unacceptably binding on their autonomy. The process, after all, was not created to facilitate broad-based state discretion. HHS has chosen to, in effect, extend waivers indefinitely, but this action has further called into question the "experimental" nature of the waivers, opening the policy up for further intervention by the courts. In the end, then, the waiver strategy led to congressional action, action that has been complicated by Congress's prior inaction.

A final problem with the waiver strategy is that it is based on Congress's abdication of its legislative responsibility. The problem of poverty and dependence is, at its base, a national problem (as the difficulties arising from interstate movement—the "welfare magnet" problem—demonstrates), and a solution, regardless of its type, will have to come from the people's representatives in Washington.

Congress's lack of involvement has allowed the process of experimentation to be conducted without any general direction or structure that would culminate in national action, despite the fact that the process must end up back in Congress's lap. By handing off the issue to the states, members of Congress have been able to put off the long, arduous task of developing a congressional majority around the direction that welfare policy should take. This weakness is as true of legislation that would extend waiver authority or transfer AFDC funds to the states in the form of block grants as it is of current policy.

Congress is currently debating proposals for comprehensive reform in AFDC. Some of these proposals are serious efforts to alter the substance of the program, but most are little more than thinly veiled attempts to avoid making the basic ethical choices regarding welfare policy. The waiver process has prepared the way for more substantive proposals, by bringing Democrats to accept the idea of enforcing some standards on the welfare population. What the process has not done is help Congress think about all the solutions that are needed to solve the problem, many of which require changing policy outside of AFDC. The welfare problem will be difficult to solve if we don't change welfare from without and replace it with guaranteed employment, child support, and other nonwelfare programs. The waiver strategy, however, has encouraged Congress to think that the welfare problem can be solved from within AFDC. For a number of reasons, it cannot.

AFDC is itself the problem, and sixty years of experience with the program and various solutions based upon its perpetuation have all proven quite limited. AFDC was created to solve a much different problem than the one the nation now faces, and the program's federal structure is one of the principal elements that cripples it. The waiver strategy, and the block grant approach, which is its kissing cousin, attempt to solve dependency by reinforcing the states' role in the program; these approaches are a sign of the continuing immaturity of welfare politics. The evasion of congressional responsibility, which dissensus politics predicts, is no longer possible in the case of AFDC.

8
Missed Opportunity: Dissensus, Devolution, and Collapse of the Clinton Welfare Plan

By the late 1980s, the acute level of ideological conflict that had previously characterized welfare policy-making was beginning to diminish. Washington was celebrating the coming of a "new welfare consensus," the emergence of a cross-ideological agreement on the need for stricter enforcement of behavioral norms, and increased resources to help the poor conform to those norms. In 1992, the country put a Democrat in the White House who promised to "end welfare as we know it" by terminating cash welfare after two years, requiring recipients to work after two years. The ground, it seemed at the time, had been cleared for substantial and permanent change in the nation's welfare programs.

What went wrong? How could this consensus, which brought American elites in line with the public, collapse? How could the Republican party, fearful of the consequences of attacking the central value questions of welfare head-on, opt for a reform in intergovernmental relations, accompanied by a sharp cut in resources? How did the ideologues wrest control of the welfare issue from the center, resurrecting dissensus from its still fresh grave? How did the Clinton administration blow its chance at comprehensively reforming welfare and lose an opportunity to remove an albatross from around the neck of the Democratic party? In this chapter I will answer these questions and relate the argument presented earlier to the events of 1991–1995.

I suggest that the welfare consensus of the late 1980s and early 1990s was real but tenuous. Ideological convergence in American politics is difficult to maintain, especially when the intellectual consensus that supports it rests on a thin political foundation. When a convergence occurs, it is critical that it is translated into policy and cemented into institutions quickly. Every day that a consensus is not implemented increases the possibility of a return to the politics of dissensus. This pattern ultimately sank the Clinton welfare plan. A strategy that was tenable early in his administration became less so as the administration dragged out the process, until ultimately the president lost his congressional majority and with it his ability to maintain the consensus.

These events bolster my analysis (see Chapter 7) of the relation between dissensus and devolution. Dissensus led to the waiver policy, as pressure for change shifted the policy venue out of the clearly ineffectual legislative track. However, the limits of the waiver strategy soon became clear, as experience with state discretion began to create its own politics. Republican governors, eager to implement much stricter welfare programs, were emboldened by their additional autonomy and sought to take the AFDC money and run. Republican senators, eager to avoid a divisive debate on work and (especially) illegitimacy, welcomed the opportunity to "reform" welfare while avoiding its central moral and administrative issues.

ENDING DISSENSUS: THE VIEW FROM THE LEFT

By the time of President Clinton's election in 1992, the ideological landscape on the left had changed dramatically in relation to the situation a decade before. A substantial, ideologically self-confident center was forming, institutionalized in the Progressive Policy Institute and the Democratic Leadership Council.[1] The most important figures on the left were now socially moderate, perhaps somewhat conservative, even as they held out hope for a dramatic expansion of the welfare state. Welfare reform that combined authority and opportunity had become acceptable and in some parts of the left even grudgingly popular. Only a few on the ideological fringes of the left retained their unremitting hostility to "ending welfare as we know it."[2]

The critical work in the evolution of the left was, curiously, a book by a prominent conservative. There is no way to overestimate the effect that Charles Murray's book *Losing Ground* had on the intellectual debate on poverty. Murray's modest proposal, the outright elimination of cash welfare, opened intellectual space not only on the right but on the left as well, by making it difficult to avoid the fundamental quandaries of social policy.[3] In addition, it created momentum for proposals that would alleviate need and open opportunity without suffering from the defects inherent in cash welfare. William Julius Wilson took up the challenge of Murray's work in his equally influential book *The Truly Disadvantaged,* in which he argues that targeted programs such as welfare are insufficient to remedy the real causes of poverty, such as structural unemployment and the lack of education and training programs. Although he did not suggest the elimination of welfare, his approach broke through the left's targeted, cash-oriented tactic of fighting poverty. His work melded a social democrat's suspicion of the free market and advocacy of strong government programs for the poor and working class with a conservative's concern for the consequences of family instability and social deviance. By connecting the egalitarian and hierarchical aspects of American culture, and suggesting that only nontargeted programs could cure the ills of the inner city, Wilson helped to reconnect egalitarians to the American cultural consensus. Since Murray and Wilson reopened the debate on poverty and redirected the discussion to alternatives to welfare, there has been a remarkable intellectual renaissance at the center of the American political spectrum.

What killed reform in the early 1970s was the absence of a viable, intellectually self-confident group of moderates who could resist the pull of the left and right. In the absence of a separate centrist agenda, enough of the middle cleaved off to the extremes to defeat radical reform. By the early 1990s, it was possible, as it was not at the time of the FAP debate, for comprehensive change in welfare to be crafted by a group in the center and in opposition to extremists on both sides. The largest strides toward cultural integration had been made on the left, perhaps because the level of cultural alienation was most acute on that end of the ideological spectrum.

At the level of ideology, the emergence of the *American Prospect* as a prominent journal of nonradical liberal thought has been critical. The *American Prospect* published two very influential articles, one by Theda Skocpol and the other by Christopher Jencks, that extended Wilson's arguments and made the case for welfare replacement more explicit. Skocpol argues:

> The message of history is clear. Those who want to help the poor should not try to devise new programs finely targeted to low-income people or the "underclass." They should forget about reforming means-tested public assistance programs like AFDC. Rather, they should aim at bypassing and ultimately replacing "welfare" with new policies that address the needs of the less privileged in the context of programs that also serve middle-class and stable working class citizens.[4]

Jencks, after exhaustively demonstrating that many welfare recipients are already working, albeit under the table, proposes that we use this fact as the foundation for transforming the nation's poverty programs:

> Instead of trying to reform a system that has resisted reform for as long as it has existed, liberals should try to construct a new system that focuses explicitly on helping all parents who work in low-wage jobs. Rewarding work is consistent with American values. And trying to help low-wage workers with families is consistent with widespread legislative concern about the current condition of children.[5]

Other examples of this type of thinking among nonradicalized liberals are not hard to find. Mickey Kaus's book *The End of Equality* proposed, from a neoliberal, communitarian point of view, a program of government-run, poverty-line jobs as a replacement for welfare. David Ellwood, in his work *Poor Support,* outlined a strategy for guaranteed child support, two years of transitional assistance, and then government jobs (if necessary) and an enhanced earned income tax credit (EITC), as a substitute for welfare. When these approaches are reduced to their policy substance, it is remarkable how small the differences are between them. Finally, the emergence of the Democratic Leadership Council and its Progressive Policy Institute created a vital link between centrist academics and the Democratic party, providing intellectual and political support for dramatic change in welfare.

This intellectual renaissance made it possible for liberals to move away from their cash orientation (a purely egalitarian strategy) and to embrace a work- and family-oriented philosophy of welfare. Liberals made the two-year limit the beginning of the debate about welfare, demonstrating just how far they had come since the early 1970s. Although there were still liberal representatives who would have preferred no change in welfare to a time-limited, work-oriented system, they were dwarfed in importance by members of the Congressional Mainstream Forum, who also had the advantage of warm relationships with moderate Republicans. There was reason to think that although the radical left still stood where it had two decades earlier, there was a sufficiently large intellectual center on the left to render the radicals irrelevant.

ENDING DISSENSUS: THE VIEW FROM THE RIGHT

The story on the other side was not quite so auspicious. By the end of the 1980s, there were signs that a large segment of conservative opinion was moving to the center on welfare. One prominent example was the American Enterprise Institute's publication of *The New Consensus on Family and Welfare*.[6] This work, which included the views of a broad range of scholars from the center to the right, reflected a culturally integrative worldview, as it argued that "no person should be involuntarily poor without having assistance from others. No able adult should be allowed voluntarily to take from the common good without also contributing to it."[7] The fashion in right-wing circles was the rise of "big government conservatism,"[8] and Lawrence Mead, whose thought centers on the need to integrate the obligation to work into welfare, was the popular conservative thinker on welfare issues. The substantial support of Republicans for the 1988 Family Support Act suggested that conservatives were willing to engage Democrats if the latter admitted the necessity of an emphasis on work and family.[9]

The optimism that FSA created dwindled, ironically, the nearer comprehensive welfare reform appeared. The most disturbing indication that conservative opinion was moving away from the work-oriented solution that liberals had embraced was the rise of Charles Murray. After *Losing Ground* was published in 1984, it quickly took a prominent place in every literate conservative's library. Even so, although most conservatives accepted Murray's analysis that welfare causes illegitimacy and reduces work effort, few openly supported his proposal for the outright elimination of government support for poor single mothers. Conservatives were still attracted to the workfare strategy that Ronald Reagan pioneered in California.

The response to Murray's October 1993 article ("The Coming White Underclass") showed that important parts of the conservative Republican establishment had moved away from workfare and toward a welfare abolition strategy. In that article, Murray surveyed the evidence that white illegitimacy was increasing and would soon pose as significant a social problem as did the same condition among blacks, unless drastic policy changes were made. His prescription echoed that of *Losing Ground:*

> Restoring economic penalties translates into the first and central policy prescription: to end all economic support for single mothers. The AFDC . . . payment goes to zero. Single mothers are not eligible for subsidized housing or for food stamps . . . the signal is loud and unmistakable: From society's perspective, to have a baby that you cannot care for is profoundly irresponsible, and the government will no longer subsidize it.[10]

And Murray's bottom line: If a woman could not support her children, the government would take them away. "What about women who can find no support but keep the baby anyway?" Murray asked. "There are laws on the books about the right of the state to take away a child from a neglectful parent. . . . Society's main response, however, should be to make it as easy as possible for mothers to place their children for adoption at infancy." The final point of Murray's essay is perhaps the most dramatic: "Some small proportion of infants and larger proportion of older children will not be adopted. For them, the government should spend lavishly on orphanages. . . . Those who prattle about the importance of keeping children with their biological mothers may wish to spend some time in a patrol car or with a social worker seeing what the reality of life with welfare-dependent biological mothers can be like."[11] In effect, Murray proposed a return to the status quo ante 1900, before the rise of the mothers' pension.

What was striking about Murray's proposal was not its sweeping and callous nature, but how his arguments became the welfare reform prescription of a large number of significant Republican leaders and potential presidential candidates.

By July 1994 the welfare proposal with the most momentum was outright abolition. The situation had been very different just a few months earlier. Senator Hank Brown (Colorado) had proposed offering welfare recipients a voucher that would double their AFDC and food stamp benefits in exchange for taking a public job. Similar in form was the House GOP proposal, which applied a two-year limit, after which welfare recipients would have to work 35 hours a week at the minimum wage. Both these proposals were at least on the same page as the Clinton welfare reform. A second alternative, supported by Representative Jan Meyers of Kansas, called for freezing AFDC spending and returning all federal funds to the states in the form of a block grant.[12]

The twenty-ton gorilla of welfare reform was, however, Murray's welfare abolition approach, which received its most prominent support when Empower America, a prominent Republican think tank headed by William Bennett, Vin Weber, Jack Kemp, and Jeane Kirkpatrick, proposed the outright abolition of AFDC and food stamps for unwed mothers.[13] A January 27, 1994, article by Bennett and Peter Wehner (director of policy at Empower America) starkly presented the problem of welfare as they saw it: "The point is not tougher work provisions and job training: rather, it is to go after a system that fosters illegitimacy and its attendant social pathologies."[14] More important, perhaps, than their policy justification for such an approach was their political rationale:

> It would be politically smart for Republicans because anything less than calling for an end to welfare will probably ensure that the debate will be conducted on Clinton's terms. That's a sure political loser. On the other hand, calling for the abolishment of AFDC is an opportunity for Republicans to make a clean, principled break with an old, failed system, seize the mantle of true reform and help return our nation to an older, better time, when moral common sense was the touchstone of social policy.[15]

Bennett admitted that if the debate were conducted on the presumption that work was the key to welfare reform, Republicans would have little with which to oppose the president. Turning the issue to illegitimacy would put the president on the defensive and resurrect the Republicans' political advantage on welfare.

Looking back, the Empower America brief seems to be the turning point in the evolution of the welfare issue. Paul Offner, then an assistant to Senator Daniel Patrick Moynihan, told me: "I think the critical document was that letter that Kemp, Weber and Bennett sent to the Republicans early in '94. . . . What I remember is three very respected Republicans saying, to hell with that [work] strategy, that's a losing strategy. It was sort of the analog to what Bill Kristol did on health care."[16]

Soon after the "White Underclass" article was published, Murray participated in a series of important meetings with Republican representatives, including one arranged by the Heritage Foundation, with approximately thirty Republican representatives.[17] These meetings, along with the substantial play Murray's argument was given by Rush Limbaugh, the conservative radio talk-show host, succeeded in making a substantial portion of the Republican party dissatisfied with the work-oriented approach. Furthermore, the Empower America brief and the Murray article energized conservative activists by unshackling them from a work-centered strategy that reflected many of their principles but gave them no political advantage vis-à-vis the president. Illegitimacy became the key symbolic instrument through which conservatives began to chip away at support for the work-oriented approach.

CONGRESSIONAL LIBERALS AND THE AGONIZING WAIT FOR THE CLINTON WELFARE PLAN

Conservative opposition to the work strategy was not significant until early 1994, and even into the summer there were a number of Republicans who were still enthusiastic about the two-years-and-work strategy. Why didn't the administration propose a bill sooner to take advantage of this still-solid ideological consensus?

The struggle over health care is the most obvious answer. The first is that health care was a priority for the administration, which believed that health care and welfare could not be handled effectively at the same time. Even so, this does not explain why the White House and congressional Democrats did not put more pressure on HHS to at least get their proposal out earlier so that it could be debated, hearings could be held, and negotiations started. It is easy to understand why the welfare reform team of Bane, Ellwood, and Reed took so long to put out a proposal: The compromises were difficult, the politics of individual provisions tricky, the differences within the team real (although vastly overstated). The important question is why other actors did not push them harder for action.

Despite the suspicions of some moderate Democrats, the main resistance to pushing ahead with welfare reform did not come from Hillary Clinton and those working on health care in the White House. "The timing issue was raised before Mrs. Clinton on December 15 [1993]. She thought the welfare planners should press ahead. Her most prescient piece of advice was: 'Whatever Senator Moynihan wants, we should listen to.' "[18] This is not to say that there was no resistance within the administration, outside of the White House. Henry Cisneros, secretary of Housing and Urban Development, stated publicly in mid-1993, "I'm not a believer in artificial deadlines of that [two-year limit] nature."[19] Assistant Secretary of HUD Andrew Cuomo and Christopher Edley of OMB were both highly vocal opponents of the plan, to the point where they were widely suspected of leaking documents from the welfare reform working group, a charge that was later refuted.[20] Resistance from within the administration clearly made the working group's efforts more difficult.

Why did the administration appoint such an enormous working group to develop the welfare reform plan? Senator Moynihan, for one, found the size of the group puzzling. He stated in January 1994, "If you want a bill, 32 people on a task force can't write it. You put two people in a room over a weekend, and they write you the bill."[21] The size of the group virtually guaranteed leaks, which made it difficult for the welfare reform planners to thoughtfully consider unusual options. Furthermore, with 32 people in the group, an unmanageable number of interests and ideologies had to be considered. It may be that the consensus-building mode of decision-making which the Clintons, and those of their generation, have adopted is unsuitable for an issue as value-laden as welfare, especially given that, as Senator Moynihan argued, "in the main, the President's appointments have been people who wouldn't proceed in the way he stated in the campaign."[22] Had the president simply given the job of hashing out a plan to Ellwood and Moynihan's assistant, Paul Offner, much of the delay, rancor, and suspicion could have been avoided.

Even so, the administration did know that it faced serious opposition in Congress. The Democratic members of the House Ways and Means Human Resources committee were among the body's most liberal. Robert Matsui, probably the most intellectually involved member of the committee, refused to agree to the conference report on the 1988 Family Support Act. Azar Kattan, a former staff member for Matsui, described the situation on the committee:

> You had a bunch of these guys who were really focused on health care, and that's what everybody had run on. Bill Clinton had run on welfare, but they hadn't run on welfare, and they felt that health care was really what they had to do. Bob Matsui didn't like the president's bill: he thought that was where we should have ended up, not where Democrats should have started out, and having that be the first thing out was absolutely outrageous.[23]

Jim McDermott, a member of Ways and Means and the author of the single-payer health care reform plan in the House, also bitterly opposed the Clinton welfare plan: "It's stupid for the president to keep talking about ending welfare after two years, because it's not going to happen."[24]

Clearly, the health care–welfare timing split was as much, if not more, about ideology as about political strategy. Individual relations between subcommittee Democrats and the administration were not especially warm, partially because of the ideological suspicion between the two groups. Kattan observed:

> There was a real frustration among the Dem[ocrat]s on the committee that David [Ellwood] and Mary Jo [Bane] would come into our offices and say, we really want to work with you, and go back to their offices, and they never asked our advice, they never told us what they were doing. . . . These guys thought that they were ignored, and because of that they had no investment in its [the Clinton welfare plan] passage.[25]

Relations between the administration and the Republican minority on the Ways and Means committee, meanwhile, were very warm, according to a senior committee staff member.[26] Congressional liberals began to get the idea that the administration was pursuing a center-out strategy, building from a base of moderate Republicans and Democrats, rather than starting with those on the left, as they had done on health care. This created a damaging environment of suspicion.

When the administration finally did put out its bill, in summer 1994, opposition on the left had already begun to mount. In January 1994, Harold Ford, the chairman of the Human Resources subcommittee, "began putting forth a completely different approach. He suggested that welfare recipients—and other poor people who do not collect welfare—ought to receive at least $9 an hour for public or private sector jobs, not the $4.25-an-hour minimum wage envisioned by the Clinton administration."[27] Ford continually attacked the underlying logic of the Clinton plan, stating, "We can't expect welfare recipients to flip hamburgers at $5 an hour. That won't come out of this committee."[28] Earlier, in discussing plans such as that of Representative Rick Santorum of Pennsylvania (and by extension, Clinton's), which would create a large number of public service jobs, he said, "I will not even take that up in committee. We're not talking about workfare."[29] The Congressional Black Caucus, Hispanic Caucus, and Democratic Freshman Class were all opposed to the Clinton welfare strategy, even before it had been formally proposed.[30] Many liberals were suspicious of the underlying philosophy of the Clinton administration—that some level of behavioral standards were fundamental to welfare reform. Lynn Woolsey, a Democratic representative from California, for example, resurrected the old liberal contention that "the danger is that it is the children who may get punished for their parent's problems."[31] When an "Oxford-style" debate was held in the House on welfare reform, in May 1994, the Democrats selected Woolsey, rather than a supporter of the Clinton approach, to face Republican Gary Franks.

Ninety-three House Democrats broke from the Clinton approach early. In a November 24, 1993, letter to the administration, authored by Representatives Bernard Sanders and Patsy Mink, they rejected a number of the building blocks of the administration's framework. The letter stated that "time limits on the receipt of AFDC benefits are unacceptably arbitrary because they fail to take into account individual circumstances, the needs of dependent children, and the failure of the economy to generate decent jobs."[32] Using the same approach as Ford did, the liberal House Democrats suggested that "public sector employment created for people leaving the AFDC system must provide pay and benefits equal to other workers doing the same work, without displacing current workers or jobs." The administration was having a hard enough time figuring out how to pay for a large number of public sector jobs at the minimum wage; at a prevailing wage, it would have become fiscally impossible, a fact that the authors of the letter undoubtedly were aware of.

Although Robert Matsui shared the sentiments of the letter, he did not sign it. Kattan observed,

> He really resisted coming up with his own bill, and he finally got fed up with the administration.... He really wanted to be supportive of the administration, but he got to this point where he thought they were so misguided in what they were doing, what they were doing was so bad for the program. He was really outraged that they were considered to be the left of this debate.[33]

Matsui proceeded to introduce his own welfare reform plan, H.R. 4767, the Family Self-Sufficiency Act. In some ways, the Matsui plan echoed the Clinton approach in its requirements that teenage mothers stay at home and its slight toughening of work requirements. However, the Matsui plan pointedly refused to include a two-year limit on cash assistance, the main rhetorical draw of the Clinton approach, and the tie that bound the moderate Democrats and Republicans.[34]

Despite these rumblings from the left wing of the Democratic party, liberals were not ideologically focused on defeating the Clinton welfare plan. Left-wing groups found it difficult to mobilize their base against the proposal. Jennifer Vasiloff, executive director of the Coalition on Human Needs, observed, "We're trying our best, but not having the specifics of the Clinton proposal to react to or organize around is holding a lot of people back."[35] Even though Matsui was able to get a number of liberal groups to support his bill, prominent liberals like Marion Wright Edelman balked at openly breaking from the administration's approach. Liberals were not able to stop the administration from proceeding with its welfare reform plan, but they "might have slowed the administration down a little bit, with all those liberals saying, we don't like what you are doing."[36] Furthermore, congressional leaders, "asked Clinton in December [1993] to hold off on welfare legislation if he wants health care this year."[37]

Of greater importance, the attempt to pay for the health care bill squeezed out many of the administration's options for fiscal offsets. Representative Dan Rostenkowski, the chairman of Ways and Means, observed, "We need every dollar for health care. . . . The cupboard is bare. There are few ways of funding that are palatable."[38] When members of the administration attempted to come up with creative ways of financing the plan, they were squashed almost immediately. Secretary of Labor Robert Reich sent the president a memo, proposing to pay for the plan by cutting "welfare for the wealthy," a strategy that, at the least, had a certain rhetorical ring to it. The White House responded meekly. Gene Sperling, a White House economics adviser, soon announced, "This is not a memo that's under serious consideration, I just want to tell you. We want a no-tax budget."[39] Because of its timidity on paying for welfare reform, the panel had to seriously restrict its plan, rejecting the less costly "Cadillac" plan and opting for the "Volkswagen" plan, which included a greatly diminished child care program, for instance. In the end, even the Republicans spent more than Clinton proposed and created more work slots as well. This fiscal timidity upset both liberals and moderates in the party.

The story was quite different where the ideological center of both parties was concerned. The Congressional Mainstream Forum, the representative of the Democratic Leadership Council (DLC) in the House, actively pushed the administration to propose a strong welfare reform plan, going so far as to put forward its own outline, which would cost even more than the Clinton plan for child care and would accelerate program participation. Unlike the Matsui plan, however, the Mainstream Forum's proposal was intended to accelerate action rather than delay it. The proposal accepted all of the major elements of the Clinton approach, including time limits. Representative Dave McCurdy of Oklahoma pointed out in an article in *Roll Call,* "The Mainstream Forum's plan is so similar to the White House task force draft that differences could probably be resolved in a single day of negotiation."[40] The Progressive Policy Institute also urged Clinton to quickly propose and push through his welfare reform plan, noting the broad range of support it had in the country and in Washington.

> The Clinton plan—and its close relations, the Mainstream Forum bill and the House GOP bill sponsored by Rep. Rick Santorum—defines the vital center of the welfare debate. With New Democrats and a majority of House Republicans embracing the main tenets of the President's approach, we have—and ought to seize—a rare opportunity to forge a broad, bipartisan coalition for fundamental change.[41]

E. Clay Shaw, ranking Republican on the House Ways and Means subcommittee on Human Resources, observed in early 1993, "If there is one issue where moderate Republicans and Democrats can work together in a bipartisan manner, this is it. My hope is that the president sticks to his guns and doesn't let the liberal side of his party pull him off course."[42] Santorum, whose plan was quite similar to Clinton's and that of the Mainstream Forum, went so far as to attack Kemp for his advocacy of a complete welfare cut-off, saying it amounted to "posture for purity's sake" and that "the risk is that you're going to have millions of women and children with absolutely no support out there."[43] Those on the center-right and the center-left were, at this point, willing to defend the principles of work-based welfare reform against ideological extremists and were eagerly awaiting a presidential program that would reflect their shared philosophy.

THE RIGHT BOLTS: THE DEATH OF THE WORK STRATEGY

Even as late as summer 1994, the major Republican welfare plans were not in substantial disagreement with the fundamentals of the Clinton welfare plan. However, there were signals that the consensus of principle that tied Republicans and moderate Democrats together was starting to shred. In January 1994, Senator Hank Brown, while introducing his own reform plan, noted of the Republicans, "To the extent that you don't have unanimity, it's not dislike for what's in this bill—it is people who want it to be even more extensive."[44] Vin Weber observed, "There has always been a little bit of tension on the conservative side, between those who want the value of work and those who are always fearful that it would turn into some big government solution."[45] Representative Tom Delay was clearly in the latter group, accepting the House Republican welfare plan, while clearly looking beyond it: "I think it is very constructive for people like [Charles] Murray and others to push the debate even further to the right. Our bill is a starting point, not necessarily an ending point. As the debate continues and we find out more and more what the nation wants, we are going to be able to move further to the right."[46] The illegitimacy issue, Murray's ideological stink bomb thrown into the previously genteel welfare debate, was beginning to have its intended effect.

Even so, the administration remained positive about the prospects for its version of welfare reform. David Ellwood, the assistant secretary of HHS for Planning and Evaluation, told me in September 1995:

> If you'd been interviewing me a year ago, I would have said we were in great shape. We introduced a bill in July, which nobody thought you could get passed last year. Health reform was supposed to come first, and then the crime bill, and there were all these other things. So there was a logic to what happened. The bottom line was, it almost passed anyway. A lot of people liked it, Moynihan was positive on it, Gibbons, who was then the chair [of the Ways and Means committee] liked it. The more they looked at it, the more they liked it, by and large, and there was a lot of enthusiasm among the Democrats about it. Even the Republicans, people like Clay Shaw and others, at least for a few days, managed to say nice things about it, until they were told from on high not to say nice things. In fact, most observers at that stage said, at that stage, if you take the Republican proposal that all the House Republicans signed on to, there are some big differences, but you'd think if you locked those people in a room they ought to be able to come to agreement.[47]

Ellwood believes that "if we had introduced our bill a year earlier, it would have passed easily. It is a tragedy, because I really felt we nailed it. People, both liberal and conservative, seemed to like it when they looked at it. Both the policy and rhetoric really did focus on work and responsibility."[48] However, there were inklings that things were not completely rosy, even in summer 1994: "Their [the Republicans] reactions were quite positive, and a couple of days later, things started to change. Both the ideology and the classic politics started to take over."[49]

By September 1994, the ideological atmosphere in Washington was becoming highly polarized as a result of the Contract with America. The contract's welfare provisions did not accurately represent the thinking of the Republicans with the most influence on the issue, such as Clay Shaw of Florida. Instead, they represented the ideas of conservative welfare elites, especially policy entrepreneurs such as Robert Rector of the Heritage Foundation. Furthermore, voices on the right started to suggest that no change would be better than going along with Clinton, precisely the message of the Empower America letter. Representative James Talent of Missouri, who coauthored a bill with Senator Lauch Faircloth of North Carolina that would have gradually implemented the Charles Murray cutoff proposal, stated in October 1994, "I'd like to see Bill Clinton veto welfare reform. I think he's going to be trapped by his own rhetoric."[50] Frank Luntz, who was a critical figure in the creation of the Contract with America, predicted before the election that "welfare reform in 1995 will be what health care was in 1994—it is going to be the emotional battleground on Capitol Hill."[51] The Republicans were beginning to feel their ideological oats once again, and even before the election a critical mass of their more right-wing members were determined not to permit any compromise with Clinton or the Democratic moderates.

The elections of 1994 drove a stake through the heart of the welfare issue's ideological center, the work and opportunity moderates. Whereas a two-year limit followed by work was the center of the moderate consensus, a new proposal, driven by the right wing's use of the illegitimacy issue took center stage: cutting off welfare entirely to most young, unwed mothers. Representative Talent observed, soon after the elections: "I'm concerned that the Contract bill may not go far enough in changing the incentives in the existing welfare system. I'm going to work to make sure we do not shift the focus off of illegitimacy."[52] Robert Rector, who became as influential among Republicans in 1995 as Lawrence Mead was in 1988, threatened, "We're not going to have a debate about AFDC. We're going to have a debate about the 'War on Poverty.' "[53]

The increased role of Robert Rector was, indeed, one of the curious features of the changed ideological atmosphere of early 1995. Unlike Mead or Murray, Rector had no legitimacy within the academic community and was considered just a few years hence to be a relatively minor and intellectually tangential figure. A Senate committee staff member observed, "Robert Rector has gone, in the space of two or three years, from being a loony out there to a policy maker. He's had enormous influence."[54] Asked why, I was told that the Republicans needed someone to "say, this is bold, this is new, this will work. You don't want someone hedging. The Republicans need bold now." Rector's influence was magnified, especially in the House, by his connections with influential conservative Christian groups. A senior House Republican staff member observed that on the welfare issue,

> The conservative groups, Christian Coalition, Heritage, Concerned Women for America, Eagle Forum, Free Congress, et cetera, have enormous influence. . . . In the House, [Rep. Richard] Armey is extremely responsive. He will meet with them personally, and he has on at least two or three occasions. And he will come to the Ways and Means committee and say, guys, we have got to have this.[55]

Ultimately, the House would follow the lead of its right-wing, slashing benefits across the board, implementing a family cap, and cutting off all cash assistance to those under 18. Between the time the Republicans took control of Congress and the Ways and Means Committee began to write its bill, a new, and ultimately very powerful, alternative to both the work and opportunity, and the illegitimacy strategies, emerged. The illegitimacy strategy had succeeded in routing the Clinton approach, but it was not sufficiently popular to hold together Republicans, especially in the Senate. Decentralization, however, was an idea all Republican senators could agree with, and that prevented an angry, and possibly devastating, split within the party.

DEVOLUTION AND THE POLITICS OF CONFLICT AVOIDANCE

The movement toward decentralization in AFDC did not begin in 1995. In fact, as I argued in Chapter 7, the political momentum for shipping the program back to the states was a primary consequence of the expanded waiver policy begun by Ronald Reagan in 1986. To understand how a process strategy, represented by decentralization, ended up drowning substantive welfare reform proposals (both the Clinton plan and the illegitimacy and cut-off alternative), we must extend the discussion of waivers that we began in Chapter 7. We will see that waivers, in effect, created their own, very powerful politics.

Clinton had sent a strong message to the states in early 1993 to the effect that he would approve even waiver requests that he opposed. A senior administration official observed that the administration was unwilling to reject outright even highly dubious waivers (such as those of Massachusetts and Virginia).

> This is a president who came from state government. Who are the federal government? You've got something that was passed by large majorities of state legislatures and signed by the governor, and we know better? You really do think this is a really big mistake? It doesn't feel real democratic. It posed enormously difficult challenges for us: morally, ethically, and every other way. Because we didn't have a president who said we will use the waiver process to do what he wanted. He wanted to allow the states to have very wide latitude.

Mary Jo Bane, assistant secretary for children and families, who had studied the relationship between welfare and family structure and was firmly convinced that a family cap would have no worthwhile effect and would take money away from needy families, was trapped by the rhetoric of experimentation and state flexibility. Discussing the issue with Jason DeParle, "Mrs. Bane acknowledged that she probably would not have suggested such experiments, since she doubts their effectiveness. But when much of the public believe a policy should be tested, she said, 'it is appropriate for us to be responsive.' "[56]

Clinton's bind, therefore, was not merely political but normative. This situation points to one of the key recurrent, internal conflicts faced by the president. On the one hand, he was committed to state flexibility and genuinely believed in the states' capacity for ingenious problem-solving. On the other hand, he (and especially his wife) believed deeply in protecting the welfare of children and in expanding programs to support them. In the end, despite the fact that the administration vigorously contested provisions it disagreed with in HHS-state negotiations, "the White House always expressed concern that we work it out," according to a senior HHS official.

By granting virtual carte blanche to the governors to experiment with AFDC, Clinton was actually shifting the political momentum in their direction. Waivers thus reduced the impression that substantial welfare reform needed to come from the federal government and increased the feeling in Washington that it could simply be handed off to the states. Soon, however, the Clinton administration found that it had a positive need for the waiver process: to ward off Republican efforts to strip away AFDC's federal structure and block grant the program.

In 1988, the National Governors' Association (NGA), led by then-governor Clinton and Delaware Governor Mike Castle, drove the negotiations that culminated in the Family Support Act. Because the governors were in fundamental agreement, regardless of party, as to their priorities on welfare reform, the NGA could act as a force for consensus and as an ideological brake. When the federal government was at least partially in Democratic hands, Republican governors had incentives to cooperate with their fellow Democratic governors, who provided institutional access to parts of the federal government that they would not have had otherwise.

In 1995, however, the NGA was split, with Republican governors, led by Tommy Thompson of Wisconsin, William Weld of Massachusetts, and John Engler of Michigan, negotiating with congressional Republicans, and the Democratic governors left on the sidelines. The partisan shift created by the 1994 elections eliminated the need Republican governors had for cooperation from their fellow Democrats in the states. Soon after the 1994 elections, "the three governors essentially offered to accept limited federal funding for welfare and related social services over the next five years in return for unprecedented state control over the program."[57] In a meeting in early December, Republicans from the House and Senate, Haley Barbour of the RNC, and Republican governors struck the block grant deal. Engler described the meeting as pointing toward "a revolutionary new form of relationship between the states and the federal government."[58]

The Republican governors' rhetoric, which emphasized state autonomy over any particular approach to solving the problem, soon began to take over the debate in Congress. Senator Robert Packwood stated, "We don't want to substitute conservative mandates for liberal mandates."[59] Strong support for the principles of federalism were probably not the driving force behind this shift in priorities. Paul Offner observed, "The thoughtful people within the Republican coalition realize the last thing they want to do is get bogged down in a [shouting] match about teenage mothers and kids born to mothers on welfare. That really was a battle that would just drag them down into the gutter."[60] A senior staff member of the Ways and Means committee observed, "There is no question, none, that returning power and money and authority to the states in the form of block grants does allow you a kind of intellectual dishonesty, that you can avoid all the substantive issues and say, that is a state issue."[61] Packwood was especially interested in the block grant approach because it provided him with a conservative argument against strong anti-illegitimacy provisions. The same Ways and Means staff member observed, "He's willing to take five years [as the limit on welfare receipt], willing to get rid of the entitlement. He's willing to have some strings, but illegitimacy, no."[62]

If block grants were the mechanism by which Republicans attempted to

avoid inflaming ideological splits within the party, waivers became the administration's chief instrument for arguing against block grants. Offner observed,
"The waiver performance of . . . HHS became a key part of the Clinton strategy
to argue against block grants. . . . As the Republican drumbeat of criticism
mounted about the existing system and all its rigidity, it became more and more
difficult for Democrats and people who had concerns about some of these waivers to say, this is absurd, we're going much too far, because by then it had become
such a central part of the Democratic defense."[63] Reflecting this scheme, Governor Howard Dean of Vermont, chairman of the NGA, opined that President Clinton's expansion of waiver policy in the summer of 1995 "almost obviates the need
for legislative welfare reform."[64]

Republicans did fight back against the Democrats' use of waivers to undercut
the argument for block grants. Virginia, which proposed a very extreme two-year
welfare cutoff, nearly had its waiver request rejected. The proposal was so controversial that other governors actually encouraged the administration to reject it.
In a televised debate on welfare reform, Governor Dean stated, "As the head of
this state, I hope they don't get their waiver, because their program doesn't protect kids. . . . We need a national policy . . . and she [Shalala] is going to be making sure that Virginia doesn't get a waiver that's going to kick 5-year-olds off any
kind of support after two years."[65] Kay James, Virginia's secretary of Human
Services, shot back: "If you'll just get out of our way, stay in Vermont, we [won't
interfere] in your state." James further complained that HHS has been continuing "to inject the Clinton philosophy into the waiver process." In the end, Clinton
folded, going so far as to announce, "It's a good plan and I am proud to be supporting it."[66]

Although Virginia gave just enough ground to HHS that the latter could ra-
tionalize signing off on a waiver, Governor Weld of Massachusetts went into the
process with no intention of compromising. Because Weld was one of the main
Republican governors pushing for block grants, he had no incentive to allow the
administration to use the waiver process to sidetrack Republican welfare reform
plans. Weld's standoff with the administration thus became a largely theatrical
device, intended to embarrass the administration and weaken its arguments.

For a number of months, HHS and Massachusetts had been in conflict over
the state's hard, sixty-day cut-off of welfare assistance. "In an August 4 letter to
Weld, Health and Human Services Secretary Donna E. Shalala said that HHS
would approve Massachusetts' plan only if there is a guarantee that 'those who
diligently pursue work but are unable to find it through no fault of their own will
receive transitional assistance.' "[67] Weld jumped on HHS resistance, pulling his
waiver request and accusing the administration of having "used its waiver power
to waive away real welfare reform." Weld further observed, "The federal government does not trust the good will of the people of Massachusetts . . . and they
really should. . . . My problem would go away if we get the Republican welfare bill
passed because there won't be any more waivers because the entitlement system

will be repealed. That would solve all of my problems in one stroke."[68] Senator Bob Dole, echoing Weld's complaint, told the NGA conference in August 1995, "The answer is not more waivers. Governors should not have to play a game of 'Mother, may I?' The waiver process only perpetuates a flawed system."[69]

Republicans, who were the force behind the creation of the expanded waiver policy, had come to see it as the largest obstacle to their flavor of welfare reform. They had also come upon a foolproof rhetorical strategy for repelling arguments against their plans: "Don't you trust the governors?" In 1995, this question was virtually unanswerable. Clinton and the Democrats had lost all of their momentum in the welfare reform process and were reduced to sniping at the margins. The momentum for packaging the program up and sending it to the states had become too strong to resist, eclipsing all other alternatives, including the forgotten public consensus on work. Welfare reform, after a brief hiatus, was once again, off center.

CONCLUSIONS

It has been reported that "one of the few bits of guidance Clinton did provide [to those devising his welfare reform plan] was to be 'bold': 'if you get everything else right, but get the values wrong, we'll fail.' "[70] In the end, however, the Clinton plan died, the welfare-work consensus collapsed, and the Republicans were able to capture the momentum on the issue, because the president was insufficiently daring. He allowed his plan to be whittled down by sniping from inside and outside the administration. He permitted the drive for health care reform to delay the planning for his welfare plan and allowed health care to monopolize the lion's share of palatable fiscal offsets. Finally, he appointed an awkward 32-member panel to devise his welfare reform plan, which, rather than making the planning easier, made it more difficult by creating opportunities for leaks and requiring that multiple interests and values be appeased.

Clinton, in the end, was insufficiently bold. He assumed that by attempting to satisfy everyone, he would be able to build a consensus. He was wrong. Instead, his efforts to bring everyone on board in the short term muddied his message and alienated his most devoted followers. He was unable to build massive public support because the long period of planning sapped the legitimacy that the campaign had provided. The Republicans were thus able to carve out a new, and devastating, argument against the work option and ultimately to rout him on the issue. Once this happened, the possibility of a culturally integrative, work-based welfare reform was gone, and Clinton and his party were reduced to tactical maneuvering to preserve as much of the AFDC safety net as possible.[71]

9

Conclusion:
Finding a Way Out

We have seen how a national opinion structure, fundamentally consistent and coherent on the subject of welfare, can coexist with a profoundly conflictual political system. We have seen how politicians and activists—with differing agendas—can pull apart the public's multiple cultural commitments and set them against one another. Because of the moral and ethical issues of AFDC, and because of the high stakes when those issues are addressed as public policy, welfare in America has been reformed only sporadically, inconsistently, unsuccessfully, and, for the most part, outside of the legislative process.

Woven through this work are five central, overarching themes concerning the nature of welfare policy-making. The first, and perhaps most important, is the centrality of issues of morality and public ethics to AFDC policy-making. AFDC is dominated by ethical issues for three reasons, two peculiar to the policy area and the other of more general application. The first reason is that there are more regime-level consequences to AFDC policy-making than in most other policy areas.[1] Family, work, and personal responsibility are all matters at the core of any regime, and it is virtually impossible to address welfare without addressing these concerns. Second, those assisted by AFDC have no representation in the political process, so that their interests are advocated by people more committed to the larger issues of morality involved in welfare rather than the practical concerns of those assisted by the program. The third reason is that the American system of competing for public office is driven by the search for "wedge issues," controversies which can serve to cleave voters into rival groups. Many politicians prefer to debate welfare at the highest level of public morality because it is at that level that AFDC can serve as a wedge issue.

A second key finding of this study is that intellectuals play a central role in welfare policy-making. A primary function of intellectual elites in all political systems is to discover, interpret, and give substance to the values of the public.

This function, in part, sustains their legitimacy in a democratic system. I believe that, at least since the 1960s, America's intellectual elites have failed to serve this political function in regard to the nation's welfare system. Reform was pushed into less publicly accessible forums (such as the courts and the White House) because certain intellectuals helped to foster a political climate that emphasized the conflict in America's ideals rather than the possibilities for their integration. If substantial change in AFDC does occur, it will be largely the result of a shift in the orientation of a portion of the nation's intellectuals.

A third key claim of this study is the inefficacy of public opinion on the issue of welfare. The public's opinion on welfare and fundamental related issues shifted dramatically between the founding of ADC in 1935 and the mid-1960s, but the policy itself did not change in that period and still has not. There is no ambiguity about American public opinion. In Chapter 3, I demonstrated conclusively that the American public agrees on the basic assumptions that should govern welfare policy-making and the policies that should emerge from those assumptions. Americans believe that every competent adult has an obligation to work and that the government should both enforce that norm and make it easier to conform to. I conclude, therefore, that the disjunction between the public's desire for action and the inability of the process to deliver it is closely linked to the failure of intellectuals.

When a dissensual political context develops, the desire for action does not dissipate but disperses. The fourth theme of this study is that instead of centering on popular political forums, such as legislatures, action in dissensus politics is taken through nonpopular avenues such as the courts and the executive branch. The leaders of the welfare rights movement realized that they could not maintain the purity of their message and act within the truck and barter context of popular politics, so they directed their attention and resources to the Supreme Court. When the Reagan administration saw its welfare reform plans ignored by Congress, it chose to enact them through the executive branch fiat.

A fifth and final theme of this study is the disjunction between public desires and public policy, and between the public and elites. A simple theory of democracy would predict that if a public desire is strongly and consistently held, public policy will adapt to it. In the case of welfare, this theory has not held. Although the desire for change in the direction of replacing welfare with work has been strong since the mid-1970s, only the most halting and inadequate steps have been taken in that direction. The key factor in this process has been the unwillingness or inability of those with intellectual power and authority in this society to understand and explain the public's views and connect them to practicable policy consequences. In American democracy, the public needs elites to give form and structure to their preferences, if those preferences are to have social and political impact. Until such elite support emerges there will be a potential, rather than an actual, national consensus on AFDC.

This theory obviously conflicts with the orthodox understanding of the role of intellectuals, wherein those with learning are understood to be above or ahead of public opinion and thus uniquely capable of criticizing it for its simplicity, bigotry, or lack of imagination.[2] Criticism is one of the proper functions of intellectuals in democratic society. With this I have no quarrel. When opinion has become corrupt, angry, or thoroughly divorced from reality, intellectuals have a responsibility to propose action without reference to the desires of the public. The question, however, becomes: Is public opinion usually corrupt or is it ordinarily responsible, if integrated and reconciled in such a way that it adds up to a public philosophy? My contention is that public opinion is usually responsible, and thus the responsibility of (at least the mass of) intellectuals is a reformist and reconciling role rather than an exclusively critical one.

This role exists somewhere between the realm of politics and philosophy: that is, the classical role of political science. Political science, unlike philosophy, is grounded in a specific place, connected to a specific people, aligned with particular institutions. Its role is to build up from those institutions, ideas and a set of principles that are better and yet thoroughly grounded in that which is imminent in a given society. Unlike philosophy, political science does not judge the regime, except in the most unusual of circumstance, by standards outside of it. It seeks improvement from within the regime. In this way, it is akin to statesmanship. Indeed, political science and statesmanship of the highest kind are one and the same. What is different is the means of knowing and the immediate object to which knowledge is applied. The higher purpose of both is the same. It is my contention that the failure of American intellectuals to perform this function is one of the principal causes of the repeated collapse of welfare reform.

If, as I endeavored to demonstrate, elite dissensus is the central cause of the disjunction between public expectations and prevailing policy in AFDC, the solution to AFDC's political problems should be clear. Only a narrowing of differences among the nation's intellectually influential classes can lead to reform in the fundamentals of welfare. Furthermore, that narrowing of differences must be sufficiently substantive to lead to the dramatic shift in policy orientation that the public desires.

The purpose of the balance of this conclusion is to discuss what type of policy change would reduce the public's opposition to welfare and to contrast that change to the now-dominant paradigm of devolution. I do not intend to address all of the administrative and policy-design issues of welfare reform but to suggest the ethical and political outlines of a program sufficient to break the welfare deadlock and restore the public trust in the nation's poverty programs. The program is a measure by which to judge other, more technically developed alternatives.

WHERE TO GO FROM HERE?

Most studies in political science end where this conclusion begins. However, it is my conviction that social scientists should not merely identify important political processes and analyze their operation but must also judge them; and if they judge them harshly, they should suggest an alternative. No reader could miss my disgust with the character of the American welfare system and even more profoundly, the political system[3] that is complicit in its perpetuation. The American welfare system is what it is because of the failure of activists, of journalists, and of politicians but, perhaps most important, of students of ideas, to surrender the rhetorical and symbolic advantages the welfare issue provides them.

The American public is unhappy with the operations of its national government, confused by the decoupling of Washington's rhetoric from the social outcomes visible to them. Press accounts of the plight of the underclass, the continuing fear of crime, the generally correct impression that the welfare system does nothing to encourage upward mobility—all of these conditions render the occasional rhetoric that Washington is "doing something" about poverty empty and cynical. The inability of the national political system to change the realities of life in America (and welfare is only one, albeit important, example) has made both parties and all politicians suspect. It has made the American political system ripe for attack by opportunists and demagogues. The success of Ross Perot in the 1992 election is only the most prominent example of the limits of partisanship; at some point, the failure of American politics to deal with the substance of critical national issues such as crime, taxes, the federal deficit, and welfare will make both parties unstable and subject to attack by a third force. The essence of the Perot campaign was the suggestion that "Washington" engaged in rhetoric but was unwilling or unable to make the changes necessary to establish a decent standard of American life. "Washington" was usually code for a system of competition between parties and the separation of powers, complications that populists like Perot promise to rise above.[4] The perpetuation of the current American political system, with its party and institutional structure, depends upon its ability to deal with core, value-laden issues like welfare.

Calls for politicians to surrender partisan advantage in favor of the national interest are quite popular in academic and other do-good, progressive circles and should always be viewed with suspicion. It should be remembered that although many of those calling for such a stance have tenure, elected representatives do not. Electoral and ideological competition plays a large part in the conflictual structure of welfare politics. At some point, however, system maintenance has to take precedence over competition within that system. Threats to the legitimacy of the political system as a whole can become as dangerous to the preservation of existing power as threats to a particular actor's position in that system. Precedents for putting system maintenance over competition exist; the Tax Reform Act of 1986 and the 1983 Social Security rescue are only the most recent examples.[5] In both these cases, adversaries realized that the partisan advantage of their positions on an issue was outweighed by the damage wrought by inaction on the entire political system. In 1993, there were good reasons to think that AFDC might be the next example of national interests outweighing partisan interests. There are now, unfortunately, more grounds for doubt than hope.

THE BEGINNING OF WISDOM: WELFARE IS UNREFORMABLE

The problem with welfare reform is that if the objective is to make the program conform with public expectations and values, welfare cannot be reformed. That is, the change the public desires, and research supports, is impossible within the current institutional and historical structure of AFDC. Change within the boundaries of the current system will continue to be, as it has been in the past, ineffective, dispiriting, and insufficient to the end of political system maintenance. The problem is not some aspect of welfare: it is welfare.

I have hinted at the reason for AFDC's moral and political obsolescence, but a brief recapitulation should be helpful. AFDC was created as a means to finance state mothers' aid programs. The purpose of those programs was to permit widows of good character to keep their children out of public institutions and in the home and to allow those women to avoid the indignity of working outside the home. The primary purpose of AFDC was to allow families whose male breadwinner had died to maintain as much of their previous form and functioning as possible. AFDC made possible the preservation of "good" families in a socially normative state.

This purpose informed the larger structure of the AFDC program, much of which is still with us today. The shared state-national responsibility for AFDC is a consequence not just of the conditions that existed prior to the program's creation but also of the function that AFDC served to divide good families from those of questionable character. AFDC was a public trust provided in lieu of the foster home, and determinations of character were paramount because recipients were performing quasi-public functions (see Chapter 2).[6] The decentralized structure also permitted states with widely divergent moral cultures to operate a welfare system within the confines of federal funding.

To put it mildly, America is now a much different place than it was at the time of AFDC's founding. As I showed in Chapter 3, work is no longer normatively prohibited for women of good character. Indeed, a combination of work and family responsibilities is now the most common lifestyle for American women. The world outside AFDC has changed dramatically, but the program's expectations continue to reflect an obsolete set of norms. Grants of assistance are still provided throughout the period of active parenting, as if the purpose of AFDC continues to be allowing women to stay out of the paid workforce to care for their children.

Determining whether programs are successful is notoriously difficult, primarily because the purposes are hard to detect or are too general. AFDC does have a clear purpose: to provide support for dependent children. The problem with AFDC is not that it does not succeed at its primary purpose (although the miserly level of benefits, as described in Chapter 2, certainly does call this "success" into question), but that its primary purpose is no longer viable. Few women spend their entire lives at home caring for their children, even if their husbands are present in the household.[7] AFDC's guarantee of cash support makes sense only if one assumes that women spend their lives at home. Because the provision of cash to unattached women with children is the basic function of AFDC, there is good reason to think that transforming our support for this population would have to entail more than a reform (defined as change within the current set of institutions and policy justifications).

The second reason that AFDC is unreformable is that although it addresses a problem that is no longer central to American society, it fails to deal with the problems that are central to the AFDC population. AFDC is tied to obsolete premises about the role of women, premises that justified a welfare-centered policy strategy. In contrast, today the main problems of the AFDC population are outside of AFDC. There may be small effects on work effort or family formation resulting from the current set of incentives in the program, but the primary causes of dependency and lack of social mobility among a large percentage of those served by AFDC are beyond the reach of the program. The least we can say about AFDC is that it does not damage work effort; no one claims that it increases it, despite the fact that the failure of AFDC mothers to work is one of the key causes of their poverty. The least we can say about AFDC is that it does not increase illegitimacy; no one can claim that the program does anything to increase family formation and enforce the responsibility of fathers. No one says any of these things because AFDC is structurally incapable of serving any of these functions. It is structured on the presumption that the fathers of AFDC children are dead and that the women it serves should not work.

AFDC is, therefore, obsolete. It serves values that are no longer normative and fails to serve those that are. It has a federal form designed for discriminating among the poor, even though such discrimination is now performed by statutory differentiation rather than administrative discretion. The problems of most welfare mothers are the result of forces outside AFDC, which it is structurally incapable of addressing. And yet, it is the main social support for the women the program serves. The beginning of wisdom, therefore, is that a transformation of AFDC must go beyond reform, to the replacement of the program with a new set of supports that address the problems of today.

CRITERIA FOR STABLE CHANGE IN AID TO SINGLE MOTHERS

Simple change in AFDC is not enough to end the public's distaste for the program. If it were, the welfare reforms of 1967, 1982, and 1988 would have done the job. None of them did. Until the program is brought into better congruence with the public's deepest values, the anger, the distrust, and the suspicion that surround our nation's programs for the poor will persist.

As I completed this work, welfare reform does not appear to be headed in the direction that the public clearly desires. And yet, things can change quickly and unpredictably. There is still an opportunity for a politician or a party to take the public consensus and turn it into policy. The right kind of proposal, put forward with the appropriate rhetoric and treated as a major priority, could end the decades-old conflict over welfare policy.

If dissensus has been caused by elite conflict structured around an effort to split the three essential elements of the public mind, it stands to reason that this political deadlock can only be broken by a program that would unite these three elements. What would such a program look like?

The essential first condition of such a program is that it center upon integrating the short-term recipients of AFDC into an insurance-like system of income security. A substantial part of the AFDC population enters and exits the program rapidly and uses its support during a few, isolated periods of distress, such as divorce.[8] There is nothing in America's political culture to prevent the establishment of a system of income security for this population, one that would support single mothers and their children who are clearly not socially deviant or lacking in the ability to reintegrate themselves into the economic and social mainstream. Obviously, an important part of such a strategy would be dealing with the nation's woefully inadequate child support system. Given that AFDC rolls would be substantially reduced by guaranteeing that every child support award is actually paid,[9] and that this would provide cash to single mothers by enforcing widely accepted social standards, this element should be the most important priority.

For the short-term poor who for whatever reason cannot get child support payments from the father of their children, some other form of income security may be needed. The simplest method might be to establish a refundable children's tax credit that would be reduced when a support award was made. Such a program could build on the tax credit already on the books. Another alternative would be to allow anyone, a single mother or anyone in need, to take up to two years of social security payments in advance; in relation to the amount that was taken, the age at which that person could begin drawing assistance in old age would be recalculated. Although there may be actuarial difficulties with a program of this sort, it has the advantage of dealing with a large segment of the current welfare population in a revenue-neutral manner and through a mechanism open to everyone.

Thus, we see that dealing with the short-term AFDC population should be relatively easy. Precedents exist and mechanisms are in place to serve this group. However, programs that help the short-term poor would not be of much assistance to long-term AFDC recipients. This group is not insignificant,[10] and more to the point, it consists of those who are the focus of controversy. They are the ones who fit the welfare stereotype, and the public will justifiably ask what has been done to put an end to their welfare dependency.

As I have shown, the heart of the public's concern for the welfare dependent is their lack of self-sufficiency and their continual dependence upon the government for subsistence not generated from the sweat of their own brow. The American public unmistakably demands that people on welfare should work. It is my conviction that this demand is morally justifiable and more to the point, politically unavoidable. There are two strategies that might be used to connect the work norm with public assistance: getting people to work within the welfare system or setting up a system of work and income support outside of and serving as an alternative to the welfare system.

To understand which option is preferable, I will present a short explication of why work is central in the public's mind. The egalitarian view supports the centrality of work to the degree that work puts people on an equal social footing. In American society, work permits citizens to have social standing, is evidence of social contribution, and thus serves as an argument for public concern.[11] People who work are like others in a very important way. Work provides dignity and is essential for recognition from others. When all work, there are few categories to set some persons aside as needing special treatment. When all work, the argument for assistance is based on strength and just expectation rather than special dispensation and charity.[12]

Work is central to the individualist cultural strain because it is the mechanism by which persons demonstrate self-reliance. Work is evidence of independence, of people who earn the things of life through their own actions, who can stand apart from others and devise their own plan for life. So long as people work, they can legitimately claim that their life and their choices are no one else's business. Work supports a claim of autonomy and is an argument for being left alone. No one asks people who work what they do in their spare time, or what they spend their money on, or how they structure their family life. Work, in most cases a quintessentially public activity, is also the precondition for privacy, the highest of individualist priorities.

Finally, work is essential to the hierarchist view in America's culture. Work is crucial to the hierarchist because it structures life, provides order and regularity, ensures discipline, and supports such social values as temperance, restraint, deference to superiors, and sobriety. Work may also affect other norms important to hierarchists, such as stable family structure, by sending a signal that to support a family, work or finding a spouse who will provide support are the only alternatives. Removing the alternative of no-strings-attached government assistance should lead to more sobriety about bearing children and thus reduce somewhat the incidence of single motherhood, a family form of which hierarchists are highly suspicious. Work thus serves the egalitarian ends by establishing a foundation for social claims as well as the hierarchist purpose of supporting social responsibility.

Therefore, the question is whether work within or outside of the welfare system best supports this set of social values and priorities. My preference is solidly for the latter.[13] The primary reason for preferring work outside the welfare system is that since the early 1980s we have tried to integrate work into the AFDC system, and even the most successful programs, such as San Diego's Saturation Work Immersion Model (SWIM), have had rather modest results.[14] According to Daniel Friedlander and Gary Burtless *(Five Years After),* the differences between those participating in these work experiments are small and generally become even more so in the fourth and fifth years. SWIM, for example, generated employment rates of only 33.7 percent among the experimental group in the fifth year, as opposed to 32 percent in the controls. Other programs, such as WORK in Arkansas, were able to increase the employment rate somewhat more than SWIM but were not able to make a substantial dent in average annual earnings.[15] Even the showpiece of this approach, Riverside, California's GAIN (Greater Avenues for Independence) program has had much more of an effect on reducing welfare receipt than on long-term employment or earnings.[16] This approach, even when exquisitely administered, has been insufficient to warrant the belief that extending it could satisfy the public's desire to see a greater work emphasis in programs for the poor.

Second, work outside of the welfare system is more likely to serve a socially integrative function. Work within the welfare system can only amount to working off a welfare check at minimum wage, which in most states would mean around 20 hours a week or in states like Mississippi as little as 6 hours. It is not just the amount of work in the inside-welfare approach but its character that makes this strategy flawed. Even though people on welfare might be "working off their check," they are still on welfare, a category that sets them apart from the rest of society. Retaining this separate-group identity means retaining one world of work for poor women and an entirely separate one for everyone else. Furthermore, the structure of work within welfare makes it difficult to wrest much effort from participants (because they get their checks and are then expected to work), which reduces the disciplining effects hierarchists desire.

Work outside welfare does not have these problems. By guaranteeing work to everyone, this strategy establishes a general civic entitlement, such that the poor are not seen as receiving special favors. This program could technically be open to anyone, although it would be designed for those currently on AFDC. It would have the salutary effect, desirable to hierarchists, of eliminating once and for all the claim of persons that they cannot find work. In many cases, the claim is probably true, but it is equally likely that the lack of jobs is often an excuse. Providing work as a civic entitlement would remove that excuse. It would firmly establish a right to work, and then make work normative. There would be no alternative to work.

Making work rather than cash the final social safety net (after some form of child support or Social Security–related income support) for single mothers would also have the political advantage of entirely eliminating AFDC. As we have seen, AFDC has a certain historical dynamic, a structure that is difficult to break out of. Eliminating it and substituting guaranteed work would put us on a new path. Ending AFDC would also send a message to the public about the capacity of the government to act radically in the service of American ideals. Eliminating the program would communicate boldness and resolve; a clear political message would be sent. Work within welfare would retain the AFDC structure, the continued presence of which might overshadow the moderate application of the work norm in the public's view.

Work outside of welfare would also send a message to those on welfare. The era of the dole is over. Get married, establish paternity and get child support, or work. After no more than two years, these are the only options if you have a child. Work within welfare sends mixed messages while work outside of welfare would be clear and would be more likely to change the culture of poor communities than any other single change in policy. It would inevitably have profound impacts on illegitimate childbearing and would have the advantage of doing so without intrusion into private lives or draconian, anti-egalitarian effects on the distribution of wealth. Finally, work outside welfare would justify much more redistribution than is possible within the current system, since a slightly subminimum wage job combined with an increased EITC could guarantee that no one willing to satisfy social standards was below poverty. It is more likely that taxpayers would dig into their pocket for this sort of objective than for the mixed objectives of the current system.

There are, of course, other nonwelfare programs that could substitute for AFDC. A larger EITC has already been mentioned. Increased support for job training and education, preferably through the existing community college system, is another alternative. Selling off all public housing to the highest bidder and substituting an across-the-board rent subsidy combined with much stronger enforcement of housing discrimination laws would also have the effect of breaking up underclass communities, thus weakening the concentration effects that occur in the current system.[17] Making inroads into America's structurally high unemployment rate would have salutary effects, both by providing employment to women on welfare and by increasing what William Julius Wilson calls the "male marriageable pool," the group of men whose employment makes them suitable husbands. Guaranteeing work outside the welfare system is, however, an essential precondition for these other programs because it eliminates the impression that aid is being given to those unwilling to make their basic social contribution.

Work outside welfare has its administrative difficulties, of course, but these may be less daunting than those faced by the work inside welfare strategy. Work inside welfare preserves an enormous welfare bureaucracy, which spends the bulk of its time on the socially unhelpful task of determining eligibility. The best work system would be open to everyone. A guaranteed subminimum wage job would eliminate completely the need to establish eligibility and would avoid the social problems of work programs specifically targeted to one group. Work outside of welfare eliminates the problem of determining eligibility. It also avoids the problem of hectoring recipients into satisfying conditions of welfare receipt. People either show up for work and perform satisfactorily and are paid for their work, or they do not. The onus is on the recipient.

A major hurdle to the strategy of work outside welfare is finding the jobs and ensuring that those jobs are legitimate. If a strict no-displacement rule were applied to this program, as organized labor would wish, it would be difficult to find a sufficient number of useful positions for those currently receiving AFDC and not covered by other new programs. If displacement were permitted, there are clearly an enormous number of jobs that welfare recipients could fill, such as filing in police departments, serving as orderlies in hospitals, cleaning up parks, and serving as crossing guards.[18]

Another stumbling block to such a system is ensuring that standards are maintained, that those in these jobs put in 40 hours a week and that they perform their tasks diligently. Diligence could be assured by paying workers on a week-by-week (or even daily) basis, but would the public support dismissing single women from public jobs if they refused to perform their tasks responsibly? Although I believe most people now suffering from long-term welfare dependency would work 40 hours a week if required to do so, some will not. A norm is not a norm, however, if failure to meet it does not result in some form of punishment. If any group of citizens should be subjected to the Murray alternative of orphanages and forcible loss of custody, it is this group. The difference between this situation and Murray's is that working in a job that would always be available is almost completely a matter of choice. Failure to do so is evidence of reckless disregard for one's children's welfare.

A final argument against such a serious pro-work policy is that it would have undesirable macroeconomic effects. An orthodox Phillips curve theory would predict that reduced unemployment could only be purchased at the price of increased inflation. However, given that the jobs that would be provided by this policy are at the subminimum wage level, the possibility of bidding up wages is quite remote. Even if it did have small effects in this regard, it is unlikely that they would exceed those caused by small changes in the price of oil. Furthermore, with the Federal Reserve following a tight and responsible monetary policy, such a program is clearly not being undertaken in a time when there are other large political pressures for inflationary policy. What inflation it might cause would seem to be an insignificant price to pay for progress.

CONCLUSIONS

As I noted in Chapter 8, welfare reform has recently taken a sharp turn away from substance and into process, away from work and toward decentralization. In fact, much of what was being considered in 1995 under the guise of welfare reform was little more than a change in intergovernmental relations.[19] This movement is dangerous for two reasons. First, it does nothing to actually change welfare and may waste a golden opportunity to rip the program up from the foundations and plant something lasting and effective in its place. Second, and more disturbing, it may substantially reduce the possibility for the nation to implement the public welfare consensus at some later time, by making the states jealous of their newfound authority and unwilling to cede powers that they have so recently been given.

All policies have a way of creating their own politics. Federal retirement insurance, in the form of Social Security, created a mass interest group of the elderly, which has made change in the program virtually impossible.[20] Federal aid to agriculture created a nexus of midwestern senators, farm bureaus, large and small farmers, that has made agricultural subsidies similarly resilient.[21] It is my suspicion that block granting AFDC, along with the rest of federal poverty assistance, will have a similarly paralyzing effect. The states will find that because their policy instruments are inferior to those of the federal government, they are incapable of making a substantial dent in poverty and dependency. Few states, acting alone, will be able to mobilize the substantial resources to credibly enforce and provide the opportunity to conform to the work norm. At the same time, they will find it difficult to stand aside and permit the federal government to institute a national and comprehensive solution.

Although I have grave reservations about the consequences of the devolution strategy for the poor themselves, my reservations are graver still for the effects it will have on the nation as a whole. Welfare, as I have argued, is fundamentally about what we are as a nation. When we make policy for the poor, we are expressing our basic ethical principles, declaring what it is that binds us together as a people. By eschewing national reform, Washington sends the signal that, in fact, the ties of principle that bind the American people are weak and inferior to those that separate us by race, by class, or by region.

There is nothing America needs more, in this time of "identity politics," "tribalism," and anger at the "system" than a strong shot of nation-building. Americans need to be reminded that the virtues of work and responsibility are held in common, that they pertain regardless of where we come from or where we reside. Changing welfare to express these virtues could be the instrument by which these national ties are re-cemented.

This message is, of course, untimely, especially in a era when the center appears to be weakening and the periphery strengthening. However, this trend will not last forever. Americans, although frequently tempted by the whisperings of those who would tear us apart, always return to leaders who promise a vision of a single nation, tied together by bonds of principle. Washington, Lincoln, the two Roosevelts: none were decentralizers, all believed the nation's greatness was connected to its unity. Perhaps, once the mania of devolution passes and is seen for what it is, a great national effort to transform the lives of the poor will be the instrument through which our union is rebuilt. So sayeth the optimist.

Does the leadership necessary to effect such a change exist? We have little choice but to wait and hope. Perhaps it will come from a mammoth revolt within the center, which takes over one of the two parties or creates a totally new party. Welfare is, after all, the greatest symbol of the lack of imagination, will, and courage of the two major parties.

If such a movement does not emerge, it is certain that welfare will haunt the American political system, twisting its priorities, distracting its deliberations, and cruelly denying the poor the opportunity they deserve and the moral standards the public expects.

Notes

'

1. AFDC: CONSENSUS OR DISSENSUS?

1. Note that I refer to the modern welfare state. The roots of the modern welfare state are found in the pensions given to Revolutionary War soldiers, the destruction of the principle of father right in the early nineteenth century, and later on, the creation of widely available Civil War pensions and, of greatest importance, mothers' aid programs at the state level. These issues will be discussed in greater detail in Chapter 2.

2. See Martha Derthick, *Policymaking for Social Security* (Washington, D.C.: Brookings Institution, 1979).

3. As of 1993, the federal share of AFDC expenditures was $12.27 billion for benefits and $1.518 billion for administrative costs; the state share was $10.016 billion and $1.438 billion. This is a rough gauge of the persistence of the state's role in the program (and the high levels of administrative costs an indication that other-than-redistributive goals are involved). The federal nature of AFDC is discussed in greater depth in Chapter 7.

4. Maximum monthly benefits in the median state, as of January 1994, were $366 for a three-person family, up to $577 for a six-person family. U.S., House of Representatives, Committee on Ways and Means, *Background Materials and Data on Major Programs Within the Jurisdiction of the Committee on Ways and Means* (Green Book) (Washington, D.C.: Government Printing Office, 1991), pp. 376–377. For an analysis of the public's perception of minimum needs and how it relates to existing programs to serve the poor, see: Center on Budget and Policy Priorities, *Real Life Poverty in America* (Washington, D.C.), July 1990. The relation of AFDC benefits to other programs is covered in Chapter 2.

5. In this book, I use the term "welfare" when describing public attitudes and AFDC when I am discussing the program itself. When I discuss studies that break public attitudes down (between food stamps, AFDC, Medicaid, etc.), I will be more specific, but most public opinion polls use the term "welfare," and for the most part I will as well.

6. Joel Handler and Ellen Hollingsworth, *The "Deserving Poor": A Study of Welfare Administration* (New York: Academic Press, 1971), p. 16. Handler's later works, especially *The Moral Construction of Poverty,* make essentially the same argument as *The "Deserving*

Poor." As an exposition of Handler's ideas, however, the latter is preferable, since it focuses more on the essential political dynamics of welfare policy.

7. Ibid., p. 19.

8. Ibid., p. 30.

9. Ibid., p. 34.

10. Michael Katz, *In the Shadow of the Poorhouse: A Social History of Welfare in America* (New York: Basic Books, 1986), p. 17.

11. Ibid., p. 25.

12. Frances Fox Piven and Richard Cloward, *Regulating the Poor* (New York: Pantheon, 1971).

13. Ibid., pp. 3–4.

14. Ibid., p. 7.

15. Ibid., pp. 7–8.

16. Ibid., p. 40.

17. Ibid., p. 274.

18. Lawrence Jacobs, "The Politics of American Ambivalence Toward Government," in James Morone and Gary Belkin, eds., *The Politics of Health Care Reform* (Durham, N.C.: Duke University Press, 1994), p. 396.

19. Benjamin Page and Robert Shapiro, "Effects of Public Opinion on Policy," *American Political Science Review,* 1983, v. 77, pp. 188–189.

20. James Davison Hunter, *Culture Wars* (New York: Basic Books, 1991), p. 42.

21. Ibid., p. 59.

22. But not inevitably so, for in Marxism the revolution will usher in the era of classless, and thus apolitical, society. See Karl Marx, "Economic and Philosophical Manuscripts of 1844," in Marx and Engels, *Collected Works,* v. 3. (London: Lawrence and Wishart, 1975), pp. 295–297.

23. For more on this strain of elite theory, see Ettore A. Albertoni, *Mosca and the Theory of Elitism* (Oxford: Basil Blackwell, 1987); James Meisel, *The Myth of the Ruling Class* (Ann Arbor: University of Michigan Press, 1962); and Tom Bottomore, *Elites and Society* (London: Routledge, 1993), especially chaps. 1 and 2.

24. Niccolo Machiavelli, *The Discourses* (London: Penguin Books, 1983), Book 1, ch. 16, p. 156.

25. The most powerful critic of Mills (and there have been many) is Daniel Bell, *The End of Ideology* (New York: Free Press, 1962), pp. 47–74.

26. C. Wright Mills, *The Power Elite* (Oxford: Oxford University Press, 1956).

27. Daniel Bell, *The Cultural Contradictions of Capitalism* (New York: Basic Books, 1976), ch. 6. I agree with Bell that these elite conceptions must be overcome by a culturally integrative ideal, which structures public demands and imposes civic responsibilities. I discuss this idea in more depth in Chapter 9.

28. Martha Derthick and Paul Quirk, *The Politics of Deregulation* (Washington, D.C.: Brookings Institution, 1985), p. 238.

29. Timothy Conlan, David Beam, and Margaret Wrightson, "Policy Models and Political Change: Insights from the Passage of Tax Reform," in Marc Landy and Martin Levin, eds., *The New Politics of Public Policy* (Baltimore: Johns Hopkins Press, 1995), p. 130.

30. Gary Mucciaroni, *Reversals of Fortune* (Washington, D.C.: Brookings Institution, 1995). Mucciaroni observes that of the four policy areas he examined—tax reform, deregu-

lation, trade protection, and agriculture subsidies—in only the latter case did producer groups successfully defend their interests. He observes that "on balance, these groups now find themselves on the short end of the stick as often as not" (p. 181).

31. As this book is being completed, the first stirrings of an intellectual consensus evolving to challenge an entrenched interest-group structure are appearing in the case of subsidized grazing on Western lands and the broad area of "corporate welfare." Like deregulation and tax reform just a few years before they were completely restructured, change in both of these areas now seems impossible.

32. Michael Thompson, Richard Ellis, and Aaron Wildavsky, *Cultural Theory* (Boulder: Westview, 1990), p. 7.

33. As one reader noted, this may have special relevance to the politics of the urban underclass. Even so, given that this group does not actively participate in politics and is not an important part of our national debate on welfare issues, I will set them aside.

34. I should emphasize that these are not natural or inevitable categorizations. One can slice ideological categories in a number of different ways without abusing reality. Two alternative structures deserve note, which also go beyond the rather stale liberal-conservative continuum. One possible approach is to change the dimensions to the level of moralism on the vertical axis (higher level of moral regulation on the north pole, less on the south), and degree of individual responsibility for socioeconomic status on the horizontal (less responsibility on the west, more on the east). This change gives a breakdown with modern fusionist conservatism on the NE corner, free market individualism on the SE, liberal-radicalism on the SW, and populism-communitarianism on the NW. Although this might seem more helpful (and might be a useful complement to the Wildavsky-derived categories), what it really amounts to is cutting the hierarchist position in half and leaving the rest intact, dividing the position into fusionist conservatism and communitarianism. The free market position corresponds closely to individualism, and the liberal-radical position to egalitarianism. It seems better to preserve the succinct Wildavsky categories, while making a point of addressing the real splits within it (which largely have to do with whether hierarchy is challenged by markets, the communitarian position, or consistent with them, the fusionist position). For a somewhat similar schema, see Lawrence Mead, *Beyond Entitlement* (New York: Free Press, 1986), ch. 11.

Another reasonable schematic is that of Rogers Smith, who suggests that American history is characterized by liberal, republican, and cultural nationalist strains (as opposed to the position of Samuel Huntington and Louis Hartz, who see only liberalism and nonideological exceptions and alternatives. I agree with Smith that American history cannot be categorized in the simplistic manner of Huntington and Hartz, but I see American liberalism as, from its earliest period, attempting to reconcile the three basic cultural alternatives I borrow from Wildavsky. To a certain degree, the republic position parallels the egalitarian, the liberal the individualist, and the cultural nationalist the hierarchist—but only loosely. Smith's categories do not have much room for the real roots of American communitarianism, religion and the family, which are at the heart of the hierarchist position, rather than race. See Rogers Smith, "The 'American Creed' and American Identity: The Limits of Liberal Citizenship in the United States," *Western Political Quarterly,* June 1988, v. 41, no. 2, pp. 225–251.

35. The Algerians in France and the Turks in Germany are a particularly useful example of such a phenomenon.

36. Samuel Huntington, *American Politics: The Promise of Disharmony* (Cambridge: Belknap Harvard, 1981), p. 16.

37. These two issues will be addressed in Chapters 3 and 4.

2. THE DEVELOPMENT OF THE AFDC PROGRAM

1. Patricia Ruggles and Richard Michel, "Participation Rates in the Aid to Families with Dependent Children Program: Trends for 1967 Through 1984," April 1987, Urban Institute, unpublished manuscript.

2. Ibid., p. 31.

3. Robert Moffitt, "Historical growth in Participation in Aid to Families with Dependent Children: Was There a Structural Shift?" *Journal of Post-Keynesian Economics,* Spring 1987, v. 10, p. 362. Although I am convinced of the value of Moffitt's overall argument, I have not found much evidence of any "legislative decisions" of the magnitude of those made by the Supreme Court. This is why I identify the causal factors in the shift as "nonpopular."

4a. U.S. Bureau of the Census, *Statistical Abstract of the United States: 1993* (Washington, D.C.: Government Printing Office, 1993-), p. 61.

4b. Ibid., p. 469.

4c. Greg Duncan, *Years of Poverty, Years of Plenty* (Ann Arbor: Institute for Social Research, 1984), p. 75.

5. U.S. House of Representatives, Committee on Ways and Means, *Overview of Entitlement Programs,* WMCP: 101-29, 1990, p. 553.

6. Ibid.

7. Charles Murray's *Losing Ground* (New York: Basic Books, 1984) is the most well known.

8. All racial statistics were acquired from the files of the U.S. Department of Health and Human Services, Administration for Children and Families, AFDC Information Measurement Branch, Division of Program Evaluation, Office of Family Assistance.

9. U.S. Bureau of the Census, *Historical Statistics of the United States: Colonial Times to 1970* (Washington, D.C.: Government Printing Office, 1971), Series B 28-35, p. 52.

10. *Ibid.,* Series A 320-334, p. 42.

11. Richard Sterner, *The Negro's Share: A Study of Income, Consumption, Housing, and Public Assistance* (New York: Harper & Row, 1943), p. 282.

12. Ibid., pp. 282–283.

13. U.S. Bureau of the Census, *Historical Statistics,* Series A 172-194, p. 22.

14. Ibid., Series A 276-287, p. 40.

15. Theda Skocpol, *Protecting Soldiers and Mothers* (Cambridge: Belknap Press, 1992), p. 458.

16. U.S. Congress, Senate, *Conference on the Care of Dependent Children: Proceedings,* 60th Cong., 2nd sess., 1909, S. Doc. 721 (Serial Set 5400).

17. Quoted in Jamil Zainaldin, "The Emergence of Modern American Family Law: Child Custody, Adoption, and the Courts, 1796–1851," *Northwestern University Law Review,* 1979, v. 74, p. 1055.

18. Mason Thomas, "Child Abuse and Neglect. Part I: Historical Overview, Legal Matrix and Social Perspectives," *North Carolina Law Review,* 1970, v. 49, p. 311.

19. U.S. Congress, Senate, *Conference on the Care of Dependent Children: Proceedings,* pp. 9–10.

20. Skocpol, *Protecting Soldiers and Mothers,* p. 428.

21. Ibid., p. 430.

22. Christopher Howard, "Sowing the Seeds of 'Welfare': The Transformation of Mother's Pensions, 1900–1940," *Journal of Policy History,* 1992, v. 4, p. 193.

23. Skocpol, *Protecting Soldiers and Mothers,* p. 430.

24. Mark Leff, "Consensus for Reform: The Mothers' Pension Movement in the Progressive Era," *Social Service Review,* September 1973, v. 47, p. 410.

25. Skocpol, *Protecting Soldiers and Mothers,* p. 457.

26. Ibid., p. 472.

27. Ibid., p. 474.

28. Howard, "Sowing the Seeds of 'Welfare,' " p. 199.

29. Skocpol, *Protecting Soldiers and Mothers,* p. 451.

30. Howard, "Sowing the Seeds of 'Welfare,' " p. 198.

31. Welfare is defined as noncontributory cash assistance to single mothers.

32. Robert Stevens, ed., *Statutory History of the United States: Income Security* (New York: Chelsea House, 1970), pp. 172–173.

33. These terms may need clarification. By the financial function of the states, I mean their ability to maintain control of their own budgets, and by control I intend to suggest the capacity to regulate personal and public behavior.

34. See U.S. Congress, Senate, 74th Cong., 1st sess., 1935, S. Rep. 628, 29, 36; U.S. Congress, House, 74th Cong., 1st sess., 1935, H.R. Rep. 615, 18, 24.

35. Reprinted in U.S. Congress, Senate, Committee on Finance, *Hearings on the Economic Security Act,* 74th Cong., 1st sess., S1130, p. 236.

36. *Report of the Committee on Economic Security,* p. 35, reprinted in National Conference on Social Welfare, *The Report of the Committee on Economic Security of 1935* (Washington, D.C.: National Conference on Social Welfare, 1985).

37. Joel Handler, "The Transformation of Aid to Families with Dependent Children," *NYU Review of Law and Social Change,* 1987, v. 16, p. 461.

38. Senate, Report 628, p. 19.

39. Social Security Board's Third Annual Report, quoted in Josephine Brown, *Public Relief: 1929–1939* (New York: Henry Holt, 1940) pp. 371–372.

40. Ibid.

41. Senate, Report 628, p. 234.

42. Advisory Council on Social Security, *Final Report, 1937–1938,* pp. 17–18. Reprinted in National Conference on Social Welfare, *The Report of the Committee on Economic Security of 1935.*

43. Linda Gordon, *Pitied But Not Entitled* (New York: Free Press, 1994), p. 295.

44. Information drawn from U.S. Department of Health and Human Services, Administration of Children and Families, *Overview of the AFDC Program: Fiscal Year 1992,* "Summary of Legislative History," pp. 25–26.

45. Ibid., p. 28.

46. Ibid., p. 30.

47. Ibid., p. 27.

48. James Patterson, *America's Struggle Against Poverty: 1900–1980* (Cambridge: Harvard University Press, 1981), p. 87.

49. Ibid., p. 88; and Martha Derthick, *The Influence of Federal Grants* (Cambridge: Harvard University Press, 1970), p. 78.

50. June Axinn and Herman Levin, *Social Welfare: A History of the American Response to Need* (New York: Harper & Row, 1975), p. 236.

51. Memorandum for the Commissioner of Social Security from Secretary Flemming, January 16, 1961. Quoted in Charles Reich, "Midnight Welfare Searches and the Social Security Act," *Yale Law Journal,* 1963, v. 73, p. 1358.

52. "Welfare's Condition X," *Yale Law Journal,* 1967, p. 1227.

53. Ibid.

54. *Message on the Public Welfare Program,* delivered February 1, 1962. Quoted in Axinn and Levin, *Social Welfare,* pp. 256, 262.

55. Ibid., p. 259.

3. THE COLLAPSE OF ONE CONSENSUS, THE RISE OF ANOTHER

1. Alexander Hamilton, James Madison, and John Jay, *The Federalist Papers* (New York: Mentor, 1961), p. 82.

2. An intensely insightful discussion of the Founders' ideas concerning public opinion, and how they distinguished the idea from more "popular opinion," can be found in Robert Nisbet, "Popular Opinion Versus Public Opinion," in Nathan Glazer and Irving Kristol, eds., *The American Commonwealth, 1976* (New York: Basic Books, 1976), ch. 8.

3. On level of information, see Robert Erikson, Norman Luttbeg, and Kent Tedin, *American Public Opinion* (New York: Macmillan, 1988), p. 42. For a broad and nuanced argument about the nature of public opinion, which distinguishes when such opinion is and is not coherent, see W. Russell Neuman, *The Paradox of Mass Politics* (Cambridge: Harvard University Press, 1986). The classic statement of incoherence and instability in policy preferences is Philip Converse, "The Nature of Belief Systems in Mass Publics," in David Apter, ed., *Ideology and Discontent* (New York: Free Press, 1964), pp. 206–261.

4. Benjamin Page and Robert Shapiro, *The Rational Public* (Chicago: University of Chicago Press, 1992), p. 386.

5. Ibid., pp. 391–394.

6. Paul Sniderman and Michael Hagen, *Race and Inequality: A Study in American Values* (Chatham, N.J.: Chatham House, 1985), p. 16.

7. Question (National Opinion Research Center [NORC]–General Social Survey [GSS]): "We are faced with many problems in this country, none of which can be solved easily or inexpensively. I'm going to name some of these problems, and for each one I'd like you to tell me whether you think we're spending too much money on it, too little money, or about the right amount. . . . Are we spending too much, too little, or about the right amount on . . . welfare?"

8. Fay Cook and Edith Barrett, *Support for the American Welfare State* (New York: Columbia University Press, 1992), p. 62.

9. My conviction on this score has been reinforced when I told college-educated professionals that the subject of my study was AFDC. I was met numerous times with the response "What is that?" When I told them, instead, that I was looking at "welfare," they suddenly recognized what I meant and were able to express quite consistent and coherent opinions on the subject.

10. Cook and Barrett, *Support for the American Welfare State,* p. 261.

11. For a discussion of the changes in the AFDC population, benefit levels, and overall spending, see Chapter 2. For a wonderful journalistic account of the rise of poverty as a public issue, see Nicholas Lemann, *The Promised Land* (New York: Vintage, 1992), "Washington."

12. Out-of-control spending for social programs, including welfare, without adequate fiscal support from the federal government, was one reason for the 1975 bankruptcy of New York City, which culminated in the city's loss of financial sovereignty.

13. See Chapter 5.

14. James Kluegel, "Macro-economic Problems, Beliefs about the Poor and Attitudes Toward Welfare Spending," *Social Problems,* February 1987, v. 35, p. 89.

15. Juliet Schor's *The Overworked American* (New York: Basic Books, 1991) is instructive on this point. Schor calculates that the average working woman puts in 65 hours a week in combined domestic and paid work while their husbands are working evenings and weekends, not to mention second jobs, at much higher levels than in previous decades. See especially pp. 20–21.

16. See note 7. "Spend more on improving the conditions of blacks, spend more on problems of big cities."

17. Gerald Wright, "Racism and Welfare Policy in America," *Social Science Quarterly,* Fall 1977, p. 722.

18. Evidence for the decline in racial prejudice can be found in Howard Schuman, Charlotte Steeh, and Lawrence Bobo, *Racial Attitudes in America* (Cambridge: Harvard University Press, 1985); and Paul Sniderman and Michael Hagen, *Race and Inequality: A Study in American Values* (Chatham, N.J.: Chatham House, 1985), pp. 3–6.

19. Paul Sniderman and Thomas Piazza, *The Scar of Race* (Cambridge: Belknap Press/Harvard, 1993), p. 97.

20. This concept may even be the characteristic element of American culture: a non-tragic view of the world, where people are not at the whim of fortune or destiny but have the capacity to shape, and not just be shaped, by their environment. The public wants to help people expand their control over the world (which is why the quasi–Social Darwinist views of the right are flawed) but also expects them to exercise whatever control is possible within the sphere of their current circumstances, which is why the left is in error as well.

21. Donald Kinder and Tai Mendelberg, "Cracks in American Apartheid," *Journal of Politics,* May 1995, v. 57, no. 2, pp. 415. When Kinder and Mendelberg used a more questionable measure, "total effect," which measures "opinion through its effects on other determinants of opinion" (p. 416), they found a more substantial effect, although one still in the lower range of the issues in question.

22. Question (National Election Study): "I'll read the name of a person and I'd like you to rate that person using something called the feeling thermometer. You can choose any number between 0 and 100. The higher the number, the warmer or more favorable you feel toward that person, the lower the number, the colder or less favorable. You could rate the person at the 50 degree mark if you feel neither warm nor cold toward them. If we come to a person whose name you don't recognize, you don't need to rate that person. Just tell me and we'll move on to the next one. . . . And still using the thermometer, how would you rate the following . . . blacks . . . people on welfare . . . poor people?"

23. A contributing factor to this recipient-program divergence in opinion may be the numbers of respondents who had themselves received some form of welfare. Greg Duncan's work using the Panel Study of Income Dynamics showed that 25.2 percent of the population had received some form of welfare income (which includes Food Stamps as

well as AFDC) for at least one of the previous ten years (1969–1978), while 8.7 percent were dependent for at least one of those years on welfare for more than 50 percent of their family income. It may be that those who have received welfare are as opposed to the program as the general population but have less animus toward people on welfare than those who have never received such assistance. See Greg Duncan, *Years of Poverty, Years of Plenty* (Ann Arbor: Institute for Social Research, 1984), p. 75.

24. See note 7. This seeming anomaly is discussed in detail by Tom Smith, "That Which We Call Welfare by Any Other Name Would Smell Sweeter," *Public Opinion Quarterly,* 1987, v. 51, pp. 75–83.

25. Question (NORC-GSS): "Here are some opinions other people have expressed about welfare. For each of the following statements, please tell me whether you strongly agree, agree, disagree, or strongly disagree. Welfare . . . makes people work less than they would if there wasn't a welfare system . . . helps people get on their feet when facing difficult situations such as unemployment, a divorce, or a death in the family . . . encourages young women to have babies before marriage . . . helps keep people's marriage together in times of financial problems . . . helps prevent hunger and starvation . . . discourages young women who get pregnant from marrying the father of the child."

26. The classic example of this professional skepticism is found in David Ellwood and Lawrence Summers, "Is Welfare Really the Problem?" *Public Interest,* Spring 1986, pp. 57–78.

27. These findings are supported by Cook and Barrett's study, which found that a substantial majority thought that the program makes recipients dependent and does not help them to be independent (two different ways of getting at the same issue). Still, more than a majority continued to believe, despite their suspicions about dependency, that "society benefits" from AFDC. These data further support my contention that the American public wants to continue to help the AFDC population but in a substantially different way. Cook and Barrett, *Support for the American Welfare State,* pp. 118–121.

28. Question (NORC-GSS): "Now I will [give] a list of reasons some people give to explain why there are poor people in this country. Please tell me whether you feel each is very important, somewhat important, or not important, in explaining why there are poor people in this country . . . failure of society to provide good schools for many Americans . . . loose morals and drunkenness . . . failure of industry to provide enough jobs . . . lack of effort by the poor themselves."

29. Shanto Iyengar, "Framing Responsibility for Political Issues: The Case of Poverty," *Political Behavior,* 1990, v. 12, no. 1, pp. 19–40.

30. In Figure 3.7, class is structured educationally, with lower-class individuals defined as those with an associate of arts (two-year college) degree or below, and upper-class members as those with a bachelor of arts or science degree or more.

31. Jeffry Will, "The Dimensions of Poverty: Public Perceptions of the Deserving Poor," *Social Science Research,* 1993, v. 22, pp. 322–323.

32. In 1986, the typical AFDC benefit, as defined by the Department of Health and Human Services (HHS), was $383.09. U.S. Department of Health and Human Services, AFDC Information and Measurement Branch, *Overview of the AFDC Program,* Fiscal Year 1992, p. 11.

33. Ibid., p. 324.

34. An example of this kind of study is Center on Budget and Policy Priorities, *Real Life Poverty in America,* Washington, D.C., July 1990.

35. The only comparably persistent and high levels of support are for Social Security and Medicare. See Page and Shapiro, *The Rational Public,* pp. 118–121, 129–132.

36. Robert Shapiro, "The Polls—A Report," *Public Opinion Quarterly,* Summer 1987, pp. 272, 273, 275.

37. Question (NORC-GSS): "If you had to choose, which thing on this list would you pick as the most important for a child to learn to prepare him or her for life? . . . to work hard." A close second were ambition and having a good education. Other options were coming from a wealthy family, having well-educated parents, natural ability, knowing the right people, having political connections, a person's race, a person's religion, country of origin, being born a man or woman, or a person's political beliefs.

38. Robert Shapiro, Kelly Patterson, Judith Russell and John Young, "The Polls—A Report: Employment and Social Welfare," *Public Opinion Quarterly,* Spring 1987, v. 51, pp. 279–280.

39. Jeffry Will, "The Dimensions of Poverty," p. 325.

40. Ibid., p. 325–326.

41. Ibid., p. 330.

42. Douglas Muzzio and Richard Behn, "Thinking About Welfare: The View from New York," *Public Perspective,* February-March 1995, p. 36.

43. Ibid., p. 37.

44. This finding calls into question John Rawls's contention, most recently in *Political Liberalism* (New York: Columbia University Press, 1993), that the overlapping consensus in modern liberal states is basically neutral as regards the good life and the obligations of citizens beyond tolerance and obedience to the law. Work is a good desired in American life because it is considered a political obligation, not merely a preference, existing outside the world of politics.

45. Page and Shapiro, *The Rational Public,* p. 127.

46. Herbert McCloskey, *The American Ethos* (Cambridge: Harvard University Press, 1984), p. 108.

47. Ibid. The question was, "If you were to get enough money to live comfortably as you like for the rest of your life, would you continue to work or would you stop working?" For a fascinating discussion of the role of work in American political culture, see Judith Shklar, *American Citizenship* (Cambridge: Harvard University Press, 1991). Of course, the classic argument for the moral significance of work in modern societies is Max Weber, *The Protestant Ethic and the Spirit of Capitalism* (New York: Scribners, 1958). A more recent, and thoroughly Gallic, discussion of the transformation of the idea of work affected by modernity is Anne Godignon and Jean-Louis Thiriet, "The Rebirth of Voluntary Servitude," in Mark Lilla, ed., *New French Thought: Political Philosophy* (Princeton: Princeton University Press, 1994), pp. 226–231.

48. Theda Skocpol's *Protecting Soldiers and Mothers* (Cambridge: Belknap Press, 1992), which was discussed in Chapter 2, draws substantially from the literature on this subject. Another good source of information on the separate spheres idea is Linda Kerber, "Separate Spheres, Female Worlds, Woman's Place: The Rhetoric of Women's History," *Journal of American History,* June 1988, v. 75, no. 1, pp. 9–39.

49. Connie de Boer, "The Polls: Women at Work," *Public Opinion Quarterly,* 1977, p. 272.

50. Hazel Erskine, "The Polls: Women's Role," *Public Opinion Quarterly,* 1977, pp. 183–184. In 1935–1936, 41.68 percent of families had an income under $1,000, and 72.6 had an

income under $1,750. U.S. Bureau of the Census, *Statistical Abstract of the United States, 1939* (Washington, D.C.: Government Printing Office, 1939), table 354.

51. Ibid., p. 184.

52. Ibid.

53. Ibid., p. 186.

54. U.S. Bureau of the Census, *Statistical Abstract of the United States, 1993* (Washington, D.C.: Government Printing Office, 1993), p. 399, table 631.

55. Ibid., table 633, p. 400.

56. Question (NORC-GSS): "Now I'm going to read several more statements. As I read each one, please tell me whether you strongly agree, agree, disagree, or strongly disagree. For example, here is the statement: A working mother can establish just as warm and secure a relationship with her children as a mother who does not work."

57. Question (NORC-GSS): "Do you agree or disagree with this statement? Women should take care of running their homes and leave running the country up to men."

58. Rita Simon and Jean Landis, "Women's and Men's Attitudes About a Woman's Place and Role," *Public Opinion Quarterly,* 1989, p. 273.

59. Ibid., p. 272.

60. Shirley Wilkins and Thomas Miller, "Working Women: How It's Working Out," *Public Opinion,* October-November 1985, v. 8, p. 45.

61. Arguing for mandatory participation in work as a condition for welfare, Lawrence Mead observes, "The poor, who have more difficulty working, apparently appreciate the structure that workfare provides." Lawrence Mead, "Should Workfare Be Mandatory?: What the Research Says," *Journal of Policy Analysis and Management,* 1990, v. 9, no. 3, pp. 400–404.

62. Nancy Goodban, "The Psychological Impact of Being on Welfare," *Social Service Review,* September 1985, v. 59, p. 415.

63. Ibid., p. 418.

64. One survey in Chicago found that 67 percent of those questioned found that AFDC had a negative impact on their family life. Susan Popkin, "Welfare: Views from the Bottom," *Social Problems,* February 1990, v. 37, p. 72.

65. Ibid., p. 75. Only 18 percent of those surveyed thought that they were on welfare because of "not being able to find a job or not being able to find a job that paid enough for them to support themselves and their families."

66. Christopher Jencks and Kathryn Edin, "The Real Welfare Problem," *American Prospect,* Spring 1990, p. 34.

67. For a discussion of the larger foundations for the work norm in American culture and for why the findings in this chapter point to a more-than-policy consensus, see Chapter 9.

4. THE NATURE OF THE ELITE CULTURAL CONFLICT

1. James Q. Wilson, "New Politics, New Elites, Old Publics," in Marc Landy and Martin Levin, eds., *The New Politics of Public Policy* (Baltimore: Johns Hopkins Press, 1995), p. 257.

2. For convenience' sake, all works published by Stanley Rothman in collaboration

with Althea Nagai, Robert Lerner, and S. Robert Lichter will be referred to simply under Rothman's name.

3. M. Kent Jennings, "Ideological Thinking Among Mass Publics and Political Elites," *Public Opinion Quarterly,* 1992, v. 56, pp. 419–441; quote is from pp. 434–435.

4. Jennings found that the general public had "product-moment correlations," a measure of ideological constraint, that were much lower than party elites, ranging from .12 for the public to .46 for political elites (for seven issue positions), to .12 to .58 (for evaluations of sociopolitical groups).

5. W. Russell Neuman, *The Paradox of Mass Politics* (Cambridge: Harvard University Press, 1986), pp. 170–171.

6. Robert Lerner, Althea Nagai, and Stanley Rothman, "Elite vs. Mass Opinion: Another Look at a Classic Relationship," *International Journal of Public Opinion Research,* 1991, v. 3, no. 1, pp. 1–31. Also, see the discussion by Allen Barton and the author's response, "Comment on 'Elite vs. Mass Opinion: Another Look at a Classic Relationship,' " *International Journal of Public Opinion Research,* 1992, v. 4, no. 1, pp. 62–69.

7. Kristin Luker, *Abortion and the Politics of Motherhood* (Berkeley: University of California Press, 1984), p. 186.

8. Jane Mansbridge, *Why We Lost the ERA* (Chicago: University of Chicago Press, 1986), ch. 13.

9. The most recent example of unitary ruling-class thinking is Michael Lind, *The Next American Nation* (New York: Free Press, 1995).

10. "Gaps Between Leaders and Publics," *Society,* July-August 1995, p. 3. This divergence on foreign affairs also applies to domestic concerns with an international color, such as immigration and trade. Large differences also existed on expanding entitlements, an issue where the more substantial information of elites may play a role.

11. Robert Lerner, Althea Nagai, and Stanley Rothman, "Elite Dissensus and Its Origins," *Journal of Political and Military Sociology,* 1990, v. 18, p. 30.

12. Sidney Verba and Gary Orren, *Equality in America: The View from the Top* (Cambridge: Harvard University Press, 1985), p. 118. This difference in group opinion on equality was maintained even when demography and party affiliation were controlled for.

13. Sidney Verba, *Elites and the Idea of Equality* (Cambridge: Harvard University Press, 1987), pp. 74–80.

14. Ibid., pp. 32–33. On alienation, the difference was nearly four standard deviations (38.54, where 10 equals one standard deviation) and 2.5 for expressive individualism (25.26).

15. Verba's studies are more oriented to rights and resource issues (i.e., should women have the same rights as men, should we distribute more resources to the poor, etc.) and less to the moral issues that are a primary force in AFDC. Because of this, I rely on Rothman's studies more than those conducted by Verba, although I will use the latter when appropriate.

16. Robert Lerner, Althea Nagai, and Stanley Rothman, *American Elites* (New Haven: Yale University Press, in press). The "attitudinal items" for the four ideological dimensions were:

Collectivist liberalism: "The government should work to substantially reduce the income gap between the rich and the poor." "It is not the proper role of government to insure that everyone has a job." "Less government regulation would be good for the country." "Our environmental problems are not as serious as people have been led to believe."

Expressive individualism: "It is a woman's right to decide whether or not to have an abortion." "Lesbians and homosexuals should not be allowed to teach in public schools." "It is wrong for a married person to have sexual relations with someone other than his or her spouse." "It is wrong for adults of the same sex to have sexual relations."

System alienation: "The American legal system mainly favors the wealthy." "The American private enterprise system is generally fair to working people." "The United States needs a complete restructuring of its basic institutions." "Big corporations should be taken out of private ownership and run in the public interest." "The structure of our society causes most people to feel alienated." "The main goal of U.S. foreign policy has been to protect U.S. business interests."

Regime threat: "It is sometimes necessary for the CIA to protect U.S. interests by undermining hostile governments." "We should be more forceful in our dealings with the Soviet Union even if it increases the risk of war." "It is important for America to have the strongest military force in the world, no matter what it costs." "There is too much concern in the courts for the rights of criminals." The following items had a lower loading and therefore showed less coherence. "Our environmental problems are not as serious as people have been led to believe." "In general, blacks don't have the motivation or will power to pull themselves out of poverty." "Almost all the gains made by blacks in recent years have been made at the expense of whites." "Lesbians and homosexuals should not be allowed to teach in public schools." "Hard work will always pay off if you have faith in yourself and stick to it." "Less government regulation of business would be good for the whole country."

17. In *Habits of the Heart* (Berkeley: University of California Press, 1985), Robert Bellah describes this conflict as the division between utilitarian and expressive individualism, the former characterized by Benjamin Franklin, the latter by Walt Whitman. Utilitarian individualism emphasizes individualism and self-reliance and their joint discipline of the body and the shackling of desire. Expressive individualism, in contrast, suggests the sensual and spiritual possibilities open to the person divorced from ties of tradition. Utilitarian individualism is the ethos of bourgeois capitalism, while expressive individualism is the ethos of counterculture modernism. Another, more penetrating analysis along the same lines is Daniel Bell, *The Cultural Contradictions of Capitalism* (New York: Basic Books, 1976).

18. Rothman also studied bureaucrats, congressional aides, and judges. In the case of congressional aides and judges, the element of elite circulation due to political appointment suggests that the study's findings would fluctuate significantly over time. Finally, bureaucrats were consistently moderate on most issues but very conservative on collectivist liberalism and alienation. This finding would be consistent with bureaucrats' feeling that they represent the system others feel alienated from, and would account for their opposition to adding new responsibilities to their plate. It is my suspicion that most bureaucrats are, fundamentally, nonideological.

19. Lerner, Nagal, and Rothman, *American Elites,* ch. 3.

20. Robert Lerner, Stanley Rothman, and S. Robert Lichter, "Christian Religious Elites," *Public Opinion,* March-April 1989, v. 11, pp. 54–58.

21. Robert Lerner, Althea Nagai, and Stanley Rothman, "Marginality and Liberalism Among Jewish Elites," *Public Opinion Quarterly,* Fall 1989, v. 53, pp. 330–352.

22. A similar finding—that American law is dominated by an individualistic, rights orientation—is discussed in Mary Ann Glendon, *Rights Talk* (New York: Free Press, 1991). If a strong individualistic orientation characterizes modern lawyers, this suggests a dramatic

shift since the early years of the Republic. Tocqueville describes American lawyers in the early nineteenth century as possessing a "taste for regularity and order" and a strong attachment to "authority." Alexis de Tocqueville, *Democracy in America I* (New York: Vintage, 1960), p. 289. This shift, from a hierarchical to an individualistic ethos, is crucial to an understanding of the changing role of law in American life.

23. Peter Lewis, "On the Net: Dissecting the Information Revolution," *New York Times,* August 28, 1995, p. D3.

24. For an enthusiastic discussion of the bourgeois virtues, see Donald McCloskey, "Bourgeois Virtue," *American Scholar,* Spring 1994, v. 63, no. 2, pp. 177–191.

25. Verba and Orren, *Equality in America,* p. 74.

26. One can describe these ideological splits as cultural but in a fusionist fashion. Conservatives are typically hierarchist/individualist, and liberals are egalitarian/individualist.

27. David Frum, *Dead Right* (New York: New Republic/Basic Books, 1994).

28. Althea Nagai, Robert Lerner, and Stanley Rothman, *Giving for Social Change* (Westport, Conn.: Praeger, 1994), p. 133.

29. Ibid., p. 134. When politicization is measured by politicized grants as a percentage of all grants, only the Eli Lilly Foundation was close to even-handed, giving 55 percent of its politicized grants to liberals. When politicization was measured by politicized dollars as a percentage of all grant dollars, the Rockwell International Foundation appears even-handed, giving 58 percent of its grants to conservatives.

30. Ibid., pp. 134, 137, 138.

31. Sidney Blumenthal, *The Rise of the Counter-Establishment* (New York: Times Books, 1986), ch. 2.

32. James Allen Smith, *The Idea Brokers* (New York: Free Press, 1991), p. 182.

33. Ibid., pp. 151–152. Liberal-leaning foundations, however, provide over half their funding to conservative or neutral think tanks.

34. Almost all liberal foundations tend to be egalitarian, while the conservative ones tend to be an amalgam of hierarchical and individualistic. Some of the conservative foundations can more clearly be defined as hierarchical, such as the Bradley Foundation, while the corporate conservative foundations, such as the Amoco Foundation, tend to be more individualistic. It may be that the partisanship of the foundations' founders acts as a constraining factor, keeping the naturally unstable liberal-conservative division from breaking down.

35. The Christian Coalition, which could be thought of as a interest group, does some idea-oriented work. Whether one considers it a think tank or a movement or interest group is not particularly relevant for my purposes.

36. A good example of this consensus is Arthur Schlesinger, *The Vital Center* (Cambridge: Houghton Mifflin, 1949), ch. 11.

37. Smith, *The Idea Brokers,* p. 231.

38. Irving Kristol, quoted in Blumenthal, *The Rise of the Counter-Establishment,* p. 149.

39. Oscar Lewis, "The Culture of Poverty," in Daniel Patrick Moynihan, *On Understanding Poverty* (New York: Basic Books, 1968), p. 193.

40. Ibid., p. 195.

41. Edward Banfield, *The Unheavenly City Revisited* (Boston: Little, Brown, 1974), p. 61.

42. Ibid., pp. 260–269.

43. Ibid., p. 270. He also suggested reduction in unemployment and the removal of bar-

riers to low-skill and low-wage work, although these are less clearly related to his analysis of the central problem. The idea that poor children are in primary need of a shift in cultural milieu is the grounding of the recent support for orphanages as an instrument in the battle against poverty. See James Q. Wilson, "Culture, Incentives, and the Underclass," in Henry Aaron, Thomas Mann, and Timothy Taylor, eds., *Values and Public Policy* (Washington, D.C.: Brookings Institution, 1994).

44. Lawrence Mead, "Poverty: How Little We Know," *Social Service Review,* September 1994, p. 334.

45. Lawrence Mead, *The New Politics of Poverty* (New York: Basic Books, 1992), p. 145.

46. Marvin Olasky, *The Tragedy of American Compassion* (Washington, D.C.: Regnery Gateway, 1992). Olasky emphasizes that the main issue is not necessarily public versus private but theistic versus atheistic, value-driven versus value-less, and between the idea that poverty is a sickness of the soul, to be cured through love, versus the idea that it is a condition of the wallet, to be cured through redistribution.

47. Nathan Glazer, *The Limits of Social Policy* (Cambridge: Harvard University Press, 1988), p. 13.

48. Myron Magnet, *The Dream and the Nightmare* (New York: William Morrow, 1993), p. 123.

49. Steven Rhoads's *The Economist's View of the World* (Cambridge: Cambridge University Press, 1985) is the best analysis of the strengths, as well as the weaknesses, of the economic approach to policy.

50. That honor, if honor it is, goes to George Stigler. See "The Economics of Minimum Wage Legislation," *American Economic Review,* 1946, pp. 358–365.

51. Milton Friedman, *Capitalism and Freedom* (Chicago: University of Chicago Press, 1962), p. 192.

52. Arthur Okun, *Equality and Efficiency: The Big Tradeoff* (Washington, D.C.: Brookings Institution, 1975), p. 80.

53. See George Stigler and Gary Becker, "De Gustibus Non Est Disputatum," *American Economic Review,* March 1977, pp. 76–90. Critiques of preference stability include Cass Sunstein, "Preferences and Politics," *Philosophy and Public Affairs,* Winter 1991, pp. 3–34; Mark Sagoff, "Values and Preferences," *Ethics,* January 1986, pp. 301–316; Timur Kuran, "Private and Public Preferences," *Economics and Philosophy,* 1990, no. 6, pp. 1–26; and George Akerlof and William Dickens, "The Economic Consequences of Cognitive Dissonance," *American Economic Review,* June 1982, pp. 307–319.

54. Charles Murray, *Losing Ground* (New York: Basic Books, 1984), p. 146.

55. Ibid., pp. 212–216.

56. George Gilder, *Wealth and Poverty* (New York: Basic Books, 1981), p. 118. Gilder, it must be admitted, is a very strange individualist, primarily because of his strong moral convictions. However, Gilder emphasizes that only a free market system, freed from the distortions of the welfare state, provides the proper material and spiritual incentives to social mobility. This belief suggests that his underlying principles are individualistic.

57. Two instructive, recent studies of Paine's political and social thought are A. J. Ayer, *Thomas Paine* (New York: Atheneum, 1988) and John Keane, *Tom Paine: A Political Life* (Boston: Little Brown, 1995).

58. The best exposition of this idea of equality is R. H. Tawney, *Equality* (New York: Barnes and Noble, 1964).

59. Herbert Gans, *More Equality* (New York: Vintage, 1974), p. 27.

60. One characteristic illustration of this tendency is Andrew Hacker, "The Crackdown on African-Americans," *Nation,* July 10, 1995, pp. 46–47. Hacker believes that popular outcries against illegitimacy and welfare are actually efforts to regulate blacks and return them to a formally subjugated social status.

61. Nancy Fraser and Linda Gordon, "A Genealogy of Dependency: Tracing a Keyword of the U.S. Welfare State," *Signs,* Winter 1994, v. 20, p. 331.

62. Herbert Gans, "The War Against the Poor," *Dissent,* Fall 1992, v. 39, p. 462.

63. Richard Cloward and Frances Fox Piven, "A Class Analysis of Welfare," *Monthly Review,* February 1993, p. 27.

64. Laurence Lynn, "Rejoinder to Mead," *Journal of Policy Analysis and Management,* 1990, v. 9, no. 3, p. 407.

65. June Axinn and Amy Hirsch, "Welfare and the 'Reform' of Women," *Families in Society: The Journal of Contemporary Human Services,* November 1993, p. 571.

5. THE FAILURE OF COMPREHENSIVE REFORM

1. Jane Mansbridge, *Why We Lost the ERA* (Chicago: University of Chicago Press, 1986), p. 179.

2. Ibid., p. 180. Mansbridge notes that the process of movement-building drives this purification. Since a movement seeks not only to change the world outside but also to preserve and expand the world inside, it needs to constantly distill its ideology: "Becoming 'us' involves purifying your beliefs. The dynamic that binds activists to the movement entails idealism, radicalism, and exclusion. It works against the inclusive policy of accommodation and reform." This helps explain why, as the debate on FAP progressed, the demands of the NWRO grew more rigid rather than more flexible. Coming to agreement would have weakened the stability of the group.

3. A very insightful discussion of Secretary Wirtz's alternative strategy for the War on Poverty is Judith Russell, "The Making of American Anti-poverty Policy: Willard Wirtz and the Other War on Poverty," paper delivered at the 1993 American Political Science Association convention, September 2–5, 1993. Margaret Weir also points to the conflict of visions for the War on Poverty in *Politics and Jobs* (Princeton: Princeton University Press, 1992), ch. 3.

4. Nathan Glazer and Daniel Patrick Moynihan, *Beyond the Melting Pot: The Negroes, Puerto Ricans, Jews, Italians, and Irish of New York City* (Cambridge: MIT Press and Harvard University Press, 1963).

5. Report reprinted in Lee Rainwater and William Y. Yancey, *The Moynihan Report and the Politics of Controversy* (Cambridge: MIT Press, 1967), p. 66.

6. Ibid.

7. Ibid., p. 76.

8. Daniel Patrick Moynihan, "A Family Policy for the Nation," *America,* September 18, 1965. Reprinted in Rainwater and Yancey, *The Moynihan Report and the Politics of Controversy,* p. 385.

9. Ibid., p. 387.

10. Ibid., p. 392.

11. Ibid., p. 388.

12. Glenn Loury, "The Family, the Nation, and Senator Moynihan," *Commentary*, June 1986, p. 23.

13. Address delivered October 29, 1965, at Abbott House, Westchester County, New York. Reprinted in Rainwater and Yancey, *The Moynihan Report and the Politics of Controversy*, pp. 403–404.

14. James Farmer, "The Controversial Moynihan Report," December 18 (syndicated column). Reprinted in Rainwater and Yancey, *The Moynihan Report and the Politics of Controversy*, p. 410.

15. Ibid.

16. Ibid.

17. Herbert Gutman, *The Black Family in Slavery and Freedom* (New York: Vintage Books, 1976), p. xvii.

18. William Julius Wilson, *The Truly Disadvantaged* (Chicago: University of Chicago Press, 1987).

19. Richard Cloward and Lloyd Ohlin, *Delinquency and Opportunity* (Glencoe: Free Press, 1960), p. 86.

20. Ibid., p. 173.

21. Ibid., p. 211.

22. See Allen Matusow, *The Unraveling of America: A History of Liberalism in the 1960s* (New York: Harper & Row, 1984), ch. 4; and Daniel Patrick Moynihan, *Maximum Feasible Misunderstanding* (New York: Free Press, 1970). The report on the black family discussed earlier was, in part, an attempt to provide intellectual support for an alternative strategy to that of Ohlin. Moynihan would continue to oppose Cloward and Ohlin's community organization strategy in his later life, as we shall see later in this chapter.

23. Herbert Gans, "The Positive Functions of Poverty," *American Journal of Sociology* 1972, v. 78, no. 2, pp. 275–289.

24. Reprinted in Richard Cloward and Frances Fox Piven, *The Politics of Turmoil* (New York: Pantheon Press, 1972), p. 89.

25. Ibid., p. 95.

26. See Frances Fox Piven and Richard Cloward, "Dissensus Politics: A Strategy for Winning Economic Rights," reprinted in Cloward and Piven, *The Politics of Turmoil*.

27. Cloward and Piven, *The Politics of Turmoil*, p. 170.

28. Daniel Patrick Moynihan, *The Politics of a Guaranteed Income* (New York: Random House, 1973), p. 67.

29. Leslie Lenkowsky, *Politics, Economics, and Welfare Reform: The Failure of the Negative Income Tax in Britain and the United States* (Washington, D.C.: American Enterprise Institute, 1986), p. 65.

30. Ibid., p. 23.

31. Vincent and Vee Burke, *Nixon's Good Deed: Welfare Reform* (New York: Columbia University Press, 1974), ch. 3.

32. Ibid., p. 42.

33. Ibid., p. 69.

34. Ibid., p. 70. The Speenhamland program was an early guaranteed income, known as a rate in wages. See Walter Trattner, *From Poor Law to Welfare State* (New York: Free Press, 1984), pp. 50–51.

35. Nixon's motivations may have been more cynical than my discussion suggests. In the recently published H. R. Haldeman, *The Haldeman Diaries: Inside the White House* (New York: Putnam, 1994), it is revealed that Nixon told his chief of staff "to be sure it's [FAP] killed by Democrats and that we make big play for it, but don't let it pass, we can't afford it." Whether this is an accurate account of Nixon's feelings on the matter or whether it was one of the rants that Nixon was capable of in times of stress is hard to determine. In order to give this one comment pride of place in interpretations of the administration's purpose in supporting FAP, documentation beyond this one comment would be necessary.

36. Christopher Leman, *The Collapse of Welfare Reform: Political Institutions, Policy, and the Poor in Canada and the United States* (Cambridge: MIT Press, 1980), p. 79. Leman emphasizes that both the chairman and the ranking Republican on Ways and Means supported FAP. Not one Republican on the committee opposed the bill.

37. Moynihan, *Politics of a Guaranteed Income,* p. 400.

38. Steven Smith and Christopher Deering, *Committees in Congress* (Washington, D.C.: Congressional Quarterly Press, 1984), p. 95. For more on Ways and Means' special role in the House, see Richard Fenno, *Congressmen in Committees* (New York: Little, Brown, 1973).

39. Moynihan, *Politics of a Guaranteed Income,* p. 426.

40. Paul Peterson and Mark Rom, *Welfare Magnets* (Washington, D.C.: Brookings Institution, 1990), p. 15.

41. Leman, *The Collapse of Welfare Reform,* p. 81.

42. Although NWRO had done so earlier in the process. Ibid., p. 79.

43. Moynihan, *Politics of a Guaranteed Income,* p. 451.

44. Moynihan states that this would have cost $20 billion a year, four times the cost of the administration's proposal.

45. To provide a sense of proportion to these figures, consider that in 1970 the average poverty-line cutoff for a family of four was $3,968, and in 1975 it was $5,500. In that same year, the minimum wage was $1.60 an hour, or $3,200 a year. In 1974 the minimum wage was increased to $2.00 an hour, or $4,000 a year. U.S. Bureau of the Census, *Statistical Abstract of the United States, 1993* (Washington, D.C.: Government Printing Office, 1993), Tables 735 and 675.

46. The litigation strategy of the welfare rights movement and the response of the Supreme Court will be the subject of Chapter 6.

47. "Social Security Raised; Welfare Pay Restricted," *CQ Almanac,* 1967, p. 893.

48. U.S. Congress, House of Representatives, Committee on Ways and Means, *Social Security Amendments of 1967,* 90th Cong., 1st Sess., 1967, H. Rep. 544.

49. Chief among them is Lawrence Mead, *Beyond Entitlement* (New York: Free Press, 1986), ch. 5. In fact, the weakness of work requirements is, for Mead, the primary reason all major attempts at changing welfare have failed. I think his interpretation is valid when applied to Carter's Program for Better Jobs and Income. However, the fact remains that FAP would have passed had the three liberal senators on the Finance Committee voted it out of committee. There was a short window of opportunity for a program such as FAP; it was the opposition of radical egalitarians that closed it. Later on, hierarchists kept it shut.

50. Laurence Lynn, *The President as Policymaker: Jimmy Carter and Welfare Reform* (Philadelphia: Temple University Press, 1981). See also Leman, *The Collapse of Welfare Reform,* pp. 94–112.

6. THE ROLE OF THE SUPREME COURT IN AFDC

1. Benjamin Ginsberg and Martin Shefter, *Politics by Other Means* (New York: Basic Books, 1990).

2. See in particular Justice David Souter's argument in *Planned Parenthood v. Casey,* 112 S. Ct. 2791 (1992).

3. Never in the debate over FAP, for example, did Nixon ever suggest that his negative income tax amounted to income by right. This was why, flimsy as they may have been, FAP's work requirements were so significant. They represented the line between norm-driven and norm-less public assistance.

4. See Arnold Meltsner, *Policy Analysts in the Bureaucracy* (Berkeley: University of California Press, 1976).

5. Quoted in Winifred Bell, *Aid to Dependent Children* (New York: Columbia University Press, 1965), p. 78.

6. Theda Skocpol, *Protecting Soldiers and Mothers* (Cambridge: Belknap Press, 1992), p. 467.

7. Ibid., p. 468.

8. U.S. Congress, Senate, 74th Cong., 1st sess., 1935, S. Rep. 628, p. 19.

9. Ibid., pp. 29, 36; and U.S. House, 74th Cong., 1st sess., 1935, H.R. Rep. 615, pp. 18, 24.

10. As we shall see later in the chapter, Reich was as concerned for the security of licenses and other publicly created property as he was for relief, and he conceptualized all of them as forms of public assistance.

11. Charles Reich, "Midnight Welfare Searches and the Social Security Act," *Yale Law Journal,* 1963, v. 73, p. 1350.

12. Ibid., p. 1359.

13. Charles Reich, "The New Property," *Yale Law Journal,* April 1964, v. 73, no. 5, pp. 739–743.

14. John Stuart Mill, "On Liberty," in *Three Essays* (New York: Oxford University Press, 1975).

15. Reich, "The New Property," p. 778.

16. Ibid., p. 779.

17. Ibid., p. 786.

18. See H. H. Gerth and C. Wright Mills, eds., *From Max Weber: Essays in Sociology* (New York: Oxford University Press, 1946), especially pp. 295–301.

19. The keenest analysis of this phenomenon is by Theodore Lowi, *The End of Liberalism* (New York: W. W. Norton, 1969).

20. Martha Davis, *Brutal Need: Lawyers and the Welfare Rights Movement, 1960–1973* (New Haven: Yale University Press, 1993), p. 28.

21. Edward Sparer, "The Role of the Welfare Client's Lawyer," *UCLA Law Review,* 1965, v. 13, p. 367.

22. Ibid.

23. Davis, *Brutal Need,* p. 59.

24. Ibid., p. 60.

25. Ibid., p. 64.

26. The center did not want the Court to directly address the racial disparity, for this could be done by removing whites from the rolls. The center's objective was the elimination of administrative discretion.

27. Sparer opposed litigating this case because it would be argued before an "unsympathetic judge" and was being handled by lawyers who were not capable of putting together an adequate case.

28. *Smith v. Board of Commissioners of District of Columbia,* 259 F. Supp., at 423–425 (1966).

29. The district court's use of the rights-privilege distinction in this case suggests that considering it a "canard" for explaining the caution of the courts in AFDC is, at the least, excessive. The canard argument can be found in Shep Melnick, "The Politics of the New Property" in Ellen Paul and Howard Dickman, *Liberty, Property and the Future of Constitutional Development* (Albany: SUNY Press, 1990).

30. *King v. Smith,* 392 U.S. 309.

31. Ibid., at 1126.

32. Ibid.

33. Ibid., at 1127.

34. Discussed in Chapter 2.

35. Ibid., at 1139.

36. Ibid., at 1134.

37. Ibid., at 1135.

38. See Sec. 402, part (b)(1) of the Social Security Act, which states that plans will be approved "except that it shall not approve any plan which imposes a condition of eligibility for aid to dependent children, a residence requirement which denies aid with respect to any child residing in the state (1) who has resided in the State for one year immediately preceding the application for such aid."

39. *Shapiro v. Thompson,* 394 U.S. 618.

40. Ibid., at 619.

41. 7 How 283 (1849); 383 U.S. 745 (1966); and 390 U.S. 570, (1968) respectively.

42. *Edwards v. California,* 314 U.S. 172 (1941).

43. Ibid., at 177.

44. Ibid., at 182.

45. Ibid., at 183.

46. *Shapiro v. Thompson,* at 622.

47. Ibid., at 624.

48. *Goldberg v. Kelly,* 397 U.S. 254.

49. Ibid., at 299.

50. Ibid., at 305.

51. Ibid., at 305–306.

52. *Dandridge v. Williams,* 397 U.S. 471.

53. Ibid., at 503.

54. *Townsend v. Swank,* 404 U.S. 282.

55. *Dandridge v. Williams,* at 498.

56. *New York State Department of Social Services v. Dublino,* 413 U.S. 405 (1973).

57. See Chapter 2.

58. These are discussed in R. Shep Melnick, *Between the Lines* (Washington, D.C.: Brookings Institution, 1994), p. 128.

59. *Brown v. Board of Education,* 349 US 294 (1954). *Swann v. Charlotte-Mecklenburg Board of Education,* 402 US 1 (1971). *Milliken v. Bradley,* 418 US 717 (1974).

60. *Roe v. Wade,* 410 US 113 (1973). *Harris v. McRae,* 448 US 297 (1980).

7. THE PERSISTENCE OF AFDC'S FEDERAL FORM

1. Tocqueville states the matter succinctly: "It is not the administrative, but the political effects of decentralization that I most admire in America. In the United States the interests of the country are everywhere kept in view; they are an object of solicitude to the people of the whole Union, and every citizen is as warmly attached to them as if they were his own." Alexis de Tocqueville, *Democracy in America I* (New York: Vintage Books, 1960), p. 98.

2. See especially David Mayhew's classic work, *Congress: The Electoral Connection* (New Haven: Yale University Press, 1974). R. Shep Melnick argues that a similar pattern occurs in the relation between Congress and the courts: "In effect, members of Congress can say, 'We have passed legislation to educate the handicapped, help the states, and protect the Constitution. For that we should be praised. And if you don't like any specific result, blame the courts.' " Melnick, "Separation of Powers and the Strategy of Rights," in Marc Landy and Martin Levin, eds., *The New Politics of Public Policy* (Baltimore: Johns Hopkins Press, 1995), pp. 44–45.

3. This strategy will be discussed in more detail in the conclusion. It is my contention that the 1995 welfare debate shows the political pressures inherent in the system for pushing controversial issues like welfare down to the states.

4. L. Harmon Zeigler, "Interest Groups in the States," in Virginia Gray, Herbert Jacob, and Kenneth Vines, eds., *Politics in the American States* (Boston: Little, Brown, 1983).

5. Public Welfare Amendments of 1962, Pub. L. No. 87-543, tit. 1, at 122, 76 Stat. 172, 192 (codified as amended at 42 U.S.C. at 1315 (1988)).

6. Ibid.

7. These will be discussed in more detail at the end of this chapter.

8. President Ronald Reagan, *Public Papers of the Presidents: 1986* (Washington, D.C.: Government Printing Office, 1988), February 4, 1986, p. 128.

9. Domestic Policy Council, Low Income Opportunity Working Group, *Up From Dependency: Report to the President by the Domestic Policy Council* (Washington, D.C.: Government Printing Office, 1986), p. 58.

10. Ibid., p. 42.

11. Ibid., p. 48.

12. Ibid., p. 51.

13. Ibid., p. 58.

14. Michael Wiseman, "The New State Welfare Initiatives," Institute for Research on Poverty, Discussion paper No. 1002-93, April 1993, p. 10.

15. All quotes from Chuck Hobbs are from an interview I conducted June 13, 1994.

16. Message from the president of the United States, "Proposed Legislation—Low Income Opportunity Improvement Act of 1987." 100th Cong., 1st sess., H. Doc. 100-39.

17. Michael Fishman and Daniel Weinberg, "The Role of Evaluation in State Welfare Reform Waiver Demonstrations," in Charles Manski and Irwin Garfinkel, eds., *Evaluating Welfare and Training Programs* (Cambridge: Harvard University Press, 1992), p. 117.

18. Certain proposals, such as the guaranteed work strategy suggested by Mickey Kaus in *The End of Equality* (New York: Basic Books, 1992), could not be attempted even under the most elastic definitions or timetables for cost neutrality. That is, welfare proposals that sought an end other than reduction in cost or caseload were effectively pushed out of the realm of consideration, leaving ideological room for dramatic conservative proposals or marginal, essentially administrative-bureaucratic liberal changes.

19. Interview conducted in June 1994.

20. That is, the federal government would not provide the federal contribution for any expenditures in excess of what would have occurred in the absence of an experiment; neutrality had to be practiced in each year of the project.

21. In a pre-post, as opposed to an experimental method, certain variables for an entire population are compared over time, both before (pre-) and after (post-) the treatment has been administered.

22. Fishman and Weisberg, "The Role of Evaluation," pp. 130–131.

23. Wiseman, "The New State Welfare Initiatives," p. 12.

24. Daniel Patrick Moynihan, *The Politics of a Guaranteed Income* (New York: Random House, 1973), p. 438.

25. See for example Michael Kelly, "Clinton Presents Hard Line to Bring in North Carolina," *New York Times*, October 27, 1992, p. A12.

26. President George Bush, *Public Papers of the Presidents: 1992* (Washington, D.C.: Government Printing Office, 1993), p. 162.

27. Ibid.

28. Ibid.

29. Ibid., p. 589.

30. Ibid., p. 2019.

31. Interview with Gail Wilensky, August 24, 1995.

32. President George Bush, *Public Papers of the Presidents*, p. 577.

33. Ibid.

34. Ibid., pp. 577–578.

35. Ibid., p. 578.

36. Interview conducted in June 1994.

37. Interview with senior HHS Official, August 1994.

38. Interview with Gail Wilensky, August 24, 1995.

39. For the official "New Democrat" position on welfare reform, which mirrors the Clinton administration's proposal almost to the letter, see Will Marshall and Martin Schram, eds., *Mandate for Change* (New York: Berkeley Books, 1993), ch. 10. The book was the work of the Progressive Policy Institute of the Democratic Leadership Council, of which Clinton was a founding member and former chairman.

40. David Osborne, *Laboratories of Democracy* (Boston: Harvard Business School Press, 1988).

41. *Weekly Compilation of Presidential Documents: Administration of Bill Clinton*, v. 2, no. 5, February 2, 1993, p. 125.

42. Ibid., p. 126.

43. Ibid., p. 128.

44. These figures come from the "Summary of Waiver Applications—Clinton Administration," an internal HHS document.

45. This program was also controversial because of a number of racially inflammatory statements about its intent that were made during the debate on the proposal. The general thrust of these comments were that black women on the rolls were irresponsible in their sexual behavior and the state needed to step in with some form of discipline. HHS has chosen to ignore these comments and accept the program on its face.

46. U.S., Department of Health and Human Services, "Work and Responsibility Act of 1994: Detailed Summary," June 13, 1994, p. 2.

47. A two-year time limit can mean anything from requiring recipients to enter training

programs after two years to forcing them to work for their welfare checks after that period (the most common interpretation) or denying outright any assistance after this period.

48. *New York State Department of Social Services v. Dublino,* 413 U.S. 405 (1973).

49. See Mickey Kaus, "Tommy's New Tune," *New Republic,* September 18/25, 1995, pp. 25–26.

50. Don AuCoin and Doris Sue Wrong, "Governor's Plan Requires Work For Welfare Money," *Boston Globe,* January 11, 1995, p. 19.

51. This incident will be discussed in greater detail in Chapter 8.

52. Interview with Gail Wilensky, August 24, 1995.

53. *Beno v. Shalala,* 30 F.3d 1057 (9th Cir. 1994).

54. Ibid., p. 1067–1068.

55. Ibid., p. 1069.

56. Ibid., p. 1069–1072.

57. Interview with Gail Wilensky, August 24, 1995.

58. *C. K. v. Shalala,* 883 F. Supp. 991 (D.N.J. 1995).

8. MISSED OPPORTUNITY: DISSENSUS, DEVOLUTION, AND THE COLLAPSE OF THE CLINTON WELFARE PLAN

1. John Hale, "The Making of the New Democrats," *Political Science Quarterly,* Summer 1995, pp. 207–232.

2. See Katha Pollitt, "Subject to Debate," *Nation,* May 30, 1994, p. 740, and July 11, 1994, p. 45; David Corn, "The Welfare Trap," *Nation,* June 20, 1994, p. 859; Alexander Cockburn, "Beat the Devil," *Nation,* July 18, 1994, pp. 79–80.

3. In *Poor Support* (New York: Basic Books, 1988), David Ellwood refers to these quandaries as the "helping conundrums." The idea that help itself could have costs had a substantial pedigree, popularized by Irving Kristol as the "Law of Unintended Consequences." It was not until the late 1980s that this "law" attracted any currency on the left.

4. Theda Skocpol, "Sustainable Social Policy: Fighting Poverty Without Poverty Programs," *American Prospect,* Summer 1990, p. 67.

5. Christopher Jencks and Kathryn Edin, "The Real Welfare Problem," *American Prospect,* Spring 1990, p. 49.

6. Michael Novak, ed., *The New Consensus on Family and Welfare* (Washington, D.C.: American Enterprise Institute, 1987).

7. Ibid., p. 121.

8. See Fred Barnes and Grover Norquist, "The Politics of Less: A Debate on Big-Government Conservatism," *Policy Review,* Winter 1991, pp. 66–71. In 1991, it was still possible for Barnes, a conservative of impeccable credentials, to support Mickey Kaus's proposal to scrap welfare and replace it with minimum-wage jobs. In this article, which resulted from a Heritage Foundation debate, Barnes defended "big government conservatism," a philosophy he linked to the ideas of Jack Kemp.

9. In addition, in 1988 there was a strong professional consensus, especially among the program evaluation community, for the intellectual direction that FSA took. Furthermore, this intellectual community could point to at least a few instances where the new approach yielded measurable results. See Peter Szanton, "The Remarkable 'Quango': Knowledge,

Politics, and Welfare Reform," *Journal of Policy Analysis and Management,* Winter 1994, v. 13, pp. 590–632.

10. Charles Murray, "The Coming White Underclass," *Wall Street Journal,* October 29, 1993, p. A14.

11. Ibid.

12. In an interview in January 1995, Patrick Fagan, an important conservative social policy expert at the Heritage Foundation, told me he thought that the devolution approach was the most dangerous alternative of all to substantive reform. He indicated that he and other conservatives were not at all sympathetic and on the whole much preferred the welfare abolition strategy.

13. See "Principles for Real Welfare Reform," Empower America Issue Briefing, Washington, D.C.

14. William Bennett and Peter Wehner, ". . . And a Skeptical View of Welfare," *Boston Globe,* January 27, 1994, p. 11.

15. Ibid.

16. Interview with Paul Offner, September 1995. David Ellwood, in an interview with the author on September 8, 1995, also identified the Empower America brief (letter) as the first major crack in the welfare reform consensus.

17. Interview with Charles Murray, January 1994. Murray, along with James Q. Wilson, had met with Representative Newt Gingrich in December 1993. Murray also had meetings with Representatives Jan Meyers of Kansas and Joseph Lieberman of Connecticut soon after the article was published. Murray stated that in the meeting with the thirty Republican members of Congress, there was, initially, great resistance to his argument. "In the questions there were indications from a couple of them that they really didn't like the way I was dumping on workfare. This was typical. They kept asking about ways we could get the same effect as cutting off welfare but with less drastic [means]. . . . This whole business of getting rid of welfare is for them very discomfiting. . . . So, I think politically, the conversion job on the Republicans has been much more of an intellectual conversion than simply grabbing onto them politically."

18. David Whitman and Matthew Cooper, "The End of Welfare—Sort Of," *U.S. News and World Report,* June 20, 1994, p. 28.

19. Jason DeParle, "Clinton Aides See Problem with Vow to Limit Welfare," *New York Times,* June 21, 1993, p. A1.

20. Whitman and Cooper, "The End of Welfare—Sort Of," p. 28.

21. Ibid.

22. Jason DeParle, "Moynihan Says President Is Insincere About Reforming the Welfare System," *New York Times,* January 8, 1994, p. 8.

23. Interview with Azar Kattan, September 1995.

24. Whitman and Cooper, "The End of Welfare—Sort Of," p. 28.

25. Interview with Kattan, September 1995.

26. Interview conducted in August 1995.

27. Jeffrey Katz, "Welfare Overhaul Forces Ready to Start Without Clinton" *Congressional Quarterly,* April 2, 1994, p. 801.

28. Jason DeParle, "Crucial Lawmaker Criticizes Clinton Welfare Plan," *New York Times,* January 27, 1994, p. A12.

29. DeParle, "Clinton Aides See Problem," p. A1.

30. Katz, "Welfare Overhaul Forces Ready," p. 801.

31. Ibid.

32. Letter to the president, November 23, 1993, under the aegis of the Congressional Progressive Caucus.

33. Interview with Kattan, September 1995.

34. The Progressive Policy Institute, Washington, D.C., was aware of the danger the Matsui approach represented to comprehensive, work-based reform. In July 1994, it published a report, "The Matsui Welfare Reform Bill: Status Quo Plus," which attacked the proposal because it "throws more money at the status quo."

35. James Barnes, "Waiting for Clinton," *National Journal,* March 5, 1994, p. 517.

36. Interview with Kattan, September 1995.

37. Jeffrey Katz, "Clinton Plans Major Shift in Lives Of Poor People," *Congressional Quarterly,* January 22, 1994, p. 117.

38. Jason DeParle, "House Leaders Are Criticizing Welfare Plan," *New York Times,* May 19, 1994, p. A1.

39. Jason DeParle, "Democrats Face Hard Choices in Welfare Overhaul," *New York Times,* February 22, 1994, p. A16. The welfare working group was also forced to drop a proposal to tax casinos, soon after Nevada Senator Harry Reid announced that if it was part of the plan given to Congress, "I will become the most negative, the most irresponsible, the most obnoxious person of anyone in the Senate." Jason DeParle, "From Pledge to Plan: The Campaign to End Welfare," *New York Times,* July 15, 1994, A1.

40. Dave McCurdy, "An Invitation to Work," *Roll Call,* February 7, 1994, p. 16.

41. Will Marshall, "Replacing Welfare with Work," Progressive Policy Institute Policy Briefing, July 1994, p. 19.

42. Jeffrey Katz, "A Welcome But Unwieldy Idea? Putting An End to Welfare," *Congressional Quarterly,* February 27, 1993, p. 461.

43. Jason DeParle, "Abolishment of Welfare: An Idea Becomes a Cause," *New York Times,* April 22, 1994, p. A14.

44. Barnes, "Waiting for Clinton," p. 519.

45. Ibid.

46. Ibid.

47. Interview with David Ellwood, September 1995.

48. Ibid.

49. Ibid.

50. Jeffrey Katz, "Welfare Issue Finds Home on the Campaign Trail," *Congressional Quarterly,* October 15, 1994, p. 2958.

51. Ibid.

52. Jeffrey Katz, "Parts Of Welfare Plan Concern GOP Moderates, Governors," *Congressional Quarterly,* December 10, 1994, p. 3512.

53. Ibid.

54. Interview conducted in August 1995.

55. Interview conducted in August 1995.

56. Jason DeParle, "States' Eagerness to Experiment on Welfare Jars Administration," *New York Times,* April 14, 1994, p. A1.

57. Jeffrey Katz, "Governors Group Sidelined in Welfare Debate," *Congressional Quarterly,* May 20, 1995, p. 1423.

58. Jason DeParle, "GOP Plans to Ax Aid Programs, Give States Control," *Commercial Appeal,* December 9, 1994, p. A1.

59. Katz, "Governors Group Sidelined," p. 1423.

60. Interview with Paul Offner, September 1995.

61. Interview conducted August 1995.

62. Ibid.

63. Interview with Paul Offner, September 1995.

64. *Daily Labor Report,* August 1, 1995.

65. PBS Roundtable on Welfare, moderated by Steve Roberts, June 30, 1995.

66. President Bill Clinton, *Weekly Compilation of Presidential Documents* (Washington, D.C.: Government Printing Office, 1995), August 5, 1995. Many Democrats on Capitol Hill were shocked that Clinton would go beyond accepting Virginia's plan, which could be rationalized by his support for the principles of decentralization, to actually endorsing it.

67. *Daily Labor Report,* August 8, 1995.

68. Ibid.

69. "Excerpts from Dole and Clinton Speeches on Redoing Welfare," *New York Times,* August 1, 1995, p. A8.

70. Whitman and Cooper, "The End of Welfare—Sort Of," p. 28.

71. This loss of control over the issue explains why Senate Democrats voted in such large numbers for that body's welfare reform plan, which was, in its substance, diametrically opposed to the spirit of the DLC approach (which had been signed onto by every Senate Democrat). They voted for the proposal not out of agreement with its principle but to avoid the chances of getting something worse and to give them some leverage in House-Senate negotiations.

9. CONCLUSION: FINDING A WAY OUT

1. Although a plausible argument might be made for abortion as a competitor with welfare for the significance of its regime-level consequences, abortion is, in fact, driven more by matters of moral ultimacy (that is, above the regime) than the immediate questions of fundamental obligation that make up a political regime. Because defense policy concerns the preservation of the regime, it could be seen as a competitor as well. However, the military is seen (both by those inside and outside the armed forces) as an institution that is not supposed to reflect the society that it protects. Therefore, the shape and structure of the armed forces do not necessarily reflect opinions concerning the basic obligations and rights of citizens.

2. Julian Benda, *The Treason of the Intellectuals* (New York: Norton, 1969).

3. My use of the term "system" does not suggest some entity that exists apart from actual sets of persons. Rather, a system is a structured set of interactions and expectations that characterize a set of persons in a particular context. The "system" is in fact a set of persons with varying interests and preferences, not the monolith that the term might suggest.

4. The similarity between Perot and Alberto Fujimori, who was elected president of Peru in 1990 and staged a coup eighteen months later, is striking. I would not, of course, suggest that Ross Perot possesses a similar authoritarian temperament. A similar point is made by Harvey Mansfield in "Only Amend," *New Republic,* July 6, 1992, pp. 13–14.

5. See Jeffrey Birnbaum and Alan Murray, *Showdown at Gucci Gulch* (New York: Vintage Books, 1987); and Paul Light, *Artful Work: The Politics of Social Security Reform* (New

York: Random House, 1985). Although the Social Security reforms might not seem sufficiently comprehensive to meet this standard, they do involve what was previously a highly controversial issue, in which various actors had to suspend short-term political advantage in order to salvage an institution central to the legitimacy of the political system as a whole. Light's book captures this dynamic well.

6. Of course, children whose families were not on AFDC were not directed as a matter of course to public institutions, despite the fact that the larger structure of the program suggested that this step would be reasonable. They were simply denied assistance. This irony, if it could be called that, loomed large in the Supreme Court's decision in *King v. Smith* to strike down tests of sexual morality.

7. Married women between the ages of 20 and 24 have a 66.3 percent labor force participation rate, while those between 25 and 34 have a 70.9 percent rate, and those between 35 and 44 have a 74.8 percent rate. U.S. Bureau of the Census, *Statistical Abstract of the United States, 1993* (Washington, D.C.: Government Printing Office, 1993), Table 631.

8. Greg Duncan, *Years of Poverty, Years of Plenty* (Ann Arbor: Institute for Social Research, 1984), pp. 57–58.

9. Such a program has actually been established in Wisconsin. Called the Garfinkel Plan, after its framer, University of Wisconsin researcher Irwin Garfinkel, it is described in Irwin Garfinkel, "The Evolution of Child Support Policy," *Focus,* Spring 1988, p. 11; and in Garfinkel, *Assuring Child Support: An Extension of Social Security* (New York: Russell Sage Foundation, 1992).

10. Of all those who receive welfare in a given ten-year period, 17 percent received it for more than eight years. Although this percentage may seem small (4.4 percent of the population), this group accounts for a much larger proportion of overall welfare spending. Duncan, *Years of Poverty, Years of Plenty,* p. 92.

11. An excellent analysis of the relationship between work and political standing is Judith Shklar, *American Citizenship* (Cambridge: Harvard University Press, 1991).

12. This argument is similar to that of Lawrence Mead in *The New Politics of Poverty* (New York: Basic Books, 1992), ch. 11.

13. Much of my thinking on this subject was influenced by Mickey Kaus's important book *The End of Equality* (New York: Basic Books, 1992).

14. A useful analysis of Saturation Work Immersion Model (SWIM) and other work-oriented welfare demonstrations can be found in Judith Gueron and Edward Pauly, *From Welfare to Work* (New York: Russell Sage Foundation, 1991). For a discussion of the difficulties of the Manpower Demonstration Research Corporation (MDRC) approach in evaluating welfare reform, see Stacey Oliker, "Does Workfare Work? Evaluation Research and Workfare Policy," *Social Problems,* May 1994, v. 41, pp. 195–213.

15. Daniel Friedlander and Gary Burtless, *Five Years After* (New York: Russell Sage Foundation, 1995), pp. 88–89.

16. Stephen Freedman and Daniel Friedlander, "The JOBS Evaluation: Early Findings on Program Impacts in Three Sites," Report to the U.S. Departments of Health and Human Services and Education, Executive Summary, Manpower Demonstration Research Corporation, July 1995. The "Labor Force Attachment Model," which was tested in Atlanta, Grand Rapids, Michigan, and Riverside, California, increased earnings per month by $58, while AFDC and Food Stamp income went down. On average, total income dropped $19 a month. However, there was a 39 percent increase in employment with earnings

equivalent to at least $10,000 per year for the treatment group (13.7 percent versus 9.8 percent for the control).

17. For more on this strategy, see Douglas Massey and Nancy Denton, *American Apartheid* (Cambridge: Harvard University Press, 1993).

18. New York City, for example, is finding it very difficult to maintain its city parks and is only doing so through the assistance of volunteers and welfare recipients. Given that many city services are labor intensive and thus increasingly prohibitive in an era of strapped city budgets, an influx of former welfare recipients could help maintain the quality of life in urban centers. See Martin Douglas, "City Puts a Park in the Care of Its Citizens, *New York Times,* July 9, 1995, p. 14; and "New York Workfare Experiment Fuels Debate," *New York Times,* September 1, 1995, p. 1.

19. For this insight, I am indebted to Lawrence Mead.

20. The creators of Social Security were not unaware of the politics their policy was creating. See Martha Derthick, *Policymaking for Social Security* (Washington, D.C.: Brookings Institution, 1979).

21. Gary Mucciaroni, *Reversals of Fortune* (Washington, D.C.: Brookings Institution, 1995), ch. 4.

Bibliography

Aaron, Henry, Mann, Thomas, and Taylor, Timothy, eds., *Values and Public Policy* (Washington, D.C.: Brookings Institution, 1994).
———, *Politics and the Professors: The Great Society in Perspective* (Washington, D.C.: Brookings Institution, 1978).
Abbott, Grace, *From Relief to Social Security* (New York: Russell and Russell, 1966).
Abt Associates, *Informing the Welfare Debate: Recent Research on Policy Innovations* (Cambridge: Abt Associates, 1993).
Akerlof, George, and Dickens, William, "The Economic Consequences of Cognitive Dissonance," *American Economic Review,* June 1982, pp. 307–319.
Albertoni, Ettore A., *Mosca and the Theory of Elitism* (Oxford: Basil Blackwell, 1987).
Allsbrook, Ogden, *Aid to Dependent Children: A Grant-in-Aid Considered as a Case Study in Multi-Level Bureaucracy,* dissertation, University of Virginia, June 1966.
American Public Welfare Association, *Managing Need: Strategies for Serving Poor Families* (Washington, D.C.: APWA, July 1991).
Anderson, Martin, *Welfare* (Stanford, Calif.: Hoover Institution Press, 1978).
AuCoin, Don, and Wrong, Doris Sue, "Governor's Plan Requires Work for Welfare Money," *Boston Globe,* January 11, 1995, p. 19.
Axinn, June, and Hirsch, Amy, "Welfare and the 'Reform' of Women," *Families in Society: The Journal of Contemporary Human Services,* November 1993, pp. 563–572.
Axinn, June, and Levin, Herman, *Social Welfare: A History of the American Response to Need* (New York: Harper & Row, 1975).
Ayer, A. J., *Thomas Paine* (New York: Atheneum, 1988).
Ball, Robert, "What Are the Alternatives to Welfare?" *Public Welfare,* July 1969, v. 27, pp. 236–242.
Bane, Mary Jo, and Ellwood, David, *Welfare Realities* (Cambridge: Harvard University Press, 1994).
Banfield, Edward, *The Unheavenly City Revisited* (Boston: Little, Brown, 1974).
Barnes, Fred, and Norquist, Grover, "The Politics of Less: A Debate on Big-Government Conservatism," *Policy Review,* Winter 1991, pp. 66–71.

Barnes, James, "Waiting for Clinton," *National Journal,* March 5, 1994, p. 517.

Barrett, St. John, "The New Role of the Courts in Developing Public Welfare Law," *Duke Law Journal,* February 1970, v. 20, pp. 1–23.

Barry, Brian, "The Welfare State Versus the Relief of Poverty," *Ethics,* April 1990, v. 100, pp. 503–529.

Becker, Gary, *A Treatise on the Family* (Chicago: University of Chicago Press, 1981).

Bell, Daniel, *The Cultural Contradictions of Capitalism* (New York: Basic Books, 1976).

———, *The End of Ideology* (New York: Free Press, 1962).

Bell, Winifred, *Aid to Dependent Children* (New York: Columbia University Press, 1965).

Bellah, Robert, *Habits of the Heart* (Berkeley: University of California Press, 1985).

Bennett, Susan, and Sullivan, Kathleen, "Disentitling the Poor: Waivers and Welfare 'Reform,' " *University of Michigan Journal of Law Reform,* Summer 1993, v. 26, no. 4, pp. 741–784.

Bennett, William, and Wehner, Peter, ". . . And a Skeptical View of Welfare," *Boston Globe,* January 27, 1994, p. 11.

Berger, Brigitte and Peter, *The War over the Family* (Garden City, N.Y.: Anchor Press, 1983).

Berkowitz, Edward, *America's Welfare State* (Baltimore: Johns Hopkins, 1991).

Berkowitz, Edward, and McQuaid, Kim, *Creating the Welfare State* (New York: Praeger, 1980).

Bernstein, Jared, "Rethinking Welfare Reform," *Dissent,* Summer 1993, v. 40, pp. 277–279.

Besharov, Douglas, "Using Work to Reform Welfare," *Public Welfare,* Summer 1995, pp. 17–20.

———, "Statement Before the Subcommittee on Social Security and Family Policy," February 3, 1992 (Washington, D.C.: American Enterprise Institute, 1992).

Biemesderfer, Susan, "Welfare Reform in the Recession," *State Legislatures,* June 1992, v. 18, pp. 41–45.

Birnbaum, Jeffrey, and Murray, Alan, *Showdown at Gucci Gulch* (New York: Vintage Books, 1987).

Blash, Vincent, ed., *The Burger Court: The Counter-Revolution That Wasn't* (New Haven: Yale University Press, 1983).

Blau, Peter, and Duncan, Otis Dudley, *The American Occupational Structure* (New York: John Wiley and Sons, 1967).

Bloch, Frank, "Cooperative Federalism and the Role of Litigation in the Development of Federal AFDC Eligibility Policy," *Wisconsin Law Review,* Spring 1991, v. 1979, pp. 1–51.

Blum, Barbara, "Bringing Administrators into the Process," *Public Welfare,* Fall 1990, v. 48, pp. 4–18.

Blumenthal, Sidney, *The Rise of the Counter-Establishment* (New York: Times Books, 1986).

Bobo, Lawrence, "Social Responsibility, Individualism, and Redistributive Policies," *Sociological Forum,* 1991, v. 6, no. 1, pp. 71–92.

Bowler, Kenneth, *The Nixon Guaranteed Income Proposal* (Cambridge, Mass.: Ballinger, 1974).

Bremner, Robert, *The Discovery of Poverty in the United States* (New Brunswick, N.J.: Transaction Publishers, 1992).

Brown, Josephine, *Public Relief: 1929–1939* (New York: Henry Holt, 1940).

Burke, Vincent and Vee, *Nixon's Good Deed: Welfare Reform* (New York: Columbia University Press, 1974).

Bussiere, Elizabeth, "The Failure of Constitutional Welfare Rights in the Warren Court," *Political Science Quarterly,* Spring 1994, v. 109, pp. 105–131.

Butler, Stuart, and Kondratas, Anna, *Out of the Poverty Trap* (New York: Free Press, 1987).

Center on Budget and Policy Priorities, *Real Life Poverty in America,* Washington, D.C., July 1990.

Christensen, Craig, "Of Prior Hearings and Welfare as 'New Property,' " *Clearinghouse Review,* April 1970, v. 4, pp. 321–323, 333–351.

Cloward, Richard, and Ohlin, Lloyd, *Delinquency and Opportunity* (Glencoe: Free Press, 1960).

Cloward, Richard, and Piven, Frances Fox, *The Politics of Turmoil* (New York: Pantheon Books, 1972).

Cockburn, Alexander, "Beat the Devil," *Nation,* July 18, 1994, pp. 79–80.

Cofer, M. Donna Price, *Administering Public Assistance* (Port Washington, N.Y.: National University Publications, 1982).

Congressional Budget Office, "A Preliminary Analysis of Growing Caseloads in AFDC," December 1991, CBO Staff Memorandum.

Coniff, Ruth, "Big Bad Welfare," *Progressive,* August 1994, v. 58, p. 21.

Cook, Fay, and Barrett, Edith, *Support for the American Welfare State* (New York: Columbia University Press, 1992).

Corn, David, "The Welfare Trap," *Nation,* June 20, 1994, p. 859.

Coughlin, Richard, ed., *Reforming Welfare* (Albuquerque: University of New Mexico Press, 1989).

———, *Ideology, Public Opinion, and Welfare Policy* (Berkeley: Institute for International Studies, University of California, 1980).

Coyle, Dennis, and Wildavsky, Aaron, "Requisites of Radical Reform: Income Maintenance Versus Tax Preferences," *Journal of Policy Analysis and Management,* Spring 1987, v. 6, pp. 1–16.

Coyle, Pamela, "Rights or Responsibilities?" *ABA Journal,* April 1995, pp. 82–88.

Danziger, Sheldon, and Plotnick, Robert, "Can Welfare Reform Eliminate Poverty?" *Social Service Review,* June 1979, v. 53, pp. 244–260.

Danziger, Sheldon, and Weinberg, Daniel, eds., *Fighting Poverty: What Works and What Doesn't* (Cambridge: Harvard University Press, 1986).

Davis, Martha, *Brutal Need: Lawyers and the Welfare Rights Movement, 1960–1973* (New Haven: Yale University Press, 1993).

Dawson, Diane, "The Evolution of a Federal Family Law Policy Under Title IV-A of the Social Security Act—The Aid to Families with Dependent Children Program," *Catholic University Law Review,* 1986, v. 36, pp. 197–218.

Demkovich, Linda, "Political, Budget Pressures Sidetrack Plan for Turning AFDC over to States," *National Journal,* September 19, 1991, pp. 1671–1673.

DeParle, Jason, "GOP Plans to Ax Aid Programs, Give States Control," *Commercial Appeal,* December 9, 1994, p. A1.

———, "From Pledge to Plan: The Campaign to End Welfare," *New York Times,* July 15, 1994, p. A1.

———, "House Leaders Are Criticizing Welfare Plan," *New York Times,* May 19, 1994, p. A1.

———, "Abolishment of Welfare: An Idea Becomes a Cause," *New York Times,* April 22, 1994, p. A14.

———, "States' Eagerness to Experiment on Welfare Jars Administration," *New York Times,* April 14, 1994, p. A1.

———, "Democrats Face Hard Choices in Welfare Overhaul," *New York Times,* February 22, 1994, p. A16.

———, "Crucial Lawmaker Criticizes Clinton Welfare Plan," *New York Times,* January 27, 1994, p. A12.

———, "Moynihan Says President Is Insincere About Reforming the Welfare System," *New York Times,* January 8, 1994, p. 8.

———, "Clinton Aides See Problem with Vow to Limit Welfare," *New York Times,* June 21, 1993, p. A1.

Derthick, Martha, *Policymaking for Social Security* (Washington, D.C.: Brookings Institution, 1979).

———, *The Influence of Federal Grants* (Cambridge: Harvard University Press, 1970).

Derthick, Martha, and Quirk, Paul, *The Politics of Deregulation* (Washington, D.C.: Brookings Institution, 1985).

Domestic Policy Council, Low Income Opportunity Working Group, *Up From Dependency: A New National Public Assistance Strategy* (Washington, D.C.: Government Printing Office, December 1986).

Doolittle, Fred, "State-Imposed Nonfinancial Eligibility Conditions in AFDC: Confusion in Supreme Court Decisions and the Need for Congressional Clarification," *Harvard Journal of Legislation,* Winter 1982, v. 19, pp. 1–48.

Dumas, Kitty, "States Bypassing Congress in Reforming Welfare," *Congressional Quarterly,* April 11, 1992, pp. 950–953.

Duncan, Greg, *Years of Poverty, Years of Plenty* (Ann Arbor: Institute for Social Research, 1984).

Dye, Thomas, *Who's Running America?* (Englewood Cliffs, N.J.: Prentice-Hall, 1986).

Edelman, Murray, *Politics as Symbolic Action* (New York: Academic Press, 1971).

Ellwood, David, *Poor Support* (New York: Basic Books, 1988).

Ellwood, David, and Summers, Lawrence, "Is Welfare Really the Problem?" *Public Interest,* Spring 1986, pp. 57–78.

Epstein, Richard, "No New Property," *Brooklyn Law Review,* 1990, v. 56, pp. 747–775.

Ethridge, Marcus, and Percy, Stephen, "A New Kind of Public Policy Encounters Disappointing Results: Implementing Learnfare in Wisconsin," *Public Administration Review,* July-August 1993, v. 53, pp. 340–346.

Fenno, Richard, *Congressmen in Committees* (New York: Little, Brown, 1973).

Ferman, Louis, Kornbluth, Joyce, and Haber, Alan, eds., *Poverty in America* (Ann Arbor: University of Michigan Press, 1968).

Fraser, Nancy, and Gordon, Linda, "A Genealogy of Dependency: Tracing a Keyword of the U.S. Welfare State," *Signs,* Winter 1994, v. 20, pp. 309–336.

Freedman, Stephen, and Friedlander, Daniel, "The JOBS Evaluation: Early Findings on Program Impacts in Three Sites," Report to the U.S. Departments of Health and Human Services and Education, Executive Summary, Manpower Demonstration Research Corporation, July 1995.

Freund, Paul, *The Supreme Court of the United States* (Gloucester, Mass.: Peter Smith, 1972).

Friedlander, Daniel, and Burtless, Gary, *Five Years After: The Long-Term Effects of Welfare-to-Work Programs* (New York: Russell Sage Foundation, 1995).

Friedman, Milton, *Capitalism and Freedom* (Chicago: University of Chicago Press, 1962).

Frum, David, *Dead Right* (New York: New Republic/Basic Books, 1994).

Gans, Herbert, "The War Against the Poor," *Dissent,* Fall 1992, v. 39, pp. 461–465.

———, *More Equality* (New York: Vintage, 1974).

Garvin, Charles, Smith, Audrey, and Reid, William, *The Work Incentive Experience* (New York: Universe Books, 1978).

Germanis, Peter, "Restructuring the Welfare System: Issues and Options for Shelby County, TN." Report by Bledsoe, Hobbs and Associates, December 28, 1990.

Gerth, H. H., and Mills, C. Wright, eds., *From Max Weber: Essays in Sociology* (New York: Oxford University Press, 1946).

Giannarelli, Linda, and Clark, Sandra, "Changes in AFDC Eligibility and in AFDC Participation Rates, 1981–1990," Urban Institute unpublished manuscript, October 30, 1992.

Gilder, George, *Wealth and Poverty* (New York: Basic Books, 1981).

Gilliam, Franklin, "Race, Class, and Attitudes Toward Social Welfare Spending: An Ethclass Interpretation," *Social Science Quarterly,* March 1989, v. 70, no. 1, pp. 88–100.

Ginsberg, Benjamin, and Shefter, Martin, *Politics by Other Means* (New York: Basic Books, 1990).

Glazer, Nathan, *The Limits of Social Policy* (Cambridge: Harvard University Press, 1988).

Glazer, Nathan, and Kristol, Irving, eds., *The American Commonwealth, 1976* (New York: Basic Books, 1976).

Glazer, Nathan, and Moynihan, Daniel Patrick, *Beyond the Melting Pot: The Negroes, Puerto Ricans, Jews, Italians, and Irish of New York City* (Cambridge: MIT Press and Harvard University Press, 1963).

Glendon, Mary Ann, *Rights Talk* (New York: Free Press, 1991).

Goodban, Nancy, "The Psychological Impact of Being on Welfare," *Social Service Review,* September 1985, v. 59, pp. 403–422.

Gordon, Kermit, ed., *Agenda for the Nation* (Washington, D.C.: Brookings Institution, 1968).

Gordon, Linda, *Pitied But Not Entitled* (New York: Free Press, 1994).

Gray, Virginia, and Lowery, David, "Interest Group System Density and Diversity: A Research Update," *International Political Science Review,* 1994, v. 15, no. 4, pp. 5–14.

Gray, Virginia, Jacob, Herbert, and Vines, Kenneth, eds., *Politics in the American States* (Boston: Little, Brown, 1983).

Gross, Jane, "U.S. Court Delays Welfare Cutback," *New York Times,* December 24, 1992, p. A10.

Gueron, Judith, "Work Programs and Welfare Reform," *Public Welfare,* Summer 1995, pp. 7–16.

Gueron, Judith, and Pauly, Edward, *From Welfare to Work* (New York: Russell Sage Foundation, 1991).

Guskind, Robert, "States of Shock," *National Journal,* November 7, 1992, pp. 2576–2579.

Gutman, Herbert, *The Black Family in Slavery and Freedom* (New York: Vintage Books, 1976).

Hacker, Andrew, "The Crackdown on African-Americans," *Nation,* July 10, 1995, pp. 46–47.

Hagen, Jan, and Lurie, Irene, *Implementing JOBS: Progress and Promise* (Albany: Nelson Rockefeller Institute of Government, August 1994).

Hale, John, "The Making of the New Democrats," *Political Science Quarterly,* Summer 1995, pp. 207–232.

Handler, Joel, "Two Years and You're Out," *Connecticut Law Review,* Spring 1994, v. 26, no. 3, pp. 857–869.

———, *The Moral Construction of Poverty* (Newbury Park, Calif.: Sage Publications, 1991).

———, "The Transformation of Aid to Families with Dependent Children," *NYU Review of Law and Social Change,* 1987, v. 16, pp. 457–533.

Handler, Joel, and Hollingsworth, Ellen, *The "Deserving Poor": A Study of Welfare Administration* (New York: Academic Press, 1971).

Harrington, Michael, *The Other America* (New York: Macmillan, 1962).

Hawkesworth, Mary, "Workfare and the Imposition of Discipline," *Social Theory and Practice,* Summer 1985, v. 11, pp. 163–181.

Hertz, Susan, *The Welfare Mothers Movement* (Washington, D.C.: University Press of America, 1981).

Hochschild, Jennifer, "Equal Opportunity and the Estranged Poor," *Annals of the American Association for Political and Social Science,* January 1989, v. 501, pp. 143–155.

Hogan, Lyn, "Jobs, Not JOBS," *Progressive Policy Institute* Policy Briefing, July 17, 1995.

Holden, Matthew, *The Politics of Poor Relief* (Beverly Hills: Sage Publications, 1973).

Hopkins, Harry, *Spending to Save: The Complete Story of Relief* (New York: W. W. Norton, 1936).

Horowitz, Donald, *The Courts and Social Policy* (Washington, D.C.: Brookings Institution, 1977).

Howard, Christopher, "Sowing the Seeds of 'Welfare': The Transformation of Mother's Pensions, 1900–1940," *Journal of Policy History,* 1992, v. 4, pp. 188–227.

Hunter, James Davison, *Culture Wars* (New York: Basic Books, 1991).

Iyengar, Shanto, "Framing Responsibility for Political Issues: The Case of Poverty," *Political Behavior,* 1990, v. 12, no. 1, pp. 19–40.

Jacoby, William, "Public Attitudes Toward Government Spending," *American Journal of Political Science,* May 1994, v. 38, no. 2, pp. 336–361.

Jarrett, Robin, "Living Poor: Family Life Among Single Parent, African-American Women," *Social Problems,* February 1994, pp. 31–49.

Jencks, Christopher, "Can We Put a Time Limit on Welfare?" *American Prospect,* Fall 1992, pp. 32–40.

Jencks, Christopher, and Edin, Kathryn, "The Real Welfare Problem," *American Prospect,* Spring 1990, pp. 31–50.

Jennings, M. Kent, "Ideological Thinking Among Mass Publics and Political Elites," *Public Opinion Quarterly,* 1992, v. 56, pp. 419–441.

Johnson, Earl, *Justice and Reform* (New York: Russell Sage Foundation, 1974).

Katz, Jeffrey, "Governors Group Sidelined in Welfare Debate," *Congressional Quarterly,* May 20, 1995, p. 1423.

———, "Parts of Welfare Plan Concern GOP Moderates, Governors," *Congressional Quarterly,* December 10, 1994, p. 3512.

———, "Welfare Issue Finds a Home on the Campaign Trail," *Congressional Quarterly,* October 15, 1994, p. 2958.

———, "Welfare Overhaul Forces Ready to Start Without Clinton," *Congressional Quarterly,* April 2, 1994, p. 801.

———, "Clinton Plans Major Shift in Lives of Poor People," *Congressional Quarterly,* January 22, 1994, p. 117.

———, "A Welcome But Unwieldy Idea? Putting an End to Welfare," *Congressional Quarterly,* February 27, 1993, p. 461.

Katz, Michael, *In the Shadow of the Poorhouse: A Social History of Welfare in America* (New York: Basic Books, 1986).

Katznelson, Ira, "The Welfare State as a Contested Institutional Idea," *Politics and Society,* Winter 1988, v. 22, pp. 517–531.

Kaus, Mickey, "Tommy's New Tune," *New Rupublic,* September 18/25, 1995, pp. 25–26.

———, "Bastards," *New Republic,* February 21, 1994, pp. 16, 18.

———, *The End of Equality* (New York: Basic Books, 1992).

———, "Welfare Waffle," *New Republic,* October 12, 1992, pp. 10–13.

———, "An American Melting Pot," *Washington Monthly,* July/August 1992, pp. 26–32.

———, "The End of Equality," *New Republic,* June 22, 1992, pp. 21–27.

———, "Yes, Something Will Work: Work," *Newsweek,* May 18, 1992, p. 38.

———, "Up from Altruism," *New Republic,* December 15, 1986, pp. 17–18.

———, "The Work Ethic State," *New Republic,* July 7, 1986, pp. 22–33.

Keane, John, *Tom Paine: A Political Life* (Boston: Little, Brown, 1995).

Kelly, Michael, "Clinton Presents Hard Line to Bring in North Carolina," *New York Times,* October 27, 1992, p. A12.

Kerber, Linda, "Separate Spheres, Female Worlds, Woman's Place: The Rhetoric of Women's History," *Journal of American History,* June 1988, v. 75, no. 1, pp. 9–39.

Key, V. O., *The Administration of Federal Grants to States* (Chicago: Public Administration Service, 1937).

Keyssar, Alan, "The Long and Winding Road," *Nation,* April 26, 1993, pp. 566–570.

Kinder, Donald, and Mendelberg, Tai, "Cracks in American Apartheid," *Journal of Politics,* May 1995, v. 57, no. 2, pp. 415.

King, Anthony, ed., *The New American Political System* (Washington, D.C.: American Enterprise Institute, 1990).

Kluegel, James, "Macro-economic Problems, Beliefs About the Poor and Attitudes Toward Welfare Spending," *Social Problems,* February 1987, v. 35, pp. 82–99.

Kluegel, James, and Smith, Eliot, *Beliefs About Inequality* (New York: Aldine de Gruyter, 1986).

Knapp, Elaine, "Programs on the Edge," *State Government News,* February 1992, pp. 6–9.

Kondratas, Anna, "Welfare Policy: Is There Common Ground?" Hudson Institute Briefing Paper No. 155, August 1993.

Kotz, Nick, and Mary Lynn, *A Passion for Equality: George Wiley and the Movement* (New York: W. W. Norton, 1977).

Kozol, Jonathan, *Rachel and Her Children* (New York: Crown Publishers, 1988).

Kuran, Timur, "Private and Public Preferences," Economics and Philosophy, 1990, no. 6, pp. 1–26.

Ladd, Everett Carl, "The New Lines Are Drawn: Class and Ideology in America," *Public Opinion,* July-August 1978, pp. 48–53.

Landy, Marc, and Levin, Martin, eds., *The New Politics of Public Policy* (Baltimore: Johns Hopkins Press, 1995).

Larner, Jeremy, and Howe, Irving, eds., *Poverty: Views from the Left* (New York: William Morrow, 1968).

Law, Sylvia, "Some Reflections on *Goldberg v. Kelly* at Twenty Years," *Brooklyn Law Review,* 1990, v. 56, pp. 805–829.

Lawrence, Susan, *The Poor in Court: The Legal Services Program and Supreme Court Decision Making* (Princeton: Princeton University Press, 1990).

Lazin, Frederick, *Policy Implementation of Social Welfare in the 1980s* (New Brunswick, N.J.: Transaction Books, 1987).

Leff, Mark, "Consensus for Reform: The Mothers' Pension Movement in the Progressive Era," *Social Service Review,* September 1973, v. 47, pp. 396–417.

Legal Services of New Jersey, "Complaint for Declaratory and Injunctive Relief," U.S. District Court, District of New Jersey, Case No. 93-5354.

Leiby, James, *A History of Social Welfare and Social Work in the United States* (New York: Columbia University Press, 1978).

Leman, Christopher, *The Collapse of Welfare Reform: Political Institutions, Policy, and the Poor in Canada and the United States* (Cambridge: MIT Press, 1980).

Lemann, Nicholas, *The Promised Land* (New York: Vintage, 1992).

——, "Slumlord," *Washington Monthly,* May 1991, pp. 39–49.

——, "After the Great Society," *New Republic,* November 19, 1984, pp. 27–32.

Lenkowsky, Leslie, *Politics, Economics, and Welfare Reform: The Failure of the Negative Income Tax in Britain and the United States* (Washington, D.C.: American Enterprise Institute, 1986).

Lerner, Robert, Nagai, Althea, and Rothman, Stanley, "Elite vs. Mass Opinion: Another Look at a Classic Relationship," *International Journal of Public Opinion Research,* 1991, v. 3, no. 1, pp. 1–31.

——, "Marginality and Liberalism Among Jewish Elites," *Public Opinion Quarterly,* v. 53, pp. 330–352.

Lerner, Robert, Rothman, Stanley, and Lichter, S. Robert, "Christian Religious Elites," *Public Opinion,* March-April 1989, pp. 54–58.

Levitan, Sar, Rein, Martin, and Marwick, David, *Work and Welfare Go Together* (Baltimore: Johns Hopkins Press, 1972).

Levy, Paul, "The Durability of Supreme Court Welfare Reforms of the 1960s," *Social Service Review,* June 1992, v. 66, pp. 215–236.

Lewis, Peter, "On the Net: Dissecting the Information Revolution," *New York Times,* August 28, 1995, p. D3.

Lichter, Linda, "Who Speaks for Black America?" *Public Opinion,* August-September 1985, pp. 41–44, 58.

Light, Paul, *Artful Work: The Politics of Social Security Reform* (New York: Random House, 1985).

Lilla, Mark, ed., *New French Thought: Political Philosophy* (Princeton: Princeton University Press, 1994).

——, "A Way to Save Welfare," *New Republic,* April 14, 1986, pp. 33–36.

Lind, Michael, *The Next American Nation* (New York: Free Press, 1995).

Loury, Glenn, "The Family, the Nation, and Senator Moynihan," *Commentary,* June 1986, pp. 21–26.

Lowi, Theodore, *The End of Liberalism* (New York: W. W. Norton, 1969).

Luker, Kristin, *Abortion and the Politics of Motherhood* (Berkeley: University of California Press, 1984).

Lupu, Ira, "Welfare and Federalism: AFDC Eligibility Policies and the Scope of State Discretion," *Boston University Law Review*, 1977, v. 57, pp. 1–38.

Lurie, Irene, "JOBS Implementation in 1991: The Progress of Ten States," *Publius*, Summer 1992, v. 22, pp. 79–91.

Lynn, Laurence, "Welfare Reform and the Revival of Ideology: An Essay Review," *Social Service Review*, December 1992, v. 66, pp. 642–653.

———, "In Designing Public Welfare Programs, Should Participation in Work and Training Be Voluntary or Mandatory?" *Journal of Policy Analysis and Management*, Summer 1989, v. 9, pp. 284–306.

———, "Rejoinder to Mead," *Journal of Policy Analysis and Management*, 1990, v. 9, no. 3, pp. 405–408.

———, *Minding the Public's Business* (New York: Basic Books, 1981).

———, *The President as PolicyMaker: Jimmy Carter and Welfare Reform* (Philadelphia: Temple University Press, 1981).

Machiavelli, Niccolo, *The Prince* (Chicago: University of Chicago Press, 1985).

———, *The Discourses* (London: Penguin Books, 1983).

Magnet, Myron, *The Dream and the Nightmare* (New York: William Morrow, 1993).

Manley, John, *The Politics of Finance: The House Ways and Means Committee* (Boston: Little, Brown, 1970).

Mansbridge, Jane, *Why We Lost the ERA* (Chicago: University of Chicago Press, 1986).

Manski, Charles, and Garfinkel, Irwin, eds., *Evaluating Welfare and Training Programs* (Cambridge: Harvard University Press, 1992).

Marks, Carole, "The Urban Underclass," *Annual Review of Sociology*, 1991, pp. 445–466.

Marshall, Will, "Replacing Welfare with Work," Progressive Policy Institute Policy Briefing, July 1994.

Marshall, Will, and Schram, Martin, eds., *Mandate for Change* (New York: Berkeley Books, 1993).

Martin, George, *Social Welfare in Society* (New York: Columbia University Press, 1981).

Mashaw, Jerry, *Due Process in the Administrative State* (New Haven: Yale University Press, 1985).

Massey, Douglas, and Denton, Nancy, *American Apartheid* (Cambridge: Harvard University Press, 1993).

Matusow, Allen, *The Unraveling of America: A History of Liberalism in the 1960s* (New York: Harper & Row, 1984).

Mayhew, David, *Congress: The Electoral Connection* (New Haven: Yale University Press, 1974).

McCurdy, Dave, "An Invitation to Work," *Roll Call*, February 7, 1994, pp. 16, 28.

Mead, Lawrence, "Poverty: How Little We Know," *Social Service Review*, September 1994, pp. 322–350.

———, *The New Politics of Poverty* (New York: Basic Books, 1992).

———, "The New Paternalism: Recent State-Level Welfare Proposals," Testimony Before the Committee on Finance, U.S. Senate, February 3, 1992.

———, "The Democrats' Dilemma," *Commentary*, January 1992, pp. 43–47.

———, "Should Workfare Be Mandatory?: What the Research Says," *Journal of Policy Analysis and Management*, 1990, v. 9, no. 3, pp. 400–404.

———, "The Potential for Work Enforcement: A Study of WIN," *Journal of Policy Analysis and Management*, Summer 1988, v. 8, pp. 264–288.

——, "The New Welfare Debate," *Commentary,* March 1988, pp. 44–52.

——, *Beyond Entitlement* (New York: Free Press, 1986).

Meisel, James, *The Myth of the Ruling Class* (Ann Arbor: University of Michigan Press, 1962).

Melnick, R. Shep, *Between the Lines* (Washington, D.C.: Brookings Institution, 1994).

Milwaukee County Welfare Rights Organization, *Welfare Mothers Speak Out* (New York: W. W. Norton, 1972).

Mink, Gwendolyn, "Welfare Reform in Historical Perspective," *Connecticut Law Review,* Spring 1994, v. 26, no. 3, pp. 879–899.

Minow, Martha, "The Welfare of Single Mothers and Their Children," *Connecticut Law Review,* Spring 1994, v. 26, no. 3, pp. 817–842.

Mitchell, Brent, "States Burdened by Surge in Welfare Caseloads," *Washington Post,* July 28, 1991, p. A1.

Moffitt, Robert, "Incentive Effects of the U.S. Welfare System: A Review," *Journal of Economic Literature,* March 1992, v. 30, pp. 1–61.

——, "Historical Growth in Participation in Aid to Families with Dependent Children: Was There a Structural Shift?" *Journal of Post-Keynesian Economics,* Spring 1987, v. 10, pp. 347–363.

Morone, James, and Belkin, Gary, eds., *The Politics of Health Care Reform* (Durham, N.C.: Duke University Press, 1994).

Morris, Robert, "The Future Challenge to the Past: The Case of the American Welfare State," *Journal of Social Policy,* v. 13, no. 4, pp. 383–416.

Moynihan, Daniel Patrick, "Social Justice in the Next Century," *America,* September 14, 1991, pp. 132–137.

——, "The Liberal's Dilemma," *New Republic,* January 22, 1977, pp. 57–60.

——, *Coping: Essays on the Practice of Government* (New York: Random House, 1973).

——, *The Politics of a Guaranteed Income* (New York: Random House, 1973).

——, ed., *Toward a National Urban Policy* (New York: Basic Books, 1970).

——, *Maximum Feasible Misunderstanding* (New York: Free Press, 1970).

Mucciaroni, Gary, *Reversals of Fortune* (Washington, D.C.: Brookings Institution, 1995).

Murray, Charles, "Does Welfare Bring More Babies?" *American Enterprise,* February 1994, v. 5, pp. 54–59.

——, "The Coming White Underclass," *Wall Street Journal,* October 29, 1993, p. A14.

——, "Welfare and the Family: The U.S. Experience," *Journal of Labor Economics,* Spring 1993, v. 11, pp. S224–S262.

——, "Helping the Poor: A Few Modest Proposals," *Commentary,* May 1985, pp. 27–34.

Muzzio, Douglas, and Behn, Richard, "Thinking About Welfare: The View from New York," *Public Perspective,* February-March 1995, pp. 35–38.

Nagai, Althea, Lerner, Robert, and Rothman, Stanley, *Giving for Social Change* (Westport, Conn.: Praeger, 1994).

Neuberg, Leland, "What Defeated a Negative Income Tax? Constructing a Causal Explanation of a Politically Controversial Historical Event," paper presented at the Northeastern Political Science Association Convention, November 1995.

Neuman, W. Russell, *The Paradox of Mass Politics* (Cambridge: Harvard University Press, 1986).

Norris, Donald, and Thompson, Lyke, *The Politics of Welfare Reform* (Thousand Oaks, Calif.: Sage, 1995).

Novak, Michael, ed., *The New Consensus on Family and Welfare* (Washington, D.C.: American Enterprise Institute, 1987).

Nozick, Robert, *Anarchy, State, and Utopia* (New York: Basic Books, 1974).

O'Brien, David, *Storm Center: The Supreme Court in American Politics* (New York: W. W. Norton, 1986).

Okun, Arthur, *Equality and Efficiency: The Big Tradeoff* (Washington, D.C.: Brookings Institution, 1975).

Olasky, Marvin, *The Tragedy of American Compassion* (Washington, D.C.: Regnery Gateway, 1992).

Oliker, Stacey, "Does Workfare Work? Evaluation Research and Workfare Policy," *Social Problems,* May 1994, v. 41, pp. 195–213.

Ostow, Miriam, and Dutka, Anna, *Work and Welfare in New York City* (Baltimore: Johns Hopkins University Press, 1975).

Page, Benjamin, and Shapiro, Robert, *The Rational Public* (Chicago: University of Chicago Press, 1992).

———, "Effects of Public Opinion on Policy," *American Political Science Review,* 1983, v. 77, pp. 175–190.

Patterson, James, *America's Struggle Against Poverty, 1900–1980* (Cambridge: Harvard University Press, 1981).

Peirce, Neal, "Cold Approaches to a Hot-Button Issue," *National Journal,* April 11, 1992, p. 890.

Peterson, Paul, and Rom, Mark, *Welfare Magnets* (Washington, D.C.: Brookings Institution, 1990).

Pierce, John, *The Dynamics of American Public Opinion* (Glenview, Ill.: Scott, Foresman, 1982).

Piven, Frances Fox, and Cloward, Richard, *Regulating the Poor* (New York: Pantheon, 1971).

Plattner, Marc, "The Welfare State vs. the Redistributive State," *Public Interest,* Spring 1979, pp. 28–48.

Plissner, Martin, and Mitosfsky, Warren, "Political Elites," *Public Opinion,* October-November 1981, pp. 47–50.

Pollitt, Katha, "Subject to Debate," *Nation,* May 30, 1994, p. 740, and July 11, 1994, p. 45.

Polsky, Andrew, *The Rise of the Therapeutic State* (Princeton: Princeton University Press, 1991).

Popkin, Susan, "Welfare: Views from the Bottom," *Social Problems,* February 1990, v. 37, pp. 64–79.

Rabkin, Jeremy, *Judicial Compulsions* (New York: Basic Books, 1989).

Rae, Nicol, *Southern Democrats* (Oxford: Oxford University Press, 1994).

———, *The Decline and Fall of the Liberal Republicans* (Oxford: Oxford University Press, 1989).

Rainwater, Lee, and Yancey, William, *The Moynihan Report and the Politics of Controversy* (Cambridge: MIT Press, 1967).

Rector, Robert, "Welfare Reform, Dependency Reduction, and Labor Market Entry," *Journal of Labor Research,* Summer 1993, v. 14, pp. 283–297.

Reed, Adolph, "The Liberal Technocrat," *Nation,* February 6, 1988, pp. 167–170.

Reich, Charles, "Beyond the New Property: An Ecological View of Due Process," *Brooklyn Law Review,* 1990, v. 56, pp. 731–745.

——, "Individual Rights and Social Welfare: The Emerging Legal Issues," *Yale Law Journal,* 1965, v. 75, pp. 1245–1257.

——, "Midnight Welfare Searches and the Social Security Act," *Yale Law Journal,* 1963, v. 73, pp. 1347–1360.

Rein, Mildred, *Dilemmas of Welfare Policy* (New York: Praeger, 1982).

Rhoads, Steven, *The Economist's View of the World* (Cambridge: Cambridge University Press, 1985).

Ricci, David, *The Transformation of American Politics* (New Haven: Yale University Press, 1993).

Roberts, Dorothy, "The Value of Black Mothers' Work," *Connecticut Law Review,* Spring 1994, v. 26, no. 3, pp. 871–878.

Robins, Philip, "Explaining Recent Declines in AFDC Participation," *Public Finance Quarterly,* April 1990, v. 18, pp. 236–255.

Rochefort, David A., *American Social Welfare Policy* (Boulder: Westview Press, 1986).

Rocheleau, Bruce, "Public Perceptions of Program Effectiveness and Worth," *Evaluation and Program Planning,* 1986, v. 9, pp. 31–37.

Rodgers, Harrell, ed., *Beyond Welfare* (Armonk, N.Y.: M. E. Sharpe, 1988).

Ross, Elizabeth, "States Step Up Pace of Programs to Curtail Welfare Dependency," *Christian Science Monitor,* May 7, 1993, p. 2.

Ross, Heather, and Sawhill, Isabel, *Time of Transition: The Growth of Families Headed By Women* (Washington, D.C.: Urban Institute, 1975).

Rovner, Julie, "New Cries for Welfare Reform Target Able-Bodied Poor," *Congressional Quarterly,* March 28, 1992, pp. 809–810.

Ruggles, Patricia, and Michel, Richard, "Participation Rates in the Aid to Families with Dependent Children Program: Trends for 1967 Through 1984," Urban Institute unpublished manuscript, April 1987.

Russell, Judith, "The Making of American Anti-Poverty Policy: Willard Wirtz and the Other War on Poverty," paper delivered at the 1993 American Political Science Association Convention, September 5, 1993.

Ryan, William, *Blaming the Victim* (New York: Pantheon Books, 1971).

Sagoff, Mark, "Values and Preferences," *Ethics,* January 1986, pp. 301–316.

Sard, Barbara, "The Role of Courts in Welfare Reform," *Clearinghouse Review,* August-September 1988, v. 22, pp. 367–388.

Sawhill, Isabel, "Poverty in the U.S.: Why Is It So Persistent?" *Journal of Economic Literature,* September 1988, pp. 1073–1119

Scheer, Robert, "Welfare or Work?" *Nation,* April 25, 1994, p. 545.

Schneider, William, "Making an Election Issue of Welfare," *National Journal,* January 4, 1992, p. 54.

Schoen, Douglas, *Pat: A Biography of Daniel Patrick Moynihan* (New York: Harper & Row, 1979).

Schor, Juliet, *The Overworked American* (New York: Basic Books, 1991).

Schubert, Glendon, *Judicial Policy Making: The Political Role of the Courts* (Glenview, Ill.: Scott, Foresman, 1974).

Schuman, Howard, Steeh, Charlotte, and Bobo, Lawrence, *Racial Attitudes in America* (Cambridge: Harvard University Press, 1985).

Shapiro, Martin, *Who Guards the Guardians?* (Athens: University of Georgia, 1988).

Shapiro, Robert, "Public Opinion and the Welfare State: The United States in Comparative Perspective," *Political Science Quarterly,* Spring 1989, v. 104, pp. 59–89.

Shapiro, Robert, Patterson, Kelly, Russell, Judith, and Young, John, "The Polls—A Report: Employment and Social Welfare," *Public Opinion Quarterly,* Spring 1987, v. 51, pp. 268–281.

Shklar, Judith, *American Citizenship* (Cambridge: Harvard University Press, 1991).

Simon, William, "Legality, Bureaucracy, and Class in the Welfare System," *Yale Law Journal,* 1983, v. 92, pp. 1198–1269.

Skocpol, Theda, *Protecting Soldiers and Mothers* (Cambridge: Belknap Press, 1992).

———, "State Formation and Social Policy in the United States," *American Behavioral Scientist,* March-June 1992, v. 36, pp. 559–584.

———, "Thinking Big: Can National Values or Class Factions Explain the Development of Social Provision in the United States? A Review Essay," *Journal of Policy History,* Winter 1990, v. 2, pp. 425–438.

———, "Sustainable Social Policy: Fighting Poverty Without Poverty Programs," *American Prospect,* Summer 1990, pp. 58–70.

Smith, Eric, *The Unchanging American Voter* (Berkeley: University of California Press, 1989).

Smith, James Allen, *The Idea Brokers* (New York: Free Press, 1991).

Smith, Rogers, "The 'American Creed' and American Identity: The Limits of Liberal Citizenship in the United States," *Western Political Quarterly,* June 1988, v. 41, no. 2, pp. 225–251.

Smith, Steven, and Deering, Christopher, *Committees in Congress* (Washington, D.C.: Congressional Quarterly Press, 1984).

Smith, Tom, "The Welfare State in Cross-National Perspective," *Public Opinion Quarterly,* Fall 1987, v. 51, pp. 404–421.

———, "That Which We Call Welfare by Any Other Name Would Smell Sweeter," *Public Opinion Quarterly,* Spring 1987, v. 51, pp. 75–83.

Sniderman, Paul, *The Scar of Race* (Cambridge: Belknap/Harvard, 1993).

Sniderman, Paul, and Hagen, Michael, *Race and Inequality: A Study in American Values* (Chatham, N.J.: Chatham House, 1985).

Sommers, Paul, ed., *Welfare Reform in America* (Boston: Kluwer-Nijhoff Publishing, 1982).

Spangler, Todd, "Virginia, Maryland Support Reforms," *Washington Times,* February 4, 1993, p. B1.

Sparer, Edward, "The Role of the Welfare Client's Lawyer," *UCLA Law Review,* 1965, v. 13, pp. 361–380.

Steiner, Gilbert, *The Futility of Family Policy* (Washington, D.C.: Brookings Institution, 1981).

Sterner, Richard, *The Negro's Share: A Study of Income, Consumption, Housing, and Public Assistance* (New York: Harper & Row, 1943).

Stevens, Robert, ed., *Statutory History of the United States: Income Security* (New York: Chelsea House, 1970).

Stigler, George, "The Economics of Minimum Wage Legislation," *American Economic Review,* 1946, pp. 358–365.

Stigler, George, and Becker, Gary, "De Gustibus Non Est Disputatum," *American Economic Review,* March 1977, pp. 76–90.

Stoesz, David, and Karger, Howard, "Deconstructing Welfare: The Reagan Legacy and the Welfare State," *Social Work,* September 1993, v. 38, pp. 619–628.

Sundquist, James, ed., *On Fighting Poverty* (New York: Basic Books, 1969).

Sunstein, Cass, "Preferences and Politics," *Philosophy and Public Affairs,* Winter 1991, pp. 3–34.

Szanton, Peter, "The Remarkable 'Quango': Knowledge, Politics, and Welfare Reform," *Journal of Policy Analysis and Management,* Winter 1994, v. 13, pp. 590–632.

Tawney, R. H., *Equality* (New York: Barnes and Noble, 1964).

Taylor, Paul, "Revamping Welfare by Rationalizing It," *Washington Post,* February 26, 1992, p. A15.

Thomas, Mason, "Child Abuse and Neglect, Part I: Historical Overview, Legal Matrix, and Social Perspectives," *North Carolina Law Review,* 1972, v. 49, pp. 293–349.

Thompson, Michael, Ellis, Richard, and Wildavsky, Aaron, *Cultural Theory* (Boulder: Westview Press, 1990).

Tocqueville, Alexis de, *Democracy in America I* (New York: Vintage Books, 1960).

Trattner, Walter, *From Poor Law to Welfare State* (New York: Free Press, 1984).

Tropman, John, *American Values and Social Welfare* (Englewood Cliffs, N.J.: Prentice-Hall, 1989).

U.S. Bureau of the Census, *Statistical Abstract of the United States, 1992* (Washington, D.C.: Government Printing Office, 1992).

——, *Historical Statistics of the United States: Colonial Times to 1970* (Washington, D.C.: Government Printing Office, 1971).

U.S. Congress, House of Representatives, Committee on Ways and Means, *Overview of Entitlement Programs,* WMCP: 101-29, 1990.

U.S. Congress, Senate, Committee on Finance, *Welfare: Reform or Replacement?* S. Hrng. 100-320, February 23, 1987.

U.S. Congress, Senate, *Proceedings of the Conference on the Care of Dependent Children,* S. Doc 721, January 25–26, 1909.

——, *Studies in Public Welfare: Papers No. 5, 12,* J. Comm, 87-242, 20-307, March 12, November 4, 1973.

U.S. Department of Health and Human Services, *Work and Responsibility Act of 1994: Detailed Summary,* June 13, 1994.

U.S. Department of Health and Human Services, Administration for Children and Families, *Overview of the AFDC Program: FY 1992,* "Summary of the Legislative History."

Verba, Sidney, *Elites and the Idea of Inequality* (Cambridge: Harvard University Press, 1987).

Verba, Sidney, and Orren, Gary, *Equality in America: The View from the Top* (Cambridge: Harvard University Press, 1985).

Vermont Agency of Human Services, "A Foundation for Change: Moving Toward Family Independence," Executive Summary, November 13, 1991.

Weber, Max, *The Protestant Ethic and the Spirit of Capitalism* (New York: Scribners, 1958).

Weinberg, Joanna, "The Dilemma of Welfare Reform: 'Workfare' Programs and Poor Women," *New England Law Review,* 1991, v. 26, pp. 415–451.

Weir, Margaret, *Politics and Jobs* (Princeton: Princeton University Press, 1992).

Weir, Margaret, Orloff, Shola, and Skocpol, Theda, eds., *The Politics of Social Policy in the United States* (Princeton: Princeton University Press, 1988).

White, Lucie, "On the 'Consensus' to End Welfare: Where Are the Women's Voices?" *Connecticut Law Review,* Spring 1994, v. 26, no. 3, pp. 843–856.

Whitman, David, and Cooper, Matthew, "The End of Welfare—Sort Of," *U.S. News and World Report,* June 20, 1994, pp. 28–35.

Wiggins, Charles, "Interest-Group and Party Influence Agents in the Legislative Process: A Comparative State Analysis," *Journal of Politics,* February 1992, v. 54, no. 1, pp. 82–100.

Wildavsky, Aaron, "Democracy as a Coalition of Cultures," *Society,* November-December 1993, pp. 80–83.

———, *The Rise of Radical Egalitarianism* (Washington, D.C.: American University Press, 1991).

Wilkins, Shirley, and Miller, Thomas, "Working Women: How It's Working Out," *Public Opinion,* October-November 1985, v. 8, pp. 44–48.

Will, Jeffry, "The Dimensions of Poverty: Public Perceptions of the Deserving Poor," *Social Science Research,* 1993, v. 22, pp. 312–332.

Williams, Lucy, "The Ideology of Division: Behavior Modification Welfare Reform Proposals," *Yale Law Journal,* 1992, v. 102, pp. 719–746.

Wilson, James Q., "New Politics, New Elites, Old Publics," in Marc Landy and Martin Levin, eds., *The New Politics of Public Policy* (Baltimore: Johns Hopkins Press, 1995).

Wilson, William Julius, "Studying Inner-City Social Dislocations: The Challenge of Public Agenda Research," *American Sociological Review,* February 1991, v. 56, pp. 1–14.

———, "The Underclass: Issues, Perspectives, and Public Policy," *Annals of the American Political and Social Science Society,* January 1989, v. 501, pp. 182–192.

———, *The Truly Disadvantaged* (Chicago: University of Chicago Press, 1987).

———, "The Black Underclass," *Wilson Quarterly,* Spring 1984, v. 8, pp. 88–103.

Wiseman, Michael, "The New State Welfare Initiatives," Institute for Research on Poverty, Discussion Paper No. 1002-93, April 1993.

Witte, Edwin, *The Development of the Social Security Act* (Madison: University of Wisconsin Press, 1963).

Wolfe, Alan, "The Mothers of Invention," *New Republic,* January 4-11, 1993, pp. 28–35.

Wright, Gerald, "Racism and Welfare Policy in America," *Social Science Quarterly* (Fall 1977), pp. 718–730.

Wrong, Dennis, "21 Years Later," *New Republic,* March 17, 1986, pp. 31–33.

Wyatt, Birchard, and Wandel, William, *The Social Security Act in Operation* (Washington, D.C.: Graphic Arts Press, 1937).

Zainaldin, Jamil, "The Emergence of Modern American Family Law: Child Custody, Adoption, and the Courts: 1796–1851," *Northwestern University Law Review,* 1979, v. 74, pp. 1038–1089.

Index